MEN OF RESPECT

A SOCIAL HISTORY
OF THE SICILIAN MAFIA

Raimondo Catanzaro

Translated by Raymond Rosenthal

THE FREE PRESS

A Division of Macmillan, Inc. • *New York*

MAXWELL MACMILLAN CANADA

Toronto

MAXWELL MACMILLAN INTERNATIONAL

New York • *Oxford* • *Singapore* • *Sydney*

The Free Press
A Division of Macmillan, Inc.
866 Third Avenue, New York, N. Y. 10022

Maxwell Macmillan Canada, Inc.
1200 Eglinton Avenue East
Suite 200
Don Mills, Ontario M3C 3N1

Macmillan, Inc. is part of the Maxwell Communication
Group of Companies.

Printed in the United States of America

printing number
1 2 3 4 5 6 7 8 9 10

Library of Congress Cataloging-in-Publication Data

Catanzaro, Raimondo.
    Men of respect: a social history of the Sicilian Mafia/Raimondo
Catanzaro; translated by Raymond Rosenthal.
Translation of : Il delitto come impresa: storia sociale della mafia.
        p. cm.
    Includes bibliographical references and index.
    ISBN 0-02-905325-0
    1. Mafia—Italy—Sicily—History.   2. Sicily (Italy)—Social
conditions.   I. Title.
HV6453.I83M32323 1992
a364.1′06′09458—dc20   91-44301
                                                         CIP

For Elisa

Contents

Preface

In a statement delivered to the Italian Government's Anti-Mafia Commission on July 2, 1970, Pasquale Sciortino, one of the members of the Salvatore Giuliano band, gave the following answer to a question by the Senator Calogero Li Causi, who insisted on trying to uncover the band's relationship with the Mafia: "Look, Mafia, with us, is a small word, but it encompasses an immensity. . . . If you wish to interpret Mafia as criminality, say criminality, don't say Mafia. If you say kidnapper, then say kidnapper and not Mafia. . . . If, furthermore, you wish to tar with the Mafioso brush the individual who breaks the law and deviates from a moral principle in order to commit a serious act against a fellow man, I say: For me he's a murderer. If, on the other hand, . . . several murderers become associated, I would call it a conspiracy to commit crimes."

Two points of crucial importance for understanding the Mafia are masterfully enunciated in this passage. First, there is a great reluctance to use the term *Mafia;* second, when it is used, it is identified with other kinds of illicit behavior so that its very meaning is blurred. Even as the Mafia becomes increasingly threatening, the term itself is on the verge of losing its semantic weight.

These points have set the direction of my research, which is based on the conviction that, to understand today's Mafia, the roots of the traditional Mafia must be traced and its evolution reconstructed. If the Mafia has been able to adapt to the contortions of history—if from estate guards (*campieri*) and tenant farm managers (*gabelloti*) the mafiosi have evolved into tradesmen and building contractors, politicians and the organizers of cooperatives, drug traffickers and investment bankers—the fact that such potentialities were present from its origins must also be understood.

Contrary to those who consider the Mafia a vestige of traditional society, destined to disappear with the inevitable modernization of Sicily, and those who have recently contrasted the modern Mafia entrepreneurs with the presumed old-style mafiosi, intent exclusively on the acquisition of honor, I seek to explain the actual historical processes that produced today's Mafia. For these processes created an organization that, although seemingly traditional, is really the result of a unique combination of old and new, having survived by adapting to the times. The Mafia's power structure has developed in a way that guarantees the success of individuals who are capable of molding to its form the continuous challenges of change.

I have begun my investigation along two crucial historical paths; first, on the phenomenology of early Mafia behavior and, second, on the relationship between the economic and social preconditions of the Mafia and its genesis. The latter took place during the formation of the Italian state, when the mid-nineteenth-century social sanction of the use of private violence in Sicily combined with the state's failure to affirm its monopoly over legitimate violence. This development boded well for the then embryonic Mafia.

I have structured the remainder of this investigation around certain other fundamental matters, including two well-known codes of Sicilian and, in particular, Mafia culture: honor and instrumental friendship. I believe that these codes are not traditional; that is, they are not, as others contend, feudal throwbacks. On the contrary, they emerge from modern economic activities and networks of political and social relationships, but not as they are understood in the capitalist countries of northwestern Europe.

These cultural codes—honor and friendship—and the modern forces that shaped them imbued the Mafia with its essential competitive character. This competitiveness, combined with the socially sanctioned use of private violence, gave the Mafia its initial dynamism as a criminal enterprise. Then, as several historical circumstances converged, the Mafia successfully entered a healthy infancy. The local ruling classes in Sicily assumed control of many governmental functions, thereby weakening still further the already ineffective Italian government's peripheral administration, while private violence gained even greater ground as an instrument of social control over the peasantry.

After World War II, the Sicilian government, having tried to foster economic development, failed to eliminate the Mafia. On the contrary, its importance in Sicilian life has grown. Beneath the surface of change, the Mafia's fundamental values—honor and instrumental friendship—and competitive structures have perpetuated it, even fostering its expansion on national and international levels.

Precisely because it is not simply a vestige of the past but a dynamic and pragmatic combination of ancient and modern, the Mafia has been able to weather, and at times even effect, change.

In this study it has been necessary not only to take into account the contributions of a great number of disciplines, but also to make forays into the fields distant from my particular expertise. As a sociologist I have ventured into the lands of the infidels—especially into the rich encampments of anthropology and history—without, however, presuming to undertake specialized studies. I hope that the results of my work will justify these raids. In fact, recourse to a blend of methods and approaches is not a whim but a necessity when dealing with this kind of "border line" material.

I am grateful to Uggio Barone, Piero Bevilacqua, Salvatore Lupo, Arturo Parisi, Nino Recupero, Pietro Rossi, and Carlo Trigilia, who read early versions of the work and helped me greatly with their suggestions. Incomparable assistance was also afforded me by the careful editing of Mariolina Palazzolo, Pietro Rossi, and Daniela Timpanaro, who made my manuscript much more readable than it was at first. Salvo Scibilia's suggestions sharpened the chapter titles and subheads. And, finally, Sara Romano collaborated on some parts of the research into the documentation of the Anti-Mafia Commission and the provisions of the Court of Palermo in the formulation and implementation of the Rognoni–La Torre law, and transformed the data into charts and figures. Though I offer my gratitude to all these people, I alone bear responsibility for what I have written.

One writes a book out of the certainty of finding an order in the succession of events, and because one wishes to weave the story of what has happened in time and space with the same thread that runs through the weft of life. But to find this weft, to set down in prose the orderly series of events and their connections, fills the author with the sensation of forsaking the richly entangled complexity of the flow of life. The acuter the consciousness—the more able to seize the multiplicity of facets—all the more does the object of the study dilate in a glittering swarm, become immense, and elude intellectual manipulation. Thus, during the entire time in which ideas are put down on paper, one is tempted to believe that it might be preferable to think a book rather than write it.

But now that the book is going into print and is being relinquished to the judgment of its readers, I would like to keep it with me for one last moment, dedicating it to my daughter Elisa, in the hope that she may live in a world in which the scholar's attention will no longer be attracted by what I have written about in these pages.

I
CHARACTERISTICS

1

AN OBSCURE OBJECT OF INQUIRY

I am not the law, which is the justice of the few; but I am power, which is the law of everyone. . . . You call this Mafia; at bottom it is nothing but social revolt.
—G. A. Cesareo, *La Mafia*

Despite the century-long debate about what really defines the Mafia, the only commonly agreed upon identifying characteristic is that the Mafia exists to make profits illegally. This was clear even to writers, critics, and historians who studied the subject in the nineteenth century. Alongi, for example, used the word *industry* in connection with the sources of income—among which he listed "highway robbery, cattle rustling, extortion, and kidnapping"—of the mafiosi.[1]

But if we considered only this characteristic, we would have no basis for making a distinction between the Mafia and other criminals. While certain aspects of mafioso behavior undoubtedly link it with common organized crime, it is also true that innumerable factors prevent the former from being reduced to the latter. Yet among these I do not intend to include the one proposed by Hess, who believes mafiosi differ from everyday bandits because mafiosi engage in the kinds of activities listed above only at the beginning of their career, afterward becoming mandators—that is, higher-level operators—whereas bandits' entire lives are occupied by routine robberies, extortions, and kidnappings.[2] Although this distinction may distinguish mafiosi from bandits, it does not pertain to a comparison

3

between mafiosi and common criminals. After all, successful criminals, too, progress in their careers to executive positions in their organizations. Nor is the exacting of payoffs in exchange for "protection" exclusively a Mafia trait. For it too is typical of urban racketeering and organized crime. Even the formation of associations for the purpose of extortion or obtaining kickbacks or monopolies, long identified as a mafia enterprise,[3] is equally typical of common organized crime. Finally, the establishment of "commercial businesses" within the normal range of economic activity is characteristic of both the Mafia and other criminal organizations, distinguishing them both from free-lance bandits. However, distinctions do exist and are reflected in Sicilian history.

The birth of the Mafia just after 1860 was closely related to other forms of illegal activity through acts of resistance to the newly unified Italian state. Political opposition in Sicily during the years 1860–1867 was rather shapeless, merging Mazzinians, clericals, supporters of the Bourbons, regionalists, and autonomists.[4] In this setting bandits, Mafia, and other political opposition groups overlapped with each other, preventing the public authorities—who actually took advantage of this confusion—from distinguishing easily among what seemed to their aloof eyes ill-defined manifestations of dissatisfaction. In the profound social and political crisis that seized Sicily after the impact of unification, years went by before groups with distinct personalities emerged. Indeed, the term *mafioso* appears for the first time only in 1863 in the play *The Mafiosi of the Vicariate of Palermo,*[5] in which the redemption of the delinquents in the jails of Palermo is achieved by the good works of a nameless character who has the features of a political prisoner, certainly a *Garibaldino,* probably Francesco Crispi himself (premier 1887–91, 1893–96). So it is not surprising that the authorities not only were unable to distinguish among these groups and their distinct activities but also capitalized on this very confusion to fight by any and all means the opposition, which they branded alternately as bandits or Mafia.[6]

Ironically, all this confusion provided the embryonic Mafia with moral credentials. Its appearance as a sort of spontaneous rebellion against the injustice of the constituted order surrounded the mafiosi with the romantic aura of popular heroes and, conveniently for them, characterized their actions as morally ambiguous even as late as the 1950s.[7] Indeed, the celebration of the "Mafia spirit" in Sicilian ideology is the early Mafia's clearest and most enduring legacy.

4

The Mafia Spirit

In 1874 the prefect of Girgenti (now Agrigento), in a report to the minister of the interior, offered the following definition of the Mafia: "The Mafia can objectively be defined as the mysterious sense of fear that a man famous for crimes and brutal force inflicts on the weak, the pusillanimous, the quietists. Subjectively, it is fame that bestows impudent courage on the man who, through criminal deeds and the swift use of physical force—through intelligence and personal connections—has been able to subject those who know him by name and personally, so that he can brazenly commit crimes with the assurance of impunity, since everyone is afraid of him and no one dares to react to his brazen demands by accusing him." And, after listing a series of rules that inform Mafia behavior, he concluded: "And therefore the Mafia can be defined as criminal silence, brazen courage, impudent mendacity, betrayal of intimate personal relations, [and] resistance to all moral and civil laws."[8]

That elements of a psychological nature have been used only to describe the Mafia can also be traced to the analysis carried out by the 1875 junta for the investigation into conditions in Sicily. In the report of its president, Bonfadini, we read:

> The Mafia is not an association that has established set forms or special organisms; neither is it a temporary assemblage of delinquents for a transitory or specific purpose; it does not have statutes, it does not share profits, it does not hold meetings, it does not have acknowledged leaders, except for the strongest and most skillful. Rather, it is *the development and perfection of strong-arm tactics aimed at all evil purposes; it is the instinctive, brutal, self-serving solidarity* that brings together, at the expense of the state, the laws and the lawful organisms, all the individuals and social strata, that prefer to derive their existence and their well-being not from work but from violence, deceit, and intimidation.[9]

From one point of view the report argues that the Mafia is not a stable association; from another it denies certain fundamental qualities that distinguish the Mafia, such as its peculiar structure and the fluid, temporary nature of its coalitions. Once these features are denied, it is easy to focus attention on its down-to-earth qualities, its "instinctive, brutal . . . solidarity," depriving the phenomenon of all social moorings.

Those who define the Mafia primarily in terms of a psychological attitude have the advantage of providing some basis for differentiating between the Mafia and common Sicilian criminality, but they make the mistake of specifying patterns of behavior that not only seem to be bereft of all historical bases but are also "naturally" impervious to economic and political change. Thus, for more than one hundred years, a whole series of studies have stressed the fact that the Mafia is

> a *state of mind, a philosophy of life, a concept of society, a moral code, a particular susceptibility prevalent among Sicilians.* From the cradle they learn, or come into the world already . . . knowing, that they must help each other, line up with their friends, and fight the common enemy, also when their friends are wrong and the enemy is right; each must defend his . . . dignity at all costs and never allow the slightest insult or . . . injury to remain unavenged; all must keep the secrets and . . . distrust official authorities and all laws. In this sense a mafioso is . . . anyone who behaves with visible pride.[10]

This definition highlights a number of cultural features that reduce the entire matter to "visible pride," a sort of mentality that resides in the mafioso's innermost depths. This same impressionistic quality can be inferred from an interview given in 1966 by the then president of the Anti-Mafia Commission, Senator Pafundi, almost as though he were trying to put to rest for once and for all the government's century-long struggle to grasp the true nature of the phenomenon in order to marshal the means to fight it effectively. In fact, Senator Pafundi declared:

> *In Sicily the Mafia is a "mental state,"* it pervades everything and everyone, at all levels . . . the Mafia [is] in the blood, in the most recondite structures of society. It exists above all in the atavistic distrust of the laws and therefore in not observing them, which in the Sicilians assumes a character of infectious pleasure. It is a mentality to be found in landowners, peasants, local authorities, the police, everywhere. . . . Hence *omertà.* . . . As . . . I said before, a mental state that bewitches, fascinates, and is contagious.[11]

As Hess has pointed out, in this sort of thinking about the Mafia two elements coexist: "the psychic attitude and the moral code."[12] The mafioso is "a man to be respected," who does not tolerate injuries and avenges insults and injustices by recourse to private violence. Those who study the Mafia spirit put great emphasis on this psychic attitude, often referring to the etymology of the word *Mafia* and neglecting all its other aspects. Exemplary in this sense is the analysis by Pitré, who describes an original conception of the word in terms of beauty, boldness, pride, graciousness, perfection, and excellence.[13] This description is echoed by the novelist Sciascia, who claims to have found, "in the roster of those reconciled by an Act of Faith celebrated at Palermo in 1658 . . . the word 'Maffia' as the nickname of a sorceress: 'Catarina la Licatisa, also called Maffua.'"[14] Not coincidentally, others have described the Mafia's criminal counterpart, the Calabrian 'ndrangheta, as a term that similarly indicates individual pride, contempt for danger, and bravery.[15]

For Pitré, the Mafia "became synonymous with banditry, camorra, highway robbery, without being any one of these three things or conditions, because banditry is an open struggle with the social laws, the camorra is an illicit profit derived from economic transactions, [and] highway robbery is typical of vulgar and extremely common folk, steeped in vice, who prey on people of low rank."[16]

In adopting the above definition, Pitré at one and the same time denies the associative character of the Mafia and its illicit nature. He goes on to argue: "The Mafia is neither a sect nor an association, it has neither rules nor statutes. The mafioso is not a thief, he is not a highway robber . . . the mafioso is simply a courageous and valiant man who does not suffer a fly to sit on his nose; in this sense to be a mafioso is necessary, indeed indispensable." Pitré ends by depicting the Mafia as an ensemble of individual qualities: "Let us put together and blend a bit of self-assurance, of daring, of bravery, valor, aggressiveness, and we will obtain something that resembles the Mafia, but there is more to it. . . . The Mafia is consciousness of one's being, the exaggerated concept of individual strength, the one and only arbiter of every clash of interests and ideas; hence, intolerance toward superiority and, even worse, the highhandedness of others."[17]

The Sicilianist Ideology

It is certainly not surprising that those who celebrate the Mafia spirit link it with a kind of exaggeration of presumed aspects of the Sicilian character. Those who consider the Mafia a kind of racial stigma prevalent among backward people see the connotation in a pejorative sense, while those who support the claim of the colonized Sicilians' moral superiority to the colonizers regard it as a glorious connection—a source of pride and ethnic self-affirmation. At any rate, Pitré, in his definition, stressed the positive connotations. The same can be said about *omertà*—that is, the general habit of remaining silent with regard to Mafia actions.[18] In mafioso culture to keep one's mouth shut and hatch revenge in silence is the correct way to behave. To say little or nothing is in fact a sign of wisdom, as expressed in the proverb that says: "The man who speaks a lot says nothing, the man who speaks little is wise." The same value is also to be found in the expression according to which the mafiosi, besides being defined as "men of respect," are also "men with a taut stomach"—that is, able to keep to themselves what they know—while women cannot be trusted because they have a "loose stomach"—that is, they chatter and gossip. The step from this to the glorification of the romantic aspects of mafioso behavior is certainly not too long, especially if one considers the connection between the early Mafia and Sicilian bandits and other political opponents to the new Italian state. The fact that the three phenomena were often confused allowed any number of Sicilian intellectuals to see in the Mafia an expression of a spirit of rebellion against foreign domination of the island, and affirmation of its own special values.

Thus, from the very inception of the Mafia, Sicilianism represented its principal ideological justification. S. F. Romano makes the case boldly when he says that "Mafia spirit and Sicilianism are often melded together, more or less unconsciously, in not a few Sicilians, and especially among certain middle management strata and Sicilianist intellectuals."[19] In fact this interconnection became clear during the earliest years of the unified kingdom, when the two-volume report of the inquiry headed by Leopoldo Franchetti and Baron Sidney Sonnino into political and economic conditions in Sicily came to be regarded in Sicilian intellectual circles as slanderous and full of anti-Southern rancor and prejudice.

Sicilianist ideology takes a very clear position on the Mafia: Either it doesn't exist or if it does, it is similar to many other criminal phenomena; in any case, it was imported by the Italian state; and for that matter, it is nothing but an exaggeration of the Sicilian people's fundamentally positive qualities. Thus on the occasion of the Notarbartolo trial, the Sicilian industrialist Vincenzo Florio stated that he had never heard of the Mafia and, confronted by the prosecuting attorney, who maintained that the Mafia was being used to obtain electoral support, indignantly exclaimed that this was how people slandered Sicily. During the same period Pitré declared that "the evil weed of the Mafia" had not existed in Sicily before 1860 and that someone had brought it there.[20] And a few years before the Mafia murder of the Marchese

Notarbartolo in 1893 Luigi Capuana, the writer, actually went so far as to insist on the absence of any traces of the Mafia on the island:

> The word *Mafia*, thanks to the distortions it has suffered due to its recent worldwide popularity—already reduced to having many meanings for the Sicilians themselves—today is used to signify [first] something similar to the Neapolitan *camorra*, the Milanese *teppa*, the Roman *bagherinaggio;* [then] something that perhaps elsewhere does not have a name of its own, while the penal code and the police simply call it an association of criminals. Of that social octopus, however, that monster [whose] viscid tentacles . . . coil around and strangle the island from one end to the other—of that legendary Mafia with its solemn statutes, its formidable organization forever intent on evading the police and deceiving justice [one cannot] find a trace.[21]

In fact, it is easy to find statements openly laudatory of the Mafia, such as the straightforward declaration by Andrea Finocchiaro Aprile, the leader of the Sicilian separatist movement, who during an election rally, expressed himself in 1944 as follows: "If there were no Mafia, we would have to invent it. I'm a friend of the *mafioso* even though I personally declare that I am against crime and violence."[22]

These are not distant memories. Even recently, with regard to the broader investigatory powers into assets and bank deposits the anti-Mafia law has granted the investigative organs, shrill complaints have been heard from many sides, maintaining that an attempt was being made to hinder Sicily's economic development and block local entrepreneurial initiatives, which might compete with those of northern industrialists. Besides, the attitude of victimization is one of the typical ways by which, in the Sicilianist ideology, one passes from praise of the island's history and civilization to justification of the Mafia or to its reduction to common delinquency.[23]

The connection between Sicilianism and the Mafia seems to be supported by two arguments. The first refers to the obscure, indeterminate character of the Sicilianist ideology itself. As Romano stresses: "*Sicilianism*, before it was a well-defined political ideology of insular autonomy and independence, is in fact at its base . . . a vague mood of solidarity among the islanders against external governments, occupations and interventions, a complex and confused sentiment."[24]

Never having succeeded in presenting itself as a real political alternative to the Italian national state (and the failure of separatism in the period after World War II is proof of this), and never having succeeded in serving as the basis for even a territorial defense party,[25] Sicilianist ideology continues to encompass everything in itself: "From the glorifi-cation of the island's natural beauty to that of its civilization, from the wealth of Sicilian culture to praise of the Mafia spirit as a manifestation of the moral superiority of a people never tamed when confronted by foreign invasions and domination. And yet, to this explanation we must add another that concerns the relationship between Sicily and the Italian national context. Indeed, we cannot ignore that in a certain sense Sicilianism is one side, the defensive aspect, of that erroneous conception of the Mafia whose other side is represented by the charge that Sicily alone, even in its tradition and its culture, bears the respon-sibility for giving birth to the Mafia. As Sciascia maintains, "As soon as the state, conditioned by the opinion of the North, poses for itself the problem of the Mafia . . . as an absolutely Sicilian problem, typi-cal of Sicily psychologically and historically—therefore detaching it from itself, presenting it as beyond its responsibilities and failings—then the cultivated Sicilian class immediately responds, camouflaging criminal events with statistical indices and descriptive comparisons of individual criminal events.[26]

This statement must not be read only in light of the fact that Sicilianist ideology feeds on Sicily's exploitation by the Italian state. Rather it must be considered from the seemingly paradoxical view that the Sicilianist ideology reached a fever pitch when Marchese Notarbar-tolo, on the point of exposing a banking swindle, was murdered at the order of highly placed officials in finance and government. In the Notarbartolo case, economic, financial, and political links between mafioso groups and interests in the Italian North became painfully obvious. And on that occasion Northern public opinion seemed intent on exorcising the problem, confining all responsibility to typically Sicilian subjects and practices, while Sicily's dominant class sought shelter behind defensive praise of the presumed virtues of the island's people. Hence the Mafia cannot be defined only in terms of its spirit. It is something more—something different.

The *Cosche*

If a mafioso's acts were inspired by the Mafia spirit alone, he would certainly not agree to submit to hierarchial rules or to obeying orders.[27] The basic requirements for the existence of an organized group would conflict with his brave and prideful spirit. Yet this argument has the merit of calling attention to the risks one runs when attempting to define the Mafia as simply an association with the aim of committing crimes.[28] However, the risks inherent in this position lie in overlooking several features that are essential to a full appreciation of the Mafia: first, its historical roots in Sicilian society; second, its activities within the normal functioning of the economic system; and, finally, its practices related to political power and social control. Stated simply, without some kind of organization the Mafia could not exist. One of the Mafia's greatest paradoxes is precisely the fact that its culture, which holds the individual characteristics of being "a man" in the highest esteem, manifests itself in forms that exist only within an organization. This fact—that the Mafia is a multifaceted, complex phenomenon—did not escape those who, a century ago, studied its intricacies.

In the *Agricultural Inquiry* of 1877–85 it is reported that for the *praetor* of Ravanusa (a commune in the province of Agrigento) the term *Mafia* had several meanings. The first was "that habit of overweening power. In its second meaning, the Mafia is banditry organized to commit crimes generally against persons and property. . . . In its third meaning it is a *vast union of persons* of all castes, of all social spheres, *without apparent links,* for the purpose of taking care of common interests, whatever they might be."[29]

Despite their acumen, however, definitions of this kind do not resolve the problem of the relationship between the Mafia's structure and spirit. Does a link exist between the two? Mosca makes a sharp distinction between them: Having described the Mafia spirit as "one that considers it a sign of weakness or cowardice to have recourse to official justice, the police, and the courts for the reparation . . . of certain injuries suffered," he establishes a precise connection between the existence of such a feeling and the Mafia organization. "Where . . . custom requires men in some way not to turn to the public authorities but to private force for the prevention and repression of injuries, insults, and crimes, one can easily understand that many misfortunes must be undergone by the isolated man, who does not know how [to] and cannot rebel against the aforesaid custom, and who is not protected by friendships and numerous connections with people who have greater ability to injure, insult, and commit crimes."

It follows that the Mafia spirit confers "an extraordinary vitality" on "a great number of small associations of delinquents," the so-called Mafia *cosche,* or "cells."[30] The spread of the Mafia spirit therefore, according to Mosca, is the basic condition, a sort of petri dish, for the propagation and multiplication of Mafia organizations. But between these two polarities there exists as a kind of interface another sort of relationship. The Mafia spirit can be considered a kind of ideology held by Mafia groups. These groups demand solidarity and loyalty from their members. Since the Mafia's rules are in competition with those of the state, demanding that no recourse be made to public justice and establishing codes based on honor and private vengeance, they also insist that side by side with subordination to the rules of the group there be insubordination to the rules of the state.

Recruitment

It is impossible to understand the origins and evolution of the Mafia without acknowledging that the Mafia's power system protects a certain number of important interests and performs functions essential to the perpetuation of specific social arrangements. The Mafia could never have lasted, much less prospered, as long as it has without such a purpose. The scholars who observed the origins of the Mafia as contemporaries put forward two differing interpretations of its infiltration throughout the Sicilian social classes. According to the first, the Mafia pervades all classes. As the prefect of Girgenti observed: "The Mafia unfortunately extends to all social classes, from the baron to the sulfur miner"; and the prefect of Caltanissetta, answering questions put to him by the minister of the interior, specified that the Mafia, "is [present in] all classes, always by habit and instinct, and therefore without need *of bonds between those who are part of it,* save for exceptional cases, and with the exclusion of the generic case of the *high Mafia,* which avails itself of and surrounds itself by the *low.* . . . The poorest peasant or sulfur miner can be a *great Mafioso,* just like the richest baron, prince, or duke."[31]

On the one hand, several of these scholars advanced the idea that since the Mafia is equally widespread among all classes, there presumably does not exist a discrete and separate Mafia organization; on the other hand, a typical distinction is introduced between high and low Mafia, categories that can be defined both in class and organizational terms—the high Mafia uses the low Mafia for its own ends.

This distinction was underscored by the prefect of Palermo, in whose opinion the Mafia took root among different social groups for different reasons. He claimed that

> the Mafia actually invades all social classes; the rich man avails himself of it in order to keep his person and property untouched by the scourge

of banditry . . . the middle class falls into its arms and practices it out of fear of revenge or because it considers it a powerful means to acquire a misconceived popularity or to obtain riches, . . . last, the proletarian becomes a Mafioso with greater ease because of the natural hatred for anyone who possesses something, or occupies a higher position.

In the same report, the middle class, perhaps because it contained a large number of Sicily's lawyers was considered to be especially fertile terrain for the germination and growth of the Mafia.[32]

This picture became even more detailed when further distinctions between high and low Mafia were introduced. Authorities were well aware of the diverse dangers of both the high and the low: "The most frightening Mafia members, most frightening and most detrimental to public safety, are those who flee into the countryside to commit crimes; but even more extremely dangerous . . . , and of grave and continuous hindrance to the authorities [whose goal is to eradicate] all this evil, are those who—availing themselves of their respectable social position—by their wealth and office protect, defend, and exculpate the scoundrels, so that these men must be considered mafiosi even more than the scoundrels [themselves]."[33]

And the acute observer Alongi noted the fact that "the distinction between high and low Mafia, between the mafioso who wears a cap and the mafioso in kid gloves," had a "relative value," since it dealt with a relationship "between protector and protected, patron and client, mandator and material executor."[34]

As early as 1874, in the prefect of Trapani's report to the minister of the interior, the classes among which the Mafia arose were observed in impressive detail. In terms of occupation, they included "middlemen, barbers, goatherds, bakers, millers, and pasta makers, and lastly, . . . carriage drivers and carters."[35] What is clear is that these tradesmen and workmen were predominantly middle class and often urban middle class at that.

According to the *Agricultural Inquiry,* which suggests that the Mafia failed to take equally deep and extensive root among peasant farmers, the peasants played "a secondary role in the execution, and a paltry role in the profit [derived from Mafia acts]. . . . The peasant in general can be said to be a *tool of the Mafia,* which is recruited *among city people* but plays a secondary role in its exploits. However, those who have close relations with it, *ordinarily abandon agriculture* and switch to being cattle dealers or innkeepers, fruit and vegetable shopkeepers, and such like."[36]

So it was not among the rural landowners or peasants that the Mafia found its rank and file. The former used the Mafia; the latter were its tools. On the contrary, mafiosi came from the urban middle classes. In the agricultural inquiry into the condition of the peasants, the reporter Giovanni Lorenzoni elaborated on this: "The largest contingent comes to the Mafia from the class of the *curatoli* (guardians of the more intensively cultivated areas) and *campieri* [estate guards] and overseers in the extensive areas, as well as from the small *gabelloti* [tenant managers] and citrus and grain merchants *from the classes between peasants and landowners,* which have the greatest opportunity to exercise their high-handedness and brutality on the former, and to deceive and intimidate or otherwise subjugate the latter."[37] He continued: "In the upper classes mafiosi find people who, out of a desire to enrich themselves or lord it over others or make rapid progress in the administration or politics, enter into relationship with them . . . and thus they can become what is called a *capo mafia* [Mafia chief]. On the lower level, mafiosi easily find henchmen or material executors for their activities."[38]

Finally, Mosca reaches the same conclusion: "The social condition of the influential members of the *cosche* is somewhat superior to that of the poor section of the Sicilian population. The mafiosi are almost always small landowners or small tenants on agricultural estates, *curatoli* [custodians] or *castaldi* [stewards], middlemen, or small merchants dealing in citrus fruits, cattle, livestock, or other agricultural products."[39]

Hence the stage was set for the rise of an economically venturesome organization, existing outside the law but dependent on legitimate political means to attain its ends.

Palermo was the center of Sicilian political power, and it was to this city that people had to turn for connections. According to an inquiry conducted in 1910: "The mafiosi . . . in the city will assist their friends to obtain a position in the town administration; they will act as electoral messenger boys, they will support the candidate who is their protector or the friend of their protectors, or has put them on his payroll."[40]

But by 1910 the Mafia had already existed for some time. Was the relationship between Mafia and politics so obvious during its initial years?

Two Theories of the Mafia's Origin

Contrary to the evidence presented above, in the popular mind the Mafia remains a phenomenon of rural origin that emerged from Sicily's

14

feudal backwardness. In general, people hold the deep-rooted belief that the desolate Sicilian *latifondo*—large landed estate—removed from modern industrial development, gave birth to Mafia violence. But this is a half truth and, like all half truths, it is really closer to falsehood. There is no doubt, if we look at the map showing the spread of the Mafia in the island's communes, drawn up by Cutrera in 1900,[41] that the area of greatest concentration appears near or around the *latifondi*. Yet, if we carefully analyze these areas, we notice that, together with the communes of the inland region, with its large estates, there are also the communes of the Conca d'Oro, that is, the orange groves that encircle Palermo, where there was no large landownership, and that also include Palermo itself.

In 1875 Villari lucidly described the relationships between the Mafia, social classes, and city and countryside by pointing out that "the greatest number of crimes are committed by the inhabitants of the environs of Palermo, who for the most part are not poor, indeed are often peasants listed by the census and proprietors, who admirably cultivate their orange orchards. In the Conca d'Oro agriculture prospers; large landownership does not exist, the peasant is well off, a member of the Mafia, and he commits a great number of crimes."[42]

The Mafia's concentration in the coastal areas of Palermo and its immediate surroundings, where large landownership was not present and where a rich agriculture prospered, strongly suggests that the Mafia grew in areas characterized not by backwardness but by economic opportunities. This confirms the accurate half of the argument that locates the origin of the Mafia on the *latifondi*. These estates were not isolated from domestic or, for that matter, foreign commerce.

Therefore, more than a consequence of poverty-stricken agriculture, Mafia power appears to emerge in the relationship between the large estates and the city: "In Palermo grain is sold and capital is to be found; in Palermo there lives a pleb ready with the knife, that can, if necessary, be turned to for physical support." But this relationship between town and countryside is also a relationship between social classes. "In Palermo they are the big owners of the large landholdings or former fiefdoms, and in the environs live the well-off peasants, from whom arises . . . a class of *gabelloti*, stewards, and grain dealers. The first are often victims of the Mafia if they do not come to an agreement with it; among the second, the Mafia recruits its soldiers, the third are its captains."[43]

As early as 1875 it was clear that the Mafia's center of gravity was in the urban environment and in the communes that make up Palermo's hinterland. In the same year, Franchetti and Sonnino dwelt at length on the distinction between banditry and highway robbery as phenomena typical of the island's interior and the Mafia as typical of Palermo. In describing the Conca d'Oro, Sonnino declared: "This is the kingdom of the Mafia, whose main breeding grounds are the cities and hamlets that encircle Palermo."[44] And Franchetti maintained: "It is now well known that the Mafia's perfect type and strongest manifestations are to be found in Palermo and its environs."[45] But Franchetti and Sonnino's opinion had already been enunciated by Rasponi, the prefect of Palermo, who claimed that "the Mafia [was] commonly called city banditry."[46].

Little more than ten years after its appearance in Palermo's jails, the term *Mafia* had come to describe an urban phenomenon that emerged in the relationships between the city of Palermo and its agricultural hinterland. As Alongi pointed out a few years later, among these relationships not only those of a political but also those of a commercial nature were of considerable importance. "Palermo . . . is the center that absorbs all of Sicilian production: both the city's internal consumption and the export of all the island's products that daily flow into it. . . . It will be easy to guess at the great variety of underhanded deals that this commercial function offers the local Mafia, the many kinds of contraband, swindles, and frauds it can perpetrate with impunity, artificially raising and lowering the products' prices, discrediting this one and imposing that one, in short, monopolizing the marketplace, exchange, and credit."[47] These activities gave the Mafia its purpose and gave shape and structure to its organizations, metaphorically revealing the body within the spirit.

Criminal Organizations and Politics

Mosca identifies in the "'kid-glove' Mafia [the] protection that upperclass individuals, sometimes invested with political mandates, and the governmental authorities themselves grant the *cosche* of the Mafia."[48]

This kind of protection has ancient roots in Sicily and elsewhere. It is an expression of the typical paternalistic syndrome wherein the upper classes protect the lower in return for a commitment of loyalty—a popular practice since the ancien régime.[49] Thus the Sicilian gentry would intercede with the police authorities to protect their criminal friends and associates. In exchange the gentry obtained respect for their life and property from the mafiosi *cosche* they protected, and also protection from other *cosche*. As Mosca explained, this syndrome persisted because the Italian government continued the Bourbon tradition of making deals with criminals.[50]

However, and perhaps more to the point, Franchetti shows that although there appeared both a resignation toward and complicity with the rule of power among the general population, it was harder to understand the impotence of the upper classes in the face of crime. At first sight it appears that their resignation was nothing but complicity, plain and simple. But at this time in Sicily, it was impossible to distinguish complicity imposed by criminal terror from the kind that was "spontaneous and lucrative." Some landowners who tried to resist criminal activity suffered damage to their property and person, and many were therefore forced to comply with the Mafia, while others became wealthy by acting as willing partners in the handling of stolen goods. Ultimately it was impossible for most landowners to avoid dealing in stolen goods, and in determining whether the Mafia criminal contact was the landowner or his supervisors, bailiffs, employees, overseer, or guards.[51] Thus a criminal network of Mafia relationships was created.

Even though their structure is completely distinctive, the Mafia associations defy hard and fast descriptions. Explaining the Mafia as a system of organized protection, Romano defines it not as an "association of ruffians [but as a] . . . management group and stratagem for criminal activities that . . . does not necessarily or directly identify itself with the criminal."

According to Romano, what truly distinguished the Mafia from other criminal organizations was its relationship with politics. "Actually, it is the alliance between politics and crime, in an organic form, that historically represents the characteristic trait of the Mafia and thus differentiates it from all other criminal associations and activities, with all the ramifications that this fact implies for the control of the economic sphere, the trade union organizations, [and] the influence on the judiciary, the police, and administrative and political bodies.[52]

This definition has been echoed by other scholars, who have defined the Mafia in terms of "a range of enterprises based on extortion; an organizational and ideological apparatus aimed at influencing the police and the judiciary; and a system of political protection supplied at first by the bosses of the middle class and subsequently by party politicians.[53]

17

We can therefore begin to think of the Mafia in a variety of ways: in terms of the goals it tries to achieve—economical and political dominance; in terms of its structure—not a formal organization but rather a collection of groups, or *cosche;* in terms of its culture—its psychology of respect; and finally in terms of the means it employs to achieve its ends—violence or the threat of it.

2

CAREERS IN KILLING

In the catechism of the virtues and qualities of civilized Western man, there has entered, historically and almost as its principal element, the goal of procuring capital.
    —F. Dostoyevski, *The Gambler*

Protection and Custody

One of the factors that gave rise to the Mafia was the estate owners' need to protect their property, especially land that was easily subject to raids or acts of banditry.[1] The private protection system provided by the Mafia developed primarily as an alternative to the relative absence of public protection through the rule or law. The Mafia partly competed with state protection, partly conspired with it, and partly became its armed extension. Certainly the more efficient the Mafia became, the greater were the difficulties faced by the government in exercising its own authority. Government leaders during the mid-nineteenth century were well aware of this fact. As the minister of justice, in presenting the collected opinions of the Sicilian magistrates on the Mafia, maintained: "The Mafia at the same time gives and receives protection, and the stronger it gets, the more it sees people having recourse to it, rather than to the legitimate intervention of the authorities."[2]

In Sicily, during the periods before and after unification, people tended to use new systems of private protection for securing their land and property. Obviously, in order to be effective, such systems had to be able to confront violence with violence. Landowners therefore needed to be sure that they hired well-known toughs, capable of deterring any attempted attack on their property, or in any case capable, through their network of acquaintances, of guaranteeing the recovery of stolen goods and of making sure that damaging acts to property, wherever they appeared, would not be repeated.[3]

The need to defend property was so great that in many ways it influenced how business was organized on large estates. Indeed, many of the functions performed by the staff on large estates were devoted to protection. In particular, the overseer, the man in charge of the entire work force, was rarely a technician, experienced in the practices of agricultural production, but rather the right-hand man of the *gabelloto* or of the owner; that is, he was "a sort of watchman of the entire flat."[4]

Along with the overseer there were the guards of the estate, called *campieri*. Their superiority over the local peasants was confirmed by a few conspicuous status symbols: First, unlike the peasants, the *campieri* were authorized to carry arms; and secondly, whereas the peasants walked on foot or used a donkey or mule, the *campieri* rode about on horseback. These distinguished them as exponents of the owner's or overseer's authority—the weapons because they symbolized their power to use violence in defense of the estate, the horse because it reflected a connection between them and the higher ranks of the estate's hierarchy. But the most important symbol was their appearance:

> On a level with the overseer, these estate guards had enjoyed the reputation of being tough, which they confirmed by their arrogant air and the arms they carried. The manner in which some of them dressed, moved, and frowned expressed this toughness. Their reticence and the opaque ambiguity of the speech, gestures, and mimicry they used among themselves sharply distinguished them from the common people. Despite the fact that these rough men were at times particularly polite and cordial, in general their behavior and equipment expressed the ability and predisposition to use physical force as a means of coercion.[5]

Guards, bodyguards, and *campieri* made up the militia of protection on the estate, and they were mafiosi as were the drovers and shepherds.[6]

The owner vouched for the *campiere*, even if he was a criminal and a mafioso, because these attributes qualified him to protect the owner's property. The owner would smooth the way for the *campiere* to obtain a permit to carry arms and would protect him against all possible charges by the authorities in exchange for the protection that the *campiere* provided for his goods. In this manner the *campieri* often became "the witting sentinels of banditry; the most active instruments of abuses, intimidation, agricultural or commercial speculations of the Palermo Mafia."[7]

This private protection of property, now a century old, first ran into trouble during the suppression of the Mafia conducted during the 1920s by Prefect Mori, and then later with the disappearance of the large estates during the years after World War II. But even until the 1950s the profession of *campiere* was still one of the first steps in a Mafioso's career. The manner in which he gained this status spoke volumes about the nineteenth-century Mafia's modus operandi.

Controlled Extortion

Blok notes an interesting episode in which the hiring of a mafioso *campiere,* as though by magic, put an end to a spate of cattle rustling. Blok's source, a man who had been a *gabelloto,* reports that on his property there were "enormous dogs . . . to prevent raids and thefts. Cattle rustling was very widespread during that period. But none of the measures we took were of any use; we were robbed all the same. When we hired a mafioso *campiere* who was imposed on us . . . by the Mafia of Bisacquino, which at that time was very powerful, the thefts ended."[8]

Of course, this meant that the Mafia was effectively able to force the hiring of *campieri* and generally dictate the terms by which the property was to be protected. The typical procedure consisted of meetings with the estate's owner arranged by certain local personages who, in a too-obsequious manner, spoke to him about *trasi e nesci*—an expression that literally means "to enter and exit" and metaphorically indicates the ambiguity of the speaker's attitude and the meanings that he conveys. In other words the speech contained a threat, presented, however, in the guise of advice or disinterested warning. It went something like this: "There is nothing to be afraid of around here even if ill-intentioned people occasionally roam the countryside; these people are only nasty pranksters, and our men, who know how to command respect, force them to see the light of reason. You have only to understand who we are, trust yourself to us, and you will have nothing to fear." If after this the owner remained aloof or pretended that he did not understand, a few days later special signals would appear: some slashed trees or vines; a theft of fruit, or damage to one of the crops. And if the owner still did not understand or pretended not to, the Mafioso's tone changed to open intimidation, which took the form of a letter of extortion (*scrocco*) or a rifle shot (*chiacchiaria*). The difference was that although the *scrocco* letter was clearly an instrument of extortion, the *chiacchiaria* was still a means of negotiation, which would later result in a form of extortion. In fact—as the word itself signifies (the Sicilian verb *chiacchiaria* means "to chat," "to discuss," so that a *chiacchiaria* is a shot intended as an extreme bargaining tool)—the shot consisted in making a burst of bullets whistle a few inches from the unfortunate landowner's head, as if to say, "Since you refused to listen to the previous arguments, perhaps it will be easier for you to hear the sound of these, clean out your ears, and be convinced by them."[9]

The point here is that the career of a mafioso was thus created out of nothing. The landowner was advised to protect himself against a nonexistent threat. If the advice was not taken, the threat from which he was offered defense then came into existence. In this way the protection from violence had its origins in a threat to use violence on the part of the protector himself, who would not put it into effect provided that he was paid tributes. The advice consisted in imposing, with violence, an undesired protection; therefore the system has been correctly called "controlled extortion."[10]

Scholars have maintained that this recourse to violence essentially served to secure the positions necessary to exercise the Mafia's control over the land.[11] In reality the violence also served to ensure its control over other economic resources—that is, marketable goods. Although control over the land seemed particularly significant because of the land's importance in the hierarchy of assets, we only have to recall the cattle-rustling incident, the *scrocco* letter, and extortion by middlemen when selling agricultural or manufactured products. The latter consisted of imposing a price on products and enforcing commercial mediation by means of threats similar to those used to impose a *campiere,* and then, to top it off, removing the protection of that same *campiere,* thus leaving the estate at the mercy of thieves and bandits.[12]

All these activities depended on the Mafia's ability to exercise its system of controlled extortion. It was controlled in the sense that it could not be pushed to extremes—that is, it had to allow its victims the possibility of continuing their productive activities, otherwise, the very foundation on which the crime industry prospered would have been undermined. But control also meant that no competition could be tolerated or that competitors were to be silenced either by an agreement or by violence. Extortion therefore had a monopolistic character and had to be exercised effectively: The motive for protection had to be well founded. The owner would agree to pay tributes only if he was not forced to pay in the form of further damage to his property or his person owing to a lack of protection or inefficient protection. What is more, whoever carried out the extortion had to prevent others from invading the territory he controlled. In that particular territory he had to be the only mafioso administering extortion. He achieved this end through noninterference pacts with other mafiosi. Each one agreed to operate in a specific territory without invading that of the other; the territorial boundaries of Mafia violence served to define the monopoly of the controlled extortion system on a local basis. But these agreements to limit the areas of competition were not in themselves sufficient, for there also existed bandits. Intimidation, violence, and extortion were the common coin of both the Mafia and banditry, but the forms they took were profoundly different.[13] In securing monopolistic positions of violence within a given territory, mafiosi would often come face to face with bandits, but since the bandits were not organized, the Mafia could not reach territorial zoning agreements with them. Therefore the Mafia often took a strategically ambiguous attitude toward bandits—sometimes crushing, sometimes exploiting, and sometimes competing with them.

The Mafia and Banditry

The Mafia also sometimes tried to use the bandits—in essence, to cooperate with them. The relationships between the Mafia and banditry from 1860 on reveal how these arrangements have metamorphosed through time. Normally the Mafia used the bandits as instruments in its extortions. Often the bandits performed tasks as enforcers under the supervision of mafioso *cosca,* even if they were not an integral part of it, and the bandits almost always needed protectors and fences to hide their activities from the police. Mafiosi used the bandits to increase their prestige and reinforce their monopoly, offering in exchange protection from the authorities.[14] However, when the bandits tried to compete with the Mafia, the relationship became antagonistic. Mafiosi could never allow the bandits to take over; they presented a challenge that threatened the Mafia's monopoly of vio-

23

lence and extortion and called into question their ability to act effectively as agents of social control. In these cases the Mafia crushed the bandits, delivering them, alive or dead, to the police. This pattern has had a long history. In fact, it was still being openly discussed during the parliamentary debate on the proposed exceptional laws for Sicily, which took place in 1975.[15] Nor should one think that this kind of punitive relationship between the Mafia and banditry was unusual, emerging only in periods of social crisis or moments of intensified police action against brigandage. On the contrary, it was a normal activity. Indeed, the mafioso customarily collaborated with the justice system. In fact, he could often appear before those who accused him of illicit activities as an honest citizen who helped bring the true outlaws to justice, claiming that it was to his credit that order reigned in his community.[16]

The figure of the mafioso arm in arm with the law in the suppression of banditry recalls a distinction between the two phenomena that was originally elaborated by Hobsbawm: Although the bandit was an outlaw, the mafioso was not; he saw himself as a man of law and order.[17] The mafioso had no need to hide from the law, because in his role as a receiver of stolen goods or protector nothing could be proved against him. However, the chief difference between bandits and mafiosi lay in the fact that the former were in open conflict with the law, while the latter, even though despising the law, collaborated with the authorities so as to reinforce their roles as de facto delegates in charge of the protection of public order.

Furthermore, as has been emphasized, "what differentiates from, and in a certain sense contrasts the spirit and organization of the Mafia with banditry is the fact that the Mafia . . . never or almost never openly sets itself against the law, [or] directly proposes to break the law or protest against its ordinances, as is the case with the bandit in popular myth; but on the contrary presents itself as concerned with order and of course formal respect for the law."[18]

The reference to the folk myth of the outlaw poses a dilemma of considerable importance. According to that myth, outlaws were social bandits—that is, exemplars of social rebellion against injustice. Bandits were considered the embodiment of the peasants' need to protect themselves from oppression by the lords of the land,[19] whereas mafiosi controlled and dominated. Hence the often-ambiguous and crosscutting relationships between mafiosi and bandits bore directly on the Mafia's activity in menacing the peasants.

Peasant Repression

According to Hobsbawm, the bandit always tried to live up to the Robin Hood model: Rob the rich to give to the poor, kill only in legitimate defense or in the name of just revenge, and act almost like a shadow government in the peasants' interest, setting the prices of basic foodstuffs or stealing them from the rich to give to the poor. Despite its illegitimacy, banditry represented an incipient and ingenuous form of class struggle.

An opposite thesis was set forth by Blok, who found in Hobsbawm a tendency to idealize the figure of the bandit and to overlook the concrete links that existed between bandits and the Mafia. Bandits could not survive successfully unless they enjoyed the protection of other individuals. These individuals may have been powerful political men, public functionaries, or party men at the local level. Among all the social categories existing in Sicilian society, the peasants have always been, without a doubt, the weakest. Peasants who, having become bandits, failed to find protection, were destined to go under. On the contrary, the greater their success as bandits, the greater the sphere of protection guaranteed them. But protection implied entry into a realm of power that became farther-reaching and more compromising as the protection offered increased—a fact that forced the bandit to become more and more a political creature as he became less and less a Robin Hood. And this, according to Blok, is the story of the rise and fall of all Sicilian bandits, who began their careers in order to correct social injustices but ended up either being killed or being co-opted into one of the power groups in the regional elites. Thus, ironically, the bandits whose rule was extended became another factor in the oppression of the peasants.[20] But Hobsbawm emphasizes the fact that "between social banditry . . . and . . . the Mafia . . . there does not exist a sharp and precise line of demarcation."[21]

Until some time ago, certainly until the 1950s, the Mafia occasionally took part in social movements. This was especially true during 1860–75, when the Mafia, bandits, and political groups commingled in opposition to the Italian state. Hobsbawm again underscores the fact that "relationships between Mafia, *picciotti* (emissaries) and bandits were . . . of a certain complexity."[22] It certainly was not out of character for bandits and outlaws to organize rebellions against established power or to become part of political liberation movements. And this occurred frequently in the Sicily of the 1860s, when mafiosi and bandit chiefs became followers of Garibaldi or fought in the 1866 revolt in Palermo.[23] It is therefore undeniable that the Mafia, banditry, and republican political opposition during the years 1860–75 were allied.

Leaving aside this first period, the relationship between the Mafia and banditry followed the pattern traced by Blok. Once the Mafia differentiated itself from banditry, bandits were used by both the Mafia and the governmental authorities—sometimes competing, sometimes allied— to repress and exploit the peasants.

Often, as in the case of the bandit Salvatore Giuliano, the Mafia and the public authorities at first became allies to exploit against the peasant movement a bandit who had begun his career as a small-time smuggler during the agitated, poverty-stricken years of the Allied occupation of Sicily. Then, later, they collaborated in order to eliminate him when, having fulfilled his role, he could have become a dangerous witness to the intrigues of power.[24]

But the Mafia's repressive function must be viewed in context. Brutal and violent men could not carry out repressions alone for so long a time and so successfully. For such an activity to be truly effective, not only was a firm establishment of the Mafia groups necessary but also a sort of social sanctioning of their use of repressive violence. They gained this approval when society deemed them men of respect.

Men of Respect

In his inquiry into Sicily's political and administrative conditions, Franchetti states that in the Sicilian vocabulary a "mafioso . . . [is] not a man dedicated to crime but a man who knows how to make his rights respected, leaving aside the means that he uses to achieve this aim."[25]

Actually, the best definition of a mafioso is that he is a "man of respect." This, indeed, is the term normally used by Sicilians to refer to a man who is in a position to practice violence effectively. Furthermore, in everyday language, owing to a sort of semantic exorcism that has changed the original positive meaning into a negative one, the terms *Mafia* and *mafioso* have lost any positive connotation even among mafiosi themselves. People will call a well-known mafioso a man of honor, a man of respect, but never a mafioso. This is an infamous accusation, rejected by all.[26] On the contrary, these "men of honor" have an image of themselves as guardians of the social order and executors of justice that the constituted authorities are not in a position to guarantee. A man of respect is a man who, with a single gesture, wasting few words, is able to settle a dispute. Alongside the man of respect one speaks of an *omu di panza e di sustanza* (a courageous man who goes to the heart of things, who does not waste time in idle talk). The man of respect fears no one, cannot tolerate insults, and turns to violence when he is insulted. He is by definition the personification of a man; of what, according to Hess, is one of the two ideals of masculine personality in Sicily: on the one hand, the aristocrat free from all material necessity, and on the other, the man who personifies power through the brute exercise of strength and violence.[27] The two ideas are in a certain sense connected inasmuch as the exercise of violence is a prerequisite for financial enrichment and thus the instrument for the achievement of the idea—that is, a life free from need and from the necessity of working.

To be respected in traditional Sicilian society meant to be entitled to the deference of others, which came from fear of violence. Anyone capable of killing would not be disturbed, at least until his power was questioned by competitors. If respect and violence were connected, there existed a further connection as well, that between respect and protection. Violent men who provided protection effectively found their respect enhanced. Conversely, those who failed to perform effectively the tasks of protection lost their respect to their competitors.[28]

It is for these reasons that traditional Sicilian society is continually exposed to challenges on the part of new pretenders to mafioso power. In fact, challenges are the only way to prove that one has greater courage—is more skillful in the exercise of violence than one's competitors.

But the challenges are not direct and open. Their typical form is the ambush, murder by treachery and stealth. Murder is the honor-accruing means par excellence, which allows its perpetrator to gain control over land and people.[29]

The struggle for honor is essential in attaining access to wealth. In this most violent of struggles even the most insignificant offense takes on an exaggerated importance. In a society like Sicily's, in which the attainment of honorific titles is so important, the slightest crime becomes a mortal challenge to the person at whom it is allegedly directed. This explains the hypersensitivity that many observers have noticed in the Sicilian temperament:

> It is to be noted that the character of revenge or of offense against a specific person is a true peculiarity of Sicilian delinquency. Crimes that elsewhere would have no personal motivation . . . in Sicily take on the

appearance of revenge for a true or supposed offense that the culprit or some relative or friend of his supposedly received at the hands of the victim.[30]

The competition for honor enhanced the *sfregio,* the quantum of "spite" in all crimes, the need to have recourse to a vendetta to prove that one is superior to the person who inflicted the spiteful act. This competition is therefore resolved when one of the parties achieves a symbolic recognition of the monopoly of respect in a specific territory. Once such a position has been secured, the victim can use his name, or allow others to use it, like a sort of credit card, with deterrent effects on those who might dare to think of challenging the holder of the monopoly. Thus, for instance, "the *campiere* of respect" usually would not perform his overseer's functions in person, and often he did not even show up on the estate that had been entrusted to his custody; he simply allowed his name to be mentioned, with the declaration that the estate was under his protection.[31]

When a man of respect achieves victory through violence, he tightens the networks between himself and the other "people who matter" in the area in which he operates. The opposite happens, too. As a mafioso's reputation becomes widespread as a result of his violent actions, more people will turn to him for protection or the resolution of conflicts. In this process, which from the point of view of the individual's career can be defined as the institutionalization of Mafia power, the exercise of violence tends to become latent; respect increasingly becomes a function of the amplitude of the network of relationships the man of honor has been able to create for himself. The ampler this network, the greater the respect paid to him. But the measure of the respect does not depend on the amplitude of the connections as much as on their importance. Men of respect place themselves at the center of crucial social networks.

Mafiosi as Brokers*

Do you know how much you stand to lose if you get mixed up with the law?—because not having money you cannot answer the summons, the complaint, the lawyers. Instead, through an intermediary everyone comes to an agreement and spends less. They trust him completely, because he's a man who can bring disputes to an agreement.[32]

*English in original.

That is how, as late as 1960, a Sicilian peasant expressed his general distrust of the administration of justice in Sicily, and why people preferred recourse to the legal administrations performed by men of respect. Mediation has decisive importance in a society in which the structures of the modern state have not penetrated the society thoroughly and impartially, but rather through patronage. The mafiosi assume the control of this function and play the part of mediators or brokers. But why do they? First of all, because they hold the monopoly of honor, that is, they are men of respect, or *'ntisi* (men whose word is above discussion). The monopoly of honor implies power; and among the distinctions that derive from holding power is included that of supplanting the official powers in the administration of justice. A second reason can be found in the system of controlled extortion which is typical of Mafia criminality. Unlike pure and simple theft, extortion does not exhaust itself in a single act, but requires a continued relationship with the victim. Theft is a violation of the law and a blow at the victim. Extortion, however, demands a constant manipulation of both victim and law. Thus the monopoly of controlled extortion demands continued negotiations,[33] and historically has served to train the individual in the activity of mediation:

> In a country where the class of malefactors has the importance that it has in Sicily, and where public authority does not have or does not use sufficient force to destroy it, it becomes necessary to find a modus vivendi between the authorities and the private citizens. This, for the rest, favors the former as much as the latter; because if the malefactors were to use their destructive ability to its utmost they would soon run out of *robbable material*. . . . So there has been established a system of transaction . . . we would almost call them regular taxations on the part of the malefactors.[34]

This system of transactions operates in such a way that it is the malefactors themselves who assume the functions of protection and guardianship and act as hinges between different milieux. This brings to light a third sort of motive in the mafiosis' assumption of the job of brokers: the paucity of links between social groups and social formations on different territorial levels. The mafiosi insert themselves between owners and peasants; they maintain the links between them, but at the same time they keep them separate and prevent them from coming into direct contact, for otherwise the centrality of their function as mediators would be eliminated.

The positioning of the mafiosi between owners and peasants is the result of the long tradition of the owners' absenteeism, and therefore of the difficulty of establishing and maintaining direct relations between the two classes. A further element that helps reinforce the position of the mafiosi as mediators is the formation of the national state, its geographical and cultural distance from local society, and in particular from the peasantry. The mafiosi exploit the opportunities that are offered them as a result of this paucity of connections, and they guarantee the links between local and national society.

The function of the mediators is to act as a connecting chain between the local and national systems. According to Wolf, cultural mediators "mediate between communally oriented groups that operate in local communities and nationally oriented groups that operate through national institutions. . . . [They] entrench themselves at the critical junctures or synapses of the relationships that connect the local system with the larger universe."[35]

The mediators protect the interests of the dominant groups both on the local and national levels by manipulating the tensions and conflicts that arise among different groups. Their function is not to solve the conflicts but rather to keep them alive, so as to guarantee the perpetuation of the tensions that are the reason for their existence. Thus the mediators' power derives from their ability to operate in both of the spheres of which they are the connecting link.

These power brokers in fact perform many tasks that are not limited to single sectors of activity or networks of relationships. Their sole limitation is the fact that the junctures at which they place themselves are critical, and that they are entrenched in them; that is, they hold a de facto monopoly of them.[36] In consequence, competition for such positions is especially intense. If, furthermore, we consider that the mafiosis' specialty as power brokers consists in the "systematic use of physical violence and the threat to resort to it,"[37] we can understand how the functions of mediation are ultimately connected with all the other activities we have considered up to now. In particular, the mediating functions are performed in the areas of protection and of controlled extortion; in the exercise of control over the land; in the domination and control of the market and the use of the labor force; and, finally, in the electoral system. In cases of theft, the mafiosi mediate between the thieves and those who have been robbed; in kidnappings or threatening letters, their role is decisive. In disputes over debts or quarrels over injuries and insults, they bring about agreements between the contenders. All this takes place without the need to assume formal power positions because, in the words of Don Calò Vizzini, a famous Mafia chief during the first half of the twentieth century: "In every society there must exist a category of persons who smooth out situations when they become complicated."[38]

The broad gamut of mediatory functions performed by mafiosi is therefore linked to the monopoly of honor and to predominance in the exercise of private violence; but at the same time it finds its motive and its consequences in the role that mafiosi play in the system of economic relationships in traditional Sicilian society:

[Mafiosi] by taking over positions of supervision and management [of estates] controlled the large properties of absentee owners, and this ensured their control over the peasants who depended on the land for their survival. . . . In exchange for being allowed access to the land, the peasants periodically supplied electoral support for the national deputies, many of whom were the owners of estates managed and controlled by Mafia power brokers.[39]

If the mandatory functions are tied to honor and violence, they are also inextricably tied to the accumulation of wealth and political power. These relationships are not only phenomena of our time; they came into being, albeit in forms different from those that we witness today, together with the birth of the Mafia.

Violence and the Accumulation of Wealth

The exercise of violence is not an end in itself, but an instrument for economic gain so that the Mafia finds in illicit enrichment a reason for its institutionalization. In fact the practice of violence is rewarded by the attainment of greater economic fortune, and in the culture this relationship between violence and the accumulation of wealth is socially accepted.

This feature of the Mafia is clear from its very origins. As Alongi writes: "It is evident that in the great majority of cases the crime . . . is not an end in itself but a means to obtain illicit gains."[40]

Profiteering is tied to the role of broker played by the mafiosi. The fact that the malefactors assume duties as custodians and protectors of the landed estates had as a consequence the establishment of relations with the wealthy classes. These relations were exploited by using the possibilities of access to both spheres, that of the peasants and that of the landowners. Once these right-hand men had obtained some form of control over the land as *campieri* or as overseers and herdsmen, or through the exercise of other functions connected with estate management, they employed this privileged position in various ways to accumulate wealth.[41]

The accumulation of wealth among the Mafia is not a trait that manifests itself only in the forms of violent or extralegal accumulation, for the mafioso combines legal and illegal means to get rich:

> The mafioso . . . inserts himself into the estate as *campiere* or as administrator with the task of protecting and administering the owner's interests against the peasants. . . . Besides his salary, he also receives from the owner an allotment of land, of variable size, which he cultivates on his own account or subleases to manual laborers and poor peasants under the spurious guises of coparticipation. . . . The tendency to develop the capitalistic elements of this position is inevitable. This is characterized by the large-scale exercise of the industry of crime and violence that helps to ensure the position attained and the accumulation of capital. In substance the mafioso avails himself of a specific extralegal organization to make good use, under *privileged conditions,* of the advantages of ordinary capitalistic accumulation as well as those of the original accumulation obtained by means of violence exercised directly against the peasants.[42]

Traditional Sicilian culture endorses the use of violence for the achievement of economic goals. The inevitability of murder and violent death are its constituent elements. Recourse is even made to those who administer justice, and this is done with the conviction that only supernatural forces or other private citizens, but not the state, can mete out true justice.[43] This conception is reinforced by the conviction that violence does not lead to some material acquisition if one can have recourse to less extreme means, such as intimidation or corruption. Intimidation is another of the basic means of mafioso enrichment; as late as the second half of the nineteenth century, the system of imposing tributes on the peasants was well established, and it left the man who worked the fields an extremely small share of his own product.[44]

In order to understand how *gabelloti* and *campieri* enriched themselves on the backs of the peasants, we must keep in mind that often these mafiosi had the *gabella* (that is, custody) of not just one estate but several. We must recall the so-called *"campiere* of respect" who, as we already mentioned, did not even have to show up on the estate entrusted to him but confined himself to allowing his name to be used

32

for purposes of deterrence. Thus, by using his name and reputation as a man of respect like a credit card, the *campiere* saw to the custody of several estates and in all of them demanded the services owed him by the peasants.

The Mafia's Profitability

The condition of the peasants was further burdened by the system of communal levies and taxes, almost all of which weighed on them disproportionately. In 1879, for example, taxes were still levied on mules and donkeys, necessities for peasants, whereas almost nothing was paid on the cattle kept by landowners and *gabelloti*. Other taxes, including the infamous tax on milled goods, were all rigged in such a way that people didn't pay in proportion to their wealth, and therefore amounted to inequitable taxation of the peasants.[45] So much so that, according to a contemporary observer,

> . . . in a very large number of communes the injustice of tax distribu-
> tion to the advantage of those who rule is monstrous; the income and
> offices of the municipality serve to enrich or support people who run
> the Communal Council, their relatives, friends, and followers; they use
> the income of charitable institutions, the funds of the *Monti rumentari*
> [welfare organization for the distribution of seed grain to the peasants]
> to acquire new supporters, and assure the loyalty of the old ones.[46]

In addition to the use of violence, intimidation, and the exercise of political influence for the purpose of enrichment, there was, finally, moneymaking in legitimate professions:

> A usurious hold over money and water, tolls on all kinds of goods in
> which the mafiosi trade, the monopolization of the sale of fruits and
> vegetables, and the hindering of the construction of irrigation canals
> connected with such produce, the illicit preempting of the best loca-
> tions in the market, the cornering of the building contracts. . . . In
> practice, the sources of profit are as varied as the commercial activities
> engaged in by Sicilians.[47]

So the mafioso's career possibilities were manifold. But first we must try to understand the means by which the traditional Mafia's accumulation of wealth began. The management of the *latifondo* dur-ing the second half of the nineteenth century reveals a combination of elements that will enable us to understand the Mafia's urban-industrial and commercial developments.

The *gabelloto,* who was often a successful *campiere,* an ex-raiser of cattle, or a supervisor, was the real entrepreneur in the commercial activities of the large estate. On one hand he exploited the peasants, while on the other he realized his profit "as essentially a *usurious profit.* The *gabelloto* realizes it by pushing the exploitation of the peasants to extremes by following *customary semifeudal forms,* and also by taking advantage of the landowner's absenteeism by seizing the lion's share of the income, to which the landowner was entitled, from the peasant."[48]

New and old means of making money were combined in the estate's business. Their connection is clearest in the practice of usury. Anyone who, by legal or illegal means, put aside some money found among the peasants a stable source of income. Stability was one of the fundamental properties of modern capitalism.

The stability of legal means of moneymaking was guaranteed by agricultural contracts. But the accumulation of wealth based on the exercise of violence also tended to be stable. Take, for example, the practice of extortion for the levying of tributes owed for presumed protection. This kind of activity fits into a topology that Max Weber defined as "intermittent financing on the basis of extorted services." However, Weber himself, in a lucid reference to the Mafia and *camorra,* declares that "these services are intermittent only at the beginning, inasmuch as they are formally 'illegal'; but in practice they often assume the character of a 'periodic payment' in exchange for specific services, and especially for a guarantee of security."[49]

The fact that these services were not intermittent but rather became stable conflicted with situations in which violence was the "normal" means of promoting the accumulation of wealth. Indeed, moneymaking in the Mafia was based on the persistence of violence together with otherwise peaceful means. The simultaneous presence of these two elements distinguished the Mafia from comparable institutions in both capitalistic and feudal society.

Social Mobility

Far from being backward, the societies in which the Mafia developed were characterized by considerable mobility. In fact, there were many examples of extremely rapid upward mobility of mafiosi who rose from *campieri* to *gabelloti,* livestock owners, or landowners. The Sicilian socialist Cammareri Scurti summarized this situation almost one hundred years ago when he spoke of the "Mafia's need to enter life."[50] But while the mafioso's wish for upward mobility in nonindustrialized society was socially acceptable, achieving this mobility was sometimes a complicated affair.

According to a recently posited theory,[51] if a mafioso's wealth became excessive, it was difficult for him—or so it is claimed—to justify his role as a defender of certain moral values that eschewed excessive riches. However, for purposes of his social ascent, wealth was still considered to be of greater importance than the more honorable qualities. Since the Sicilian ideal was based on the avoidance of manual labor and on living like a gentleman, material wealth was essential.[52]

Limits to the magnitude of wealth seemed to be borne out by the history of the Sicilian Mafia. In fact, there were more cases of considerable enrichment, though obviously relative to the level of wealth for this particular period in this social setting, where even ownership of large quantities of land was not comparable to the level of wealth achieved by industrialists. However, in this traditional society, the ownership of land did not distinguish its proprietors simply in terms of wealth but also, and perhaps to an even more meaningful extent, in terms of social prestige and political power. In this sense, efforts to accumulate wealth were conditioned by the limits inherent in the hierarchy of wealth, power, and prestige typical of traditional society. In other words, one could only be so rich. Nor must we forget that the amassing of wealth by mafiosi was not just an episodic enterprise. Rather it was a constant activity, characterized, among other things, by periods of intense exploitation of the opportunities for enrichment not only by individuals but by numerous groups. For example, we only have to remember the skill of Mafia groups at inserting themselves into the land distribution during the period of agrarian reform after World War II. Not only did they negotiate the sale and apportionment of small peasant plots, but also they bought, at privileged prices, shares in large estates so as to prevent them from being distributed among the peasants.[53]

Nearly all the nineteenth-century students of the Mafia agreed that its members came mostly from the middle class. Yet, among the scholars who have recently studied the problem, Hess, for instance, makes a sharp distinction between the mafioso's professional status and his class of origin. Indeed, according to Hess, the jobs done by mafiosi ranged between peasantry and ownership, whereas their origin was almost always among the poorest classes. Hess presents the example of three famous Mafia chiefs, Vito Cascio Ferro, the son of an illiterate peasant, Calogero (Don Calò) Vizzini, the son of a small farmer, and Giuseppe Genco Russo, who was dirt poor, did not have a lira, and was a shepherd.[54] However, there exists a dilemma: By definition one could not be a Mafia leader unless one had attained the position of a man of respect, and this position was closely associated with a certain degree of material wealth achieved through the exercise of violence and the taking of honor. True, one could become a mafioso by starting out from a poor peasant's condition, but in order to make this journey one had to take a first step, which consisted in abandoning one's social position if it did not lie at one of the junctures between different social spheres.

If we examine the career of the traditional mafioso, we see how from *campiere* he became an overseer, and then a cattle breeder or *gabelloto*, and finally a landowner. In general, as he traversed the stages of this career, he moved up the social ladder on his way to a position of Mafia leadership, all the while trying to block the ascent of others.

Thus Mafia power was not a traditional kind of power that could be transmitted by succession of inheritance. The hereditary transmission of Mafia power did not bring about legitimation, nor did it lead to acceptance by others. In 1943 Calogero Lo Bue, the *gabelloto* of the town of Corleone and an important Mafia chief in the area, on his deathbed pronounced the following words, almost as though they were his testament: "When my eyes close, I will see with those of Michele Navarra."[55] This sentence, a sort of investiture of succession, aptly expresses the need for stabilization of Mafia power through a transition that reached beyond generations.

But the very nature of enrichment and of a mafioso's career rendered impossible the stabilization of Mafia activities, since they were continually subject to challenge on the part of new pretenders to the throne. Michele Navarra took into his hands the inheritance left by Calogero Lo Bue, but he was not able to utter the same words on his deathbed. A violent death by *lupara* (shotgun blast) awaited him as he was driving along in his car.

Thus tradition itself does not serve the ends of mafioso power. In its place we find fame or reputation, and they must continually be kept alive.

In the words that Giuseppe Genco Russo used to explain his career as Mafia chief: "In the course of a life things follow one after the other. When a man came, I did him a favor; when another man came, I did him a favor; and so it went on like this, a sort of habit. This is how the reach of my name expanded."[56]

Charisma and Daily Routine in Mafia Groups

The mafioso's career unfolded through a series of distinct and successive phases and marked the stages of social ascent. The first of these, the one that constituted the primary foundation of Mafia power, consisted in the young mafioso's ability to use violence successfully.[57] The use of violence created one's reputation and opened up the market of mafioso opportunity. Violence, insofar as it was socially accepted as a way to settle disputes, was a resource formally accessible to all. The man who proved that he knew how to use it earned not only esteem and respect but also obtained material wealth—in particular, the use of the land—and saw further possibilities of a career, whose latter stages were usually marked by judicial acquittals due to lack of proof. The lack of proof served to show the public that the mafioso could count not only on his ability to intimidate others but also on high-placed protections and friendships. Then there followed recognition on the part of other mafiosi and of people in general. Other mafiosi may have had recourse to this mafioso to settle a quarrel amicably, or to determine the division of a territory according to spheres of influence. As his reputation spread, people began to consider him a man of respect. These first four phases represent the securing of the mafioso's position of influence. They were followed by the protection and consolidation of that position. The mafioso typically then built a trade or profession whose reputation served to reinforce his position. Thereafter he created for himself a *cosca* and a party and aimed at legalizing his position as much as possible. During this phase, he tended to take political offices, obtained official honorific titles, and often showed himself to be a partner of the new government officials. Finally, during a phase of legitimation, the mafioso endeavored to present himself as a humble man, a common man, without special gifts save that of being the epitome of a good family man.

The distinction between the time when the mafioso secured his position and consolidated it has been described by Arlacchi, who distinguished these two moments by different terms: the first being the "violent and individualistic one, of competition among competitors to secure a dominant position and public esteem," and the second consisting in "a process of the institutionalization of honor and its transformation into a power recognized as legitimate."[58] This leads us to ask ourselves why the institutionalization of Mafia power could not achieve the normalization of that power and its stable integration within legal society.

Moving from competition to legitimation can be understood in Weberian terms as the transformation of charisma into everyday practice. At the beginning of his career the mafioso must have been able to show certain extraordinary virtues, such as strength, ferocity, and astuteness: These were gifts that made it possible for him to build a following, create a *cosca* for himself, or to set himself at the head of another *cosca*. Once his charismatic virtues were recognized, he no longer needed to exercise violence directly; he could confine himself to threatening violence, and when he turned to it as a last resort, he usually did not use it directly, but through one or more members of the *cosca*. This evolution was accompanied by the changing of his means of enrichment from robbery and looting to ordinary trade. From a commercial standpoint the mafioso's career can be divided into three phases: The first was robbery, the second was the monopoly of controlled extortion, and the third the possession of wealth, especially landownership.

This metamorphosis, however, typically did not bring with it an end to Mafia hostilities or the cessation of the proliferation of groups and individuals who chose violence as the weapon for the acquisition of resources. On the contrary, a stable passage from illegitimate to legitimate activities never existed. The Mafia "enterprise" never had time to consolidate; it never succeeded in becoming a power based on an impersonal constellation of interests, nor did it succeed in basing itself on habit and change into a traditional power. Instability has always been the essential dynamic of Mafia power.[59]

Why is it that mafioso power failed to settle in a stable and lasting manner? Why has there been continuous turnover of groups and no end to the violent competition? The reasons are most probably two. On the one hand, the basis for the institutionalization of the power of single Mafia groups resides in the acceptance of the persistence of violence as a criterion regulating competition. On the other hand, honor remains the dominant value in Sicilian agrarian society, while the family and kinship are still the principal social arrangements. Because there is nothing to free wealth from its political and social contexts, the mafioso "enterprise"—that is, the complex of activities that are directed by each individual *cosca*—is really never able to become a purely economic enterprise.

The power of the traditional mafioso resides in social recognition of his ability to use violence successfully—a formidable obstacle to the transformation of the mafioso in a more modern, rational setting. Even if within it there was a division of labor, the basis of its legitimacy was

38

to be found in the Mafia chief's abilities and not in the functioning of the organizational apparatus. The mafioso enterprise was thus founded essentially on its titular head, and this constituted a permanent weakness. In fact, it could have been easily expelled from the market by his physical elimination. Since violence was the basis of social respectability, even a mafioso whose power was recognized as socially legitimate could not exclude challengers. Only by demonstrating that he could defeat other challengers could he prove that he was in fact the legitimate possessor of power. But in order to keep his title to power, the mafioso had to behave in accordance with the model by which "the richer a man becomes, the more likely it is he will sever his bonds to the land; that is, that he will become an absentee owner."[60]

This was the relationship between men and land in Sicily, where the ownership of land was not reflected in settling on the land but in abandoning it to go and live in the city. Absenteeism as a symbol of wealth emerged from the ideal of human existence typical of traditional Sicily, in which disdain for physical labor and for the bond with the land was accompanied by the need to live a life free from the everyday concerns that derive from having to earn one's living. In traditional Sicily land was at once the source of material prosperity— that is, that which made it possible to abstain from labor—and the source of honor. The farther one was from the land that one owned, the more one embodied the ideal of honor.

This concept greatly hindered the emergence of social values that emphasized wealth in and for itself, and not as the source of power and honor. Its persistence therefore represented a barrier to the transformation of the activities of Mafia enterprise into purely economic terms. Thus the mafioso who achieved control of the land as the result of various acts of violence, and who was constantly aware of the challenges that competitors could launch against him on his own territory, could not afford to become an absentee and base his honor on the land alone. Land was not in itself an immediate source of honor: It became so only through violent usurpation and defense. The mafioso continually needed to prove the basis of his right to the title of honor.

But while mafiosi were entrepreneurs of violence, they were also social entrepreneurs. Their function consisted in manipulating norms and customs, and through this manipulation bringing together groups and individuals, furthering the development of economic and political activity and guaranteeing social control in favor of the dominant class, into whose ranks those who were most successful managed to gain entry. As social entrepreneurs mafiosi manipulated people in order to gain access to resources. The very social relationships that they fostered were resources in themselves.[61] The socially entrepreneurial mafioso wanted to make the most of both kinds of resources to which he gained access, by strategically manipulating his relatives and friends for profit. To do this he had to be economically and politically astute and, of course, socially active as well. Having to operate on several fronts simultaneously, he could not specialize exclusively in one of them but had to be able to respond continually to the changing exigencies derived from his various commitments.

The characteristics of traditional Mafia power that enabled the mafioso to capitalize on violence and on political and social networks, that enabled the *cosche* to remain a fluid and profitable organization, that prevented power from becoming strictly institutionalized, were all connected by a single thread. Only by remaining a lone individual, could the mafioso deploy his ability to create, maintain, multiply, and manipulate social relations. This ability, precisely because it was so personal, could not be codified in prescribed roles or transmitted through the organizational architecture of the enterprise. Furthermore, the need continually to broaden the scope of the networks of social relationship reinforced the impossibility of creating stable organizational structures, thereby accentuating the organization's fluid character. Thus the organization's flexibility prevented Mafia activity from petrifying into bureaucracy.

The Structure of the *Cosche*

In 1874 the prefects of western Sicily agreed that the Mafia was not in the strict sense, an organization. The prefect of Girgenti pointed out that the Mafia was not "a sect or a typical association"; and the prefect of Trapani underscored the distinction that, in his opinion, existed between Mafia and *camorra* by noting: "The members of the Camorra continue to form a sect, have their own rules, are divided into ranks, use a cunning language, even have the semblance of a jury. . . . Mafiosi do not have regulating forms or norms."[62]

Two years later Franchetti maintained that there existed a difference of an organizational nature between the Mafia and banditry, by emphasizing that "banditry is set apart from other forms of the malefactor's industry inasmuch as a band of bandits has a fixed organization with its hierarchy of clearly defined ranks, its discipline. It is composed of people dedicated to the profession of violent crime in the countryside, to the exclusion of any regular profession, even in appearance."[63]

This denial of the organizational character of the Mafia was certainly not intentional on the part of the prefects, who had difficulties combating it (when they did not lack the will to do so). Moreover, the Mafia was not composed exclusively of people dedicated to the profession of crime but combined legitimate and illegitimate activities: hence its fluid, unstable character. Prefect Rasponi was well aware of this trait when he reported to the minister of the interior that

> the criminals or malefactors . . . do not have a truly permanent association, with agreed-upon links and pacts. But they know each other, sometimes they act uniformly, also in the way they dress, and ordinarily in the ways and means that they use to pursue their goal, *and when the necessity arises they assemble, debate, discuss and assist each other so as to bring off their operation successfully. After committing a crime or carrying out a Mafia operation and having divided the loot, they disband and actually pretend that they do not know each other until another occasion brings them together again.*[64]

This passage effectively synthesizes the ephemeral, task-oriented[65] character of the Mafia. And it was precisely this lack of organizational solidarity that rendered impossible the hereditary transmission of Mafia power. Organizational functions were all entrusted to the chief of the Mafia group, and the division of labor was rudimentary. Once again Franchetti described to a T this situation in regard to the Mafia chief,

> who in that industry fills the role of capitalist, entrepreneur, and manager. He determines the unity in the management of the crimes that gives the Mafia its appearance of ineluctable and implacable force; he regulates the division of labor and function, the discipline among the workers in this industry. . . . It falls to him to judge on the basis of circumstances whether it might be appropriate to suspend violent acts for a moment or increase them and impart to them a more ferocious character, and to examine market conditions to choose what operations are to be carried out, who is to be exploited, what form of violence is to be used to obtain the best results. His is that most subtle art that decides whether it is most convenient to kill the person who balks at following Mafia orders or to make that person come to terms by the slash of a knife, the killing of livestock, the destruction of goods, or simply a warning rifle shot. A random collection or even an association

41

of common murderers of society's lowest class would not be capable of handling such subtleties and would always resort to brutal violence.[66]

These functions were typical not of a single centralized organization but of the numerous Mafia organizations called *cosche*. In fact, there is a dispersion among the various organizations in the Mafia and a very strong central authority within each of them. The relationships pass through the Mafia chief, who tendentiously maintained one-on-one relationships with the other members of the *cosca*. All of this is aptly expressed by the words that are used. In fact, *cosca* stands for the leaf of an artichoke and indicates the Mafia group, whereas the term *cacocciula* (artichoke heart) refers to the Mafia chief.[67] What is notable is the strange inversion (which for the rest corresponds perfectly to the organizational nature of the Mafia group that draws strength from the Mafia chief) by which the entire organization is described by a term that refers to a single element (the *cosca*), whereas the entire complex is described as the *cacocciula*, which refers to the figure of the single individual who heads the organization.

The reasons for the strong centralization of each Mafia *cosca* are twofold: the absence of a centralized superorganization of the Mafia, and the functions of the mafiosi as brokers. This lack of a centralized organization at the regional level reflects that same paucity of communications that made it possible for the mafiosi to place themselves at decisive junctures in the relationships between the local and national societies.[68] Now, precisely as a result of the difficulty of communicating at the national level, the bonds of organizational closeness on the local level grew stronger, especially since in this fashion they gained greater strength in defending the monopoly of Mafia management at a territorially defined level.

But, alongside this reason stands another, which derives from fundamental requirements of the broker's role. In fact, the broker exploited the lack of connections among people to establish his own domination. The structure of the Mafia *cosca* perfectly meets this requirement: Centralization set down its roots in the constellation of two-man teams comprising the Mafia chief and individual mafiosi.[69] The *cosca* is organized as a sort of confederation (an improperly named one at that, since one member—the chief of the *cosca*—is always the same) of teams. In this fashion the chief assures himself of control of the flow of communications and prevents direct communications among the *cosca* members, enabling him to perform his role as broker in regard to them, and thus effectively exercise control. So the *cosca*, even while strongly centralized, has a fluid, unstable character: It is simultaneously an "ideal center of common interests" and an ensemble of "informal concatenated relationships."[70]

What are these relationships? According to Franchetti, the situation that spawns the Mafia is defined by

an infinite number of associations that we can only call patronage relationships, because the [membership] requirements . . . are not determined—since every day members leave or join—nor do they have the stability of regulations and statutes, since relations among their members are as varied as might be those between any two private citizens. . . . Thus are formed those *vast unions* of people of all ranks, all professions, all kinds, who, *without having any apparent, continuous, and regular bond,* are always united in order to promote their mutual interest, aside from any consideration of law, justice, and public order: this is a description of the *MAFIA.*[71]

The Mafia therefore consists of a network of two-man relationships based on kinship, patronage, and friendship. These relationships "in great number and variety remain latent; each one becomes concretized on the basis of a particular need."[72] Their prominence is based on the fact that they bind individuals in a traditional society.

3

PRELUDE: CONFLICTS OF HONOR

Rifle and wife are not to be lent.

Wine is sweet, but the blood of men is sweeter.

It is good to bear witness as long as no harm comes to one's neighbor.

To command is better than to fornicate.

One influential friend is worth more than one hundred gold coins.
        —Sicilian proverbs

In the Mafia, if a man is unable to avenge his injured honor, he ceases to be considered a real man. A husband who does not react when his wife is seduced becomes an object of contempt and mockery. A man who is unable to respond with violence to *sfregi* (insults) he has suffered will forever be the object of such insults. A man who reports an injury he has suffered to the judicial authority and the police is regarded as a spy and a traitor.

Indeed, Mafia subculture has at its center a precisely defined idea of a man: "A true man is above all represented by his silence, by the secret presence of a mysterious power, and by long and hidden paths, by his being, and being known to be, at the center of other men, who, like him, operate in the shadows."[1]

A true man is thus a man of few words, capable of settling complex problems with a single gesture or commanding glance. True men are few; others are "half men, dwarfs, buggers, or quacks," according to an old saying.[2]

Mafia conduct is by definition honorific. The mafioso is the man who is able to gain respect without having to turn to the law. However, the code of honor is present not only in deeds of the Mafia; it also informs a great deal of Mediterranean culture as a whole. To understand the role honor plays in the Mafia, it is necessary to see it in its broader social contexts. As we will discover, it has come to mean different things in Sicilian society.[3]

In the first instance, honor was accorded a man who guaranteed for his family members a living standard in keeping with his social status, protected the integrity of his property, and guarded his wife's chastity and his daughters' virginity.

In popular culture these three elements were often connected. For instance, if a woman was a spendthrift or dressed in clothes that did not befit her rank, no one was surprised if she was also an adulteress. By the same token, if a man failed to guarantee the sexual integrity of the women in his family, he was likely to be considered a nincompoop.

This conception of honor was built on two principles: In the first place, women and property were of equal value;[4] in the second, people were expected to live in conformity with their social status. In traditional Sicilian society, status as well as patrimony were transmitted by inheritance, not acquired through social mobility. People were considered honorable because they were born into honorable families. Thus there was little room for a change in one's social condition. Honor, in this context, had a purely static meaning—it was a reflection of the way things were.

But, in Sicilian society, besides honorable people, as we know, there were (and still are) also "men of honor." Unlike honorable people, "men of honor" are not born but made. A man of honor was a man who, though of humble origin, managed to become rich, and who, having killed a certain number of people and having succeeded in being acquitted through lack of evidence, gained respect. His struggle for honor was therefore competition for social advancement in a society that had not yet become fully acquainted with the capitalistic market.

It must in fact be pointed out that the competition for honor was not open to everyone but took place primarily among equals.[5] In traditional Sicily, when a baron seduced the wife of a peasant or appropriated his goods, usually no conflict of honor occurred. If, however, the injuries came from men of equal rank, conflicts of honor would explode. The violence of such conflicts was particularly intense for two reasons. First of all, these conflicts were zero-sum games; that is, the man who usurped honor did so at the expense of others who stood to lose it to the same degree. Second, and more important, in a society where resources were scarce, people competed for honor because in victory they acquired symbolic capital that gave them claim to greater access to wealth. Ultimately, honor has been described as a system of stratification that defines the distribution of wealth through a "social idiom, and prescribes the behavior proper for each individual according to his location in the social hierarchy. It entails the acceptance of a dominant . . . and a subordinate position. In this way stratification by honor compels individuals of equal rank to clash, and sanctions the dependence of those who have less honor on those who have more."[6]

Honor, unlike prestige in modern market societies, defined a man's integrity.[7] It was a composite of wealth, power, prestige, and violence. This is especially clear if we consider that the source of power and of economic wealth in a society of this kind was chiefly land ownership. The extreme difficulty of becoming a landowner made the equally extreme measure of violence the chief instrument of social advancement. Thus, conflicts of honor were fought to the death.

Cultural Dualism

"Wherever there exists a consolidated structure of power, honor tends to become the appanage of the powerful."[8]

In a society such as that of traditional Sicily, people did not, as a rule, plan for upward social mobility. Each man had his place, fixed once and for all, in the social hierarchy.[9] Social positions were substantially stable, and so was the attribution of honor to individuals.

But the concept of honor as the prize in competition among equals highlights a second principle—one whose roots lie in a niche of society in which advancement of a kind could be attained through jobs that were open to competition.[10]

Competition for honor as a means of social advancement can be traced back to the failed affirmation of individualism as a guiding principle of social action. In a static society, in which patrimony and wealth were, as a rule, transmitted through inheritance and not obtained by means of commercial activities, individuals were not allowed to carve out a position for themselves by proving their worth.[11] Wealth was seen only as the product of an inheritance or as the result of violent actions. "The rich man's father is in hell and prays for him," says a Sicilian proverb, confirming in popular imagery the diabolical nature of the origin of wealth and the ability to hold on to it.

47

But precisely because the violent means for the attainment of goals were not socially approved, individual enrichment and social advancement were always seen as something extraordinary—as the result of an individual's exceptional ability to demonstrate uncommon talents and to make his mark in the social hurly-burly. This is what some critics mean when they say that society made the mafioso: In the public view, an individual's violent action crowned by success seemed to be a sort of exceptional power. What kind of people held this power? In his report on the situation of public order and the Mafia in the province of Trapani, which the prefect presented to the minister of the interior in 1874, we read that: "The Mafia appears chiefly among those classes of men who due to special social conditions often find themselves in conflict with their unruly desires."[12]

Indeed, those men who found themselves "in conflict with their unruly desires" were often those in ambiguous social situations:[13] individuals who aspired to goals that were not granted them institutionally, and who were born neither among those to whom the achievement was guaranteed by inheritance nor among those who are excluded from it altogether.

Social Bases of Dualism

In Sicily during the period from the twelfth to the seventeenth century two very important things occurred that laid the foundation on which this peculiar group emerged: a strengthening of the structure of large landownership, and the absenteeism of the barons.[14] At the beginning of this period there was the settlement of the population in agrotowns, rural towns of considerable size. As early as the middle of the fourteenth century the smaller rural villages (*casali*) had disappeared,[15] owing to the expansion of pastureland and the cultivation of wheat and grain. Sheep raising, with its nomadic character, by alternating with the cultivation of grain, brought about the disappearance of small settlements in the countryside. With them also disappeared the intratown markets, road connections, the centers of agricultural production. The upshot of all this was a simpler structure of settlements. In fact,

> faced by the millennial power of large landownership, the rural villages revealed a certain thinning out of the inhabited areas, attachment to the land (even though in a position of dependency) on the part of the

agricultural population, an extension of arboreal cultivation, a certain form of division of the land between peasants and feudal lords. However, their destruction [the rural villages'] marks the definitive victory of the large estate, the reappropriation by the estate lords, both lay and ecclesiastic, and by the municipal oligarchies, of almost all the land, the establishment of a new network of large extended farms, of farm clusters, and the expansion of areas devoted, within the framework of an agricultural system based on grains and grass, to sheep breeding. . . . This change . . . brings about the elimination of the traditional feudal system based on the small peasant holding, on hard labor, on levies in kind or money, and it determines the establishment of a new system of exploitation of the soil: a system that empties the countryside of its inhabitants.[16]

In the area of the *latifondo* in western Sicily, each agrotown became internally differentiated, but they all resembled each other: there was no division of labor nor any hierarchical order among them. Each settlement was tied to the external world mainly through the exportation of wheat. Thus, connections between the farm agrotowns having dissolved, each one of them had connections only with the regional capital or the coastal localities where there were depots for collection of the wheat to be exported.

This historical phase was characterized by the region's rise as the breadbasket of the Mediterranean, and by the transformation of the feudal class into a group of entrepreneurs of cluster farms and herds. Beginning in the middle of the fifteenth century, there clearly arose a movement toward the commercialization of grain production and the unification of the Sicilian market. With it, and inextricably linked to the commercialization of grain production, there also came into existence a way of organizing production that, by breaking the land up into small plots subleased to the peasants, made them perennially dependent on loans and usury from owners and *gabelloti* while it permitted owners and *gabelloti* to control a large share of the product, establishing a situation of exacerbated exploitation of the peasant by the owner and the big tenant:[17]

Thus a twofold movement is delineated, whose effects end by being superimposed. One leads to concentration in the cities . . . of the landed aristocrats. The second transfers into the hands of the town oligarchies an ever-larger share of the land. . . . So the great landowners have a free hand in imposing their conditions. . . . The dynamism of estate income . . . makes land into the safest investment and . . .

49

also orients the choices of the owners: As much as possible they prefer to avoid the risks of production and pass them on to their tenants and their peasants. The *gabelloti* . . . are led to act in the same fashion, and from having been important managers, who directly administer in their own name the largest farm clusters and pasturelands, they become simple intermediaries in the running of the fiefs that are divided into plots among the peasants, to whom they lend livestock, seed, the cash they need, thus adding the earnings from usury to the earnings of the land.[18]

The *latifondo* was thus controlled from the cities. That was where the owners were and also the markets for the sale or shipment of the wheat and other produce.

This style of feudalism in western Sicily has been compared with that of Poland. But the Sicilian feudal lords and landowners succeeded in appropriating 20 to 30 percent of production (as compared with 5 to 10 percent in the Polish model), which happened because the Sicilian model was based on "the alternation or coexistence of various competing forms of cultivation, whose two extremes [were] represented by the large farm clusters that employ[ed] salaried laborers, and the small farms granted to the peasants in a precarious form."[19]

As these processes evolved, society grew more complex. The expansion of large-scale landholding exacerbated the difference between the barons and the peasants, thus reinforcing one's patrimonial condition and the role of honor in bespeaking it. The simultaneous cultivation of various crops produced a situation in which the peasants were at once owners of small plots of land, small tenants, subtenants, farmhands, and day laborers. This made precise social distinctions difficult because different interests corresponded to each of the manifold aspects of their working conditions.[20] The absence of clear-cut parameters marking off the peasant's social condition resulted in the fact that no one dared discuss relative positions in the social hierarchy. Hence this situation tended to further reinforce the static images of society and of honor.

Yet the absenteeism of the barons, the consequent granting of land leases to large tenants, and the need to commercialize production brought about the rise of a particularly active group of rural entrepreneurs.

These were those "men in conflict with their unruly desires," who found themselves performing a wide range of productive, commercial, and mediating functions, who seized the opportunities for social ascent that then became available. In this fashion the same process of social transformation that rigidified the immobile side of Sicilian regional society, founded on the opposition between landowners and peasants, and that reinforced the static image of honor also created an intermediary class between barons and peasants who chose competition as the guiding criterion of their actions.

The simultaneous presence of these two images of honor must therefore be traced back to the coexistence of two different modes of social activity and their combination in the economy of western Sicily.[21]

Violence as the Regulatory Instrument of the Economy

Honor required the family to defend the integrity of its patrimony, including women, because of their productive and reproductive functions, against external attacks. In Sicily the unity and strength of the family was, from a patrimonial standpoint, threatened by various forces. To the laws that established the division of the patrimony among the heirs at the death of the family's head, and set the dowries for the daughters who married, were added the principles of the Catholic Church that, by forbidding marriage between cousins, prevented consolidation of the property.

In this sense both the church and the state exerted strong pressures limiting the power of kinship groups in the society. Thus the code of honor was reinforced as an answer to attacks on the integrity of the family and its patrimony.[22] This defensive ethos took on violent forms when Sicily's Spanish administration failed to guarantee public order.

The Spanish administration attempted to make as few changes as possible so as not to infringe on the privileges of the barons. So, almost completely immune from fiscal impositions, the barons were given a free hand in the exercise of power on their fiefs. As late as the sixteenth century four-fifths of Sicilian towns and villages were under the barons' direct control.[23] But the structure of the settlements was such that the agrotowns were isolated and surrounded by a countryside through which it was dangerous to travel because of possible attacks by bandits and robbers. But people had to travel. In the absence of effective protection of public order by the Spanish administration, the absentee barons, active in Palermo in acquiring titles and privileges so as to reach ever-higher social positions in the ranks of the aristocracy,[24] gave a free hand to the rural entrepreneurs. The latter, in turn, set up a system for the defense of goods and patrimony founded on the exercise of violence and the threat of violence in the name of, and on behalf of, the barons. Not by chance, the organization of armed bands of *campieri* and guards on the estates came about as one of the functioning structures of Mafia violence on the *latifondi,* or large estates.

It was these individuals who found themselves in a condition of disequilibrium between culturally admissible goals and available means. Although the reigning cultural norms forbade them from making plans for social advancement, their occupations on the landed estates gave them access to the means required to attain those forbidden goals. Since no legitimate channels of social mobility existed, the only way out was recourse to violence.

Hence violence became part and parcel of Sicilian culture. The peasant knew that he must abide by the *campiere*'s law for fear that if he failed to do so, he would be forced to accept an inferior plot of land. The *campiere* knew that he must protect himself from possible attacks, because the murder of a person of his position was the only way to open the position for somebody else.

These historical circumstances also account for the birth of the code of *omertà*. *Omertà,* besides being rooted in the fear of being subjected to the vengeance of the accused or his relations and friends, found even deeper roots in questions of honor that were settled by violence. The victim of an offense had to be able to mete out his own justice; if he was unable to do so, the rules of honor compelled him to accept the law of the strongest. Furthermore, third parties were not permitted to interfere. To do so would have disrupted a delicate balance of power that demanded that things be settled between the offender and the offended.[25]

Instrumental Friendship

Yet Sicilian society could not rely simply on the competitive principles of honor and violence. Indeed, violence was described as "an action that disorients the behavior of other individuals in a deliberate or in an unintentional manner. It either renders orientation in others impossible or it is intentionally directed at preventing . . . the development of stable expectations."[26]

As in all societies, there was a need for mechanisms that—in the impossibility of eliminating violence completely—would allow for life to be lived with some degree of order and predictability. It is true that honor as a code of family protection required the existence of family solidarity. But under Spanish domination Sicily was a society too complex to be based exclusively on such solidarity. It was a society that had economic and commercial relationships with the European economies and had a unified administration of its own, albeit within the spheres of the Spanish empire. The economy was based on the activities of the large estate. Long-distance commerce and the exportation of wheat required the creation of relationships based on trust, which could guarantee a regular flow of traffic. The structure of relationships that came into existence to serve this end was represented by instrumental friendship.[27]

Instrumental friendship, unlike real, emotional friendship, was based on give-and-take in the exchange of goods. In Sicilian society this voluntary exchange between individuals made them friends. Moreover, these friendships were the closest among those who interacted most frequently; hence, in small communities they also involved most the people who were competitive.[28] In other words, if it is true that in every gift there is also a pinch of poison, this voluntary exchange of favors contained elements of poison and, therefore, of danger for friendship itself.[29] Thus there emerged an ambiguous tendency to harmonize those chiefly instrumental friendships through symbolic rituals. These rituals were played out at Mafia banquets in the toasts that celebrated old friends and relations among the mafiosi.[30]

Instrumental friendship was a sort of credit account expressed in phrases like, "Tell him that I sent you," or "Go in my name." It created special bonds, which produced social networks that were described in the popular phrase, "the friends of friends."[31] These networks arose in a society that was just developing relations with the commercial centers in which Europe's capitalistic economy was forming. Thus, in Sicily, the need to deliver the goods to their destination, among other factors, contributed to the creation of networks that transcended those of merely local scope. Lacking modern networks of impersonal relationships such as those that were slowly forming in places where capitalist market activity had come into existence, the primary basis for cooperation was constituted by these coalitions based on instrumental friendships. They made possible the exchange of economic resources and political influence.[32]

Coalitions and Alliances: The Problem of Trust

Trust in the fulfillment of business obligations lay at the basis of these coalitions.[33] Temporary and oriented toward specific goals, coalitions were destined to dissolve as soon as their goals were achieved. This brought about a substantial instability in the coalitions as well as continual redefining and reblending.[34] In fact, the trust on which they were based continually needed to be reconfirmed by the specifics of each mission. If it was not, the coalition would dissolve even before attaining its goal.

The instability of the coalitions was intensified by the ambiguity of the instrumental friendships around which they were built. Though these friendships were actually always regarded with some suspicion, so, ironically, was the lack of such friendships. Without them it would have been impossible to manipulate the administrative public structures to serve one's aims, which was effectively summed up in the proverb: "Whoever has money and friendship can screw justice." However, in the former instance, friendships were considered suspect because they were often used to set up Mafia murders. Mafiosi made a habit of pretending friendship so that the targeted victim would not be suspicious. At the same time, this would deflect suspicion from the mafiosi on the part of the public and the authorities.[35] In such a society, social relationships were forever unstable because they were based on a fragile equilibrium that derived from the fact that the instrument meant to inspire trust—friendship—could not by its very nature eliminate violence. And yet, due to the profoundly unstable and contradictory nature of Sicilian social structure, instrumental friendship was the only means capable of counterbalancing violence as a regulatory force in commerce. Paradoxically, friendship and violence became the constituent principles presiding over the formation and dissolution of Mafia groups.

The emergence of the code of instrumental friendship may therefore be interpreted as a response by rural entrepreneurs of the possibilities of social advancement that opened up to them under Spanish domination.[36] The necessity to respond in these terms was undoubtedly reinforced by the characteristics of the Sicilian administrative system itself. The distribution of offices was corrupt, the administration of justice venal, and the behavior of the bureaucracy erratic.[37] In order to obtain authorizations, licenses, and concessions, one had to be able to count on the favors of people with whom one made deals for future favors, and to be capable of "lubricating," through one's own network of acquaintances, the sluggish bureaucratic mechanisms.

Nor did the Catholic Church encourage citizens to cooperate with the justice system. The *Taxae cancelleriae et poenitentiariae romanae,* published by the Archbishop of Palermo in ten successive editions between 1477 and 1533, set forth the possibility of forgiving false depositions given before magistrates, while another article allowed the person accused of a crime to keep as "a justly earned and acquired thing of his own" money deriving from the unlawful act, provided he purchased from the church a bull of settlement and made a charitable contribution, commensurate with the value of the corpus delicti.[38] This practice of settling crimes against property by means of private agreements (*componenda*) that consisted in the payment of tributes instead of restitution of part of the corpus delicti would later become one of the principal methods for the control of public order under the Bourbons, and was continued in Sicily during the first years after Italy's unification.

In the absence of the capitalistic market and the modern state, instrumental friendship in some ways helped the administration. "In a certain sense instrumental friendship nurtured temporary coalitions in the same way as the state nurtured the entrepreneurial associations of rising capitalism: It lent credibility to contracts and offered a minimum of predictability to business deals."[39]

So if conditions in Sicily were not verging on the modern, as they were throughout much of Europe, neither were they exactly feudal. These ambiguous conditions produced a society that trained certain people in competitiveness and engendered in them a particularly disinterested attitude with regard to the law. The competitiveness was played out in the market of honor, a different arena from the market per se. In fact, the code of honor ensured that the opportunities for short-term profit were formally peaceful, besides which it bound individuals to supply each other with a mutual guarantee that they would, if at all possible, abstain from recourse to violence.[40]

In this way only temporary commitments were struck, since the ever-present possibility of violence prevented the establishment of far-reaching trust and thus of long-term investments. Although trust was an essential condition for economic development and for the formation of a market society, it was not necessary that it be of an enduring quality.[41] Deep trust within the group was accompanied by a marked suspicion toward the outside. As a result, the conditions for the development of a market society were impeded. However, not only did the prevailing ad hoc coalitions allow for the assurance of a minimum of order, but their flexibility made it possible for the alliances to change course in keeping with the sudden, unpredictable reverses that took place in the ever abruptly changing market. This system has been given the name "broker capitalism,"[42] as different in its ways from both feudalism and capitalism, in which the functions of mediation assume a central role.

II
GENESIS

4

THE STATE AND THE
MARKET OF VIOLENCE

The difference in social relationships brought about by the abolition of feudalism came down to this: Just like wealth, tyrannical acts became accessible to a greater number of people, and the class of desperadoes, who before had been at the service of the barons, became independent; so in order to obtain their services it became necessary to deal with them as equals.
—L. Franchetti, *Condizioni politiche e amministrative della Sicilia*

The Power of the Sicilian Baronage

The Mafia is not so much a vestige of the past as a dynamic product of the relationship between the formation of the Italian national state and Sicily as a peripheral European society. Although the Mafia might be considered to be "the antithesis of a strong government, . . . it nevertheless could not exist without the concentration of power in the national state."[1]

Insofar as it represented the private use of violence exercised as an instrument of social control, the Mafia was in fact a means of accommodating tensions. Mafiosi were therefore the power brokers of this in society transformation, whose activity consisted in controlling the channels that linked peasants with landowners and local populations to national society.[2]

The formation of the Italian state profoundly altered Sicilian society. Throughout the entire period of Spanish domination, Sicily had been on the outer orbit of the empire and the nascent capitalistic economy.

But in 1860 Sicily came under the sway of the Italian state, setting in motion three large-scale social processes: the formation of the state, the formation of the nation, and the extension of participatory rights—that is, the institution of political citizenship.[3] To understand the genesis of the Mafia it is therefore necessary to examine these transformations in Sicilian society during the last phase of the period preceding unification, and the manner in which the political system took shape during the course of the establishment of the national state.

If by nothing else, the persistence of "feudal" elements in landownership in Sicily as late as the eighteenth and nineteenth centuries is proved by the continuing use of the term *fief* to describe the *latifondo*. But the societal and political significance of the *latifondo* cannot be adequately understood unless we consider the specific qualities that differentiate Sicily from the continental South, and characterize the central-western as compared to the eastern section of the island.

The first important characteristic of the *latifondo* in the eighteenth century was that the titles of landownership were hard to establish. In fact, there is no proof of when the Sicilian barons secured their powers over these estates. The state archives did not contain clear documentation attesting to the existence of investitures of fiefs, rights, and civic uses, or to the apportionment as public domain of certain tracts of land. Therefore it was impossible to contest in court with any probability of success the barons' title to ownership of the land, or to demonstrate that it had been usurped. This situation actually reinforced the barons' position, making it unassailable from the standpoint of legitimacy. In addition, the barons asserted their power on the basis of a concession granted by Frederick III of Aragon, going back to 1289, that allowed the free transfer of the fief. What's more, the fiefs could be transmitted by succession all the way to the sixth degree of the collateral line. For proof of the strength of Sicilian baronage it is only necessary to recall that as late as the middle of the eighteenth century the Sicilian barons were requesting that feudal succession should be extended to the seventh degree.[4]

The consequences of this anomalous situation were many. First, feudal succession to the sixth ascendant or descendant degree, and furthermore in the collateral line, made it practically impossible for the fiscal authorities to seize the barons' assets in case of a failed succession. Second, the free transfer of the fief altered the vassal relationship between barons and monarchy, immeasurably reinforcing the power of the former since title to the disposition of the fiefs was total and absolute, free from all the restraints typical of feudal concessions. Even if the barons did not sell the estates and preferred to go into debt and use them as collateral, the right to dispose freely of their land to a great extent exempted them from fiscal obligations toward the state. This was the premise for a continuous—and almost always successful—maneuver that consisted in the barons' claim of autonomy in regard to the crown. On the basis of these prerogatives the barons asserted their right to take an active part in the island's government through participation in the constitutional organs and parliament. Exquisitely descriptive of power relationships on the island was the maxim that Count d'Olivares prescribed for the viceroys of Sicily: "With the barons you are everything, without them you are nothing."

The Sicilian barons' power was augmented by their particularly high number, a result of the fact that Spain had conferred titles of nobility with great munificence. At the beginning of the sixteenth century, together with the progressive transfer of the barons to the city of Palermo and the growth of conspicuous consumption as a distinguishing sign of the aristocratic condition, the custom of selling titles of nobility and with them the privilege of tax exemption became common practice. According to a reliable source, at the end of the eighteenth century there were in Sicily "142 princes, 95 dukes, 788 marquises, 95 counts, 1,274 barons, besides an unspecified number of people who use titles abusively and yet enjoyed the benefits inherent in a noble rank."[5]

This nobility, deeply devoted to conspicuous consumption, preoccupied with maintaining class distinctions within the aristocracy, intent on concentrating several titles in the hands of single individuals, held as its fundamental principle the preservation of its status. They lived with the magnificence that befitted their rank and title. During the nineteenth century the aristocracy had progressively concentrated in the city of Palermo, and had continued to abandon the inland estates, which were increasingly leased out through the system of the *gabelle* to *borgesi,* or well-off peasants, who thus became known as *gabelloti.*[6] Absenteeism became even more prevalent during the second half of the century, to the point of being criticized by Sicilian and foreign observers. In Sicily "many of the noble landowners . . . had never visited their estates throughout their lives. They greedily ate the products of that land of theirs, which they had never visited, and there were barons who died without having ever visited their properties."[7]

Political clout and absenteeism were typical of the barons. To confirm this we need only look at the data concerning the size of feudal property and its distribution in Sicily around the middle of the century. At that time one-fourth of the land was public property, while three-fourths was feudal property. But if we consider separately the situation in central-western Sicily and that of the rest of Sicily, we see that four-fifths of public lands were concentrated in eastern Sicily. While 40 percent of the feudally owned land was located in the western part of the island, almost 90 percent of this land was instead feudally owned, without taking into account the properties located in the Palermo territory and those that represented the patrimony of the barons, since these lands, exempt from taxation, were not included in the land registry or the census. And Palermo, a city that in the eighteenth century was on a par with the chief European capitals, had a population of 180,000, almost equal to 15 percent of the island's entire population.[8]

The Disappearance of Feudalism and the Survival of the *Latifondo*

In Sicily the laws terminating feudalism were promulgated later than in the continental South. But it wasn't so much the delay in their promulgation as the substantial lack of their enforcement that resulted, over a long period of time, in the survival of the *latifondo* as the essential structure of Sicilian agriculture. In the continental South the law abolishing feudalism, promulgated in 1806, had immediately been enforced. Instead, in Sicily the law of 1812 was followed by the amendments of 1816, 1817, and 1818, so that as late as 1820 one could not say that feudalism had been abolished.

Abolitionist legislation continued with decrees and laws in 1825, 1838, and 1841, but its effects were few and were different from those hoped for.[9]

> Very few, in fact, were the lands sold by some penniless ex-baron fallen on hard times, and in great part they went to add to the large estates of other ex-feudal lords, or the property of rich *gabelloti,* who had gotten rich in the industry of large farm tenancy; thus the land changed owner but was not fragmented, and so it was vain to hope for the development of a flourishing, industrious, and free middle class.[10]

Even during the first half of the nineteenth century, the formal feudal lands constituted nine-tenths of the total.[11] Thus the *latifondo* remained the nucleus of agriculture and of the Sicilian social structure, particularly in the western section of the island. If at the beginning of the century there had been a movement toward the fragmentation of the land and of property, this movement proceeded spasmodically without continuity, and with frequent halts. Above all there a robust class of small and medium agricultural proprietors was never formed.[12]

The *latifondo* so dominated the agrarian landscape of central-western Sicily that it struck, with its appearance of desolation and solitude, the imagination of observers:

> The fief, that is, the large estate or *latifondo* through which one wanders for days without finding a house, a tree, a blade of grass, a fountain, or a flower that could reveal, I won't say activity and civilization, but the very existence of man . . .

This is how it was described by a magistrate in 1878.[13] And Sonnino, ever the attentive and painstaking observer, gave a description that—though less hyperbolic—was not substantially different.

> One can travel by horseback five or six hours from town to town and never see a tree or a bush. One climbs and descends, now passing through fields, now clambering up steep paths washed away and ruined by the rains; one crosses torrents, passes over the crests of hills; valley follows valley; but the scene is always the same: Everywhere solitude and a desolation that rends the heart. Not a single peasant house. At very long intervals, perhaps at a distance of hours, one finds a farm with an ancient and neglected appearance, built in such a way as to remind one at once of a fortress and a granary. That is the administrative center of some large estate or former fief, which sometimes serves more as a warehouse than as a place of habitation. Along the road one meets some groups of peasants returning from work on foot, or in twos or threes astride a donkey or a mangy and sore-covered mule on which they have nevertheless loaded all their farming tools—that is, the plow and hoe.
>
> However, at the approaches to the town, the entire scene is transformed; at a distance of perhaps one mile, more or less, depending on the town's importance, you find yourself suddenly in the middle of an oasis of olive trees, almond trees, vineyards, and prickly pears; and down below, at the bottom of the valley, you see the dark foliage of the citrus gardens.[14]

This passage perfectly described the condition of the agrarian landscape in central-western Sicily. Even today the agrotowns are located at great distances from one another, interspersed by enormous tracts of land on which there stand only isolated buildings for storing agricultural implements and materials, never habitations. Only at the center of the former *latifondo* are there large clusters of farmhouses, which represent the heart of the rural enterprise. In the middle of the last century the average size of the *latifondo* was between five hundred and one thousand hectares, perhaps closer to the latter than the former. Fiefs of one and two thousand hectares were frequent, and some were over six thousand.[15]

On the *latifondo* we can trace a system composed of five classes: landowners, *gabelloti*, *borgesi*, peasants, and agricultural day laborers. As for the *gabelloti*, originally they were essentially *borgesi* who "had until that time been stewards on the feudal estates, or receivers of stolen goods, or middlemen in the sale of grains or flocks, usurers, or the accomplices of criminals."[16]

The *gabelloti* often took out leases on more than one estate, and sometimes on estates placed at different altitudes due to the exigencies of sheep herding. They therefore represented the upper fraction of the class of the *borgesi*, the fraction that had grown wealthy through large land leasing. As for the peasants, many of whom were farm laborers, the abolition of feudalism, "neither brought about, nor accompanied, nor was followed by any revolution, by any general movement that suddenly changed the de facto conditions of Sicilian society. What had until then been a legal power persisted as a de facto power or tyrannical behavior, and the peasant, considered a citizen by law, remained in servitude and oppressed. The owner of the large estate still remained a baron, and not only in name: According to public opinion, the position of the owner vis-à-vis the peasant remained that of the feudal vis-à-vis his vassal.[17]

Economic Relations and the Social Classes

The abolition of feudalism and the introduction of the principle of land commercialization took place within a framework in which the conditions for change in the traditional conception of landownership and labor had not yet appeared. Nor did the abolitionist laws have the effect of changing this.

The idea of landownership was connected more closely with prestige than with the opportunity for producing wealth.[18] In the second half of the nineteenth century, property was "still considered the authentic form of dignity. The Sicilian landowner contemptuously refuses to sell his land even when he is reduced to extremities by debts or misfortunes. The transfer of a part of his property appears to him as a true *capitis diminutio*, something unseemly for himself and for his family."[19]

This was accompanied by the notion that work was "something shameful and living on an income a sign of distinction. The accumulation of money was . . . less admired than the acquisition of 're-spect.'"[20]

These cultural elements were not typical only of the aristocracy: The *gabelloti* had the same values as the Sicilian barons. For them, too, land was predominantly a symbol of prestige and power rather than a stepping-stone to the capitalistic accumulation of wealth. So it is not surprising that these cultural conditions hindered economic development and intensive exploitation of the land.

Land use consisted of very primitive cultivation—the alternation of grains and natural pastureland. Usually they followed a rotation system that varied from between three and five years, alternating fallow land with one or two consecutive years of grains (wheat and barley), which were followed by one or two years of grazing: The land's yield was very low. Moreover, the system of ownership, of large land leasing, and of agricultural contracts was such as to discourage continuous, stable forms of capital investment in the land. One could not expect such investments to be made by owners who preferred to draw an income from their property by leasing them to the *gabelloti,* who in their turn unloaded all or at least the greater part of the risks inherent in cultivation and production onto the shoulders of the peasants to whom they subleased the estates.

The tenancy contracts were of two kinds, the so-called *metatería* and the *terratico.* The first was a kind of sharecropping contract, the second a tenancy contract with dues to be paid in kind. In both the greater part of the risks fell on the tenant, and so he was never in a position to cultivate the land for a long enough time to make long-term investments in it.

The only difference between *metatería* contracts and *terratico* contracts was that in the former the payment in kind was proportionate to the harvest, while in the latter it was a fixed amount. However, because of the rotation system, and the fact that for at least a year the fallow land was unproductive, the land for grain cultivation was leased for only the one or two years during which grain was planted, because the peasant could not survive for an entire year without crops. As a consequence, there was a continuous turnover of peasants on the various plots of land on which rotation took place. Even if the same peasant had a plot of land to work every year, that plot was never the same for longer than one or two years.

Thus the *metateria* contract did not offer any of the typical advantages of sharecropping contracts, under which, on the contrary, agricultural tools and farmhouse were supplied by the owner, who also had an interest in the enterprise and made sure to choose tenants able to cultivate and fully exploit the soil. Furthermore, the *metateria* contract involved disadvantages typical of all coparticipation contracts.

Since the cultivation of grain can only provide one harvest per year, and some time after the sowing at that, it follows that the peasant required an advance of capital, usually turning to strangers or asking the owner or *gabelloto* for assistance. In both cases whoever granted the loan did so at a usurious rate, often 25 percent for a six-month loan, and, what is more, speculated on the difference between the bad quality of seed he lent and the better quality of seed he demanded in return. Besides the continuous dependency and the shouldering of all the risks of the agricultural enterprise, the peasants had to suffer the high-handedness of those who dealt with the marketing of the product, since they could not do it themselves. To that were added all the tolls and various forms of tributes that the peasants owed the owner, *gabelloto, campiere,* priest, and so on.

The *terratico* contracts, subject to the general rotation of lands on the *latifondo,* were also of short duration, with results similar to those of the *metateria* contracts. So we may conclude with Sonnino that in a situation similar to the one described: "On one hand the peasant earns the minimum necessary for his survival . . . , whereas . . . on the other the form of his contract obliges him to live the greater part of the year not on the daily fruit of his labor, but on loans, debts, almost on charity, subjected to all sorts of abuses and harassments, happy if, having worked and sweated all year long, at harvesttime he can manage to pay his debts without having to sell his mule or his hut."[21]

Defined as "rent capitalism,"[22] this system, owing to its consistent characteristic of the intensive exploitation of the agricultural labor force, placed the peasant in a "condition or situation of almost continuous dependency that robs him of all feeling of moral dignity, and all hope of improving his lot by honest work and thrift. He cares almost nothing for his [work] except for the assurance of receiving assistance when he needs it, nor does he care for the fruit that is demanded from him in exchange for this assistance: He does not count so much on the harvest as on the guarantee that in view of the harvest someone should be interested in not letting him die of starvation, and because of this he resignedly renounces obtaining just compensation for his labors."[23]

Grain cultivation demands massive concentrations of labor during the seasons of the year devoted to sowing and harvesting, whereas during other periods the need for labor is low and the laborers find no work. In addition to this the particular system, management of the estates, leased or subleased, functioned in such a way that in reality the peasants also paid the salaries of the day laborers. Both these conditions, accompanied by the fact that often a good part of the salary was paid in kind, produced a series of mixed configurations in which the ownership or lease of small plots of land existed alongside salaried labor activity.

Contrary to regions of the continental South,[24] on the *latifondo* of central-western Sicily there did not exist a class of purely salaried or hired laborers; or if they did, it was extremely small. This absence proved to be one of the primary causes of the increase in pressure on the land and the competition for its ownership that pervades the Sicilian *latifondo* in the nineteenth century and gave rise to an autonomous industry of violence.

The Violence Industry Becomes Autonomous

The abolition of feudalism essentially favored the landed bourgeoisie and those small segments of the aristocracy that were inclined to transform themselves from feudal lords into members of the bourgeoisie. Ironically for the newly freed peasants, however, it resulted in the loss of common rights that they had secured in the previous social order, while public lands were being progressively devoured by the voracity of the *gabelloti*. But it was not only the downfall of feudalism and the failed commercialization of the land that increased hunger for the land. At the beginning of the nineteenth century, there occurred a demographic shift that brought about an exceptional increase in the number of mouths to be fed. The effect of both phenomena was to intensify pressure on the land: by the peasants, who saw themselves deprived of the traditional rights they enjoyed, without receiving anything in exchange; and by the landed bourgeoisie, whose ranks began to grow immediately after the abolition of feudalism. The pressure exerted by the peasants increased the competition for work but did not find an outlet, so that the peasant's life continued to be at the mercy of the owner and *gabelloto*. The other kind of pressure produced by the continued, progressive acquisition of land, was not accompanied by a substantial transformation of the social relationships in agriculture.[25]

This kind of competition for land was unique in Europe above all because of the absence of a class of farm workers who had a relationship based exclusively on labor with the owners of agricultural enterprise. Not only did this social class fail to develop in Sicily during the period under examination, but, due to the long persistence of relationships of a feudal nature, came about only with great difficulty and in a limited manner even in other southern regions, when the progressive introduction of capitalists engendered a robust class of laborers committed to the struggle against agrarian capital. In Sicily, however, there was no such social class to fight against the landowners and the *gabelloti*. In this situation, while the peasants were intent on establishing stable bonds to the land, the *gabelloti* were not only preventing them from doing so, but were hoarding by all available means larger and larger portions of the land. As a result the social conflict did not appear as a struggle between upper and lower classes but as a competition between groups vying for possession and use of the land.

The abolition of feudalism had opened the doors to the new agrarian bourgeoisie and had given them access to the wealth produced by landownership. But owing to the persistence of land as a source of power, the increase in the number of landowners brought with it also a greater need for violence to protect property. Not only was the market for land broadened, but the market of violence broadened as well. A greater number of people gained access to the land, and thus the necessity of employing violence to defend its possession. And, while the abolition of feudalism unsuccessfully attempted to deprive landowners of the right to mete out justice and preside over public order, it also failed to enact legislative and administrative reforms to transfer authority over the exercise of legitimate violence into the hand of the state. As Franchetti emphasized, the violence market broadened and those who had specialized in its exercise thus became independent.[26]

A sort of moral authority of violence therefore took root as a regulating criterion of social relationships. Not only because traditionally it was the legitimate consequence of land ownership, but also because the emerging social class was composed of individuals who had an interest in the continuation of violence as an instrument for the acquisition of power and wealth.

The expansion of the violence market enabled those who bore title to its use to practice it to a greater and greater extent, no longer simply on behalf of others but also on their own behalf. This was enhanced by the superimposition of legislation that formally abolished private violence and conferred the status of law on a de facto situation in which social relationships were not substantially changed. The abolition of the minimum system of social order that existed before the elimination of feudalism was not replaced by a new public order based on law. Indeed, so long as the barons' right to exercise violence had been recognized, there existed a line separating the legitimate and illegitimate use of violence. That is, the use of violence had been considered legitimate only when it had been exercised in the name of the ancient class that bore title to it. The use of force was then limited and subject to specific rules: that is, it responded de facto to the norms of positive law. With the abolition of feudalism, positive law also changed, and thus came to an end the conformity between de facto situations and legal norms. The new law considered all types of violence as illegitimate save that of the state. However, this process, which was mandated by the Kingdom of Italy, had disastrous effects, because it failed to prevent violence from regulating social relationships. The public authorities proved incapable of maintaining public order.

As a consequence, the old distinction between licit and illicit violence disappeared, and all forms of violence were in the end justified, even if they were formally declared illegitimate. Indeed, a situation was created in which, ironically enough, the public violence of the state was more likely to be considered illegitimate than the private violence of the landlords, new and old. Thus the impact of the national state on the Sicilian periphery, in particular on the central-western part of the island, resulted in violence being freed from any form of regulation that had previously existed. This situation brought about a new definition of the balances among social classes and political forces:

> The importance acquired by the independent class of the lawless had the effect of assuring it the moral authority that any private force able to get the upper hand enjoys in Sicily. . . . Consequently, on the island, the lawless class finds itself in a special situation, . . . since besides being an instrument at the service of social forces existing *ab antiquo,* it has, due to the special conditions created by the new order, become a class with an industry and interests of its own, a social force that stands apart.[27]

This class, which Franchetti calls the lawless class, became, beginning with the abolition of feudalism and in the course of the formation of the Italian state, *part* of the Italian state, part of that local dominant class to which the state's public authority delegated power:

> To the ruling class of such a society the Italian state entrusted: the care of penal justice, of public order, and security by means of juries; the attributes of the police [and] or mayors, and (until 1874) the duties of the National Guard; the administration of the public weal and authority to levy taxes, through the provincial and communal councils; the charitable institutions, in short, local administrations of all kinds; [and] the administration of the public patrimony set aside as credit through the Bank of Sicily.[28]

The conquest of autonomy on the part of the violence industry and the delegation of authority to the dominant local class constituted the preconditions for the failed affirmation of the state's monopoly of violence in Sicily—and thus the essential circumstances for the social affirmation of the Mafia.

Public Order and the Administration of Justice

The Italian state arose as a federation of regional elites with different interests and a variegated political, social, and ideological configuration. Even though the South became part of the national union somewhat later than other regions, the southern elites were immediately in a position to participate fully in government. From this vantage point, it is only partly true that the state was alien to the South, because there it took on features typical of the ruling classes. This determined the emergence of two types of conflict: the first among the different, often conflicting interests of the various regional ruling groups; the second between the law, of which some of the regional elites became proponents, and the interests of other regional elites who opposed these principles. The first type of conflict was resolved on the basis of a delimitation of the territorial jurisdiction of economic interests by each group. This resolution, however, accentuated the second type of conflict, between the law and the interests of certain regional elites. In reality, it was as much a matter of conflicts between the law on one side and concrete interests on the other as of conflicts between diverging economic interests.

Giving carte blanche to the southern ruling classes in the management of their economic interests posed serious problems for the bourgeois elites of the North, since the failed affirmation of the law hindered the growth of precisely those economic interests whose proponents they were. For the southern agrarians, affirmation of law in the South would have meant the loss of their base of territorial power.

The first years of the unified state were beset by serious problems of law enforcement. There were incredible difficulties in affirming the principle according to which the state was the only entity entitled to perform that task. This becomes clear when we consider that these agents of the state had to do battle with two nongovernmental police forces that traditionally existed in Sicily: the mounted militia and the field guards. Both of these groups represented a serious obstacle and a danger to public safety in Sicily, since they were forces that in the past had worked in collusion with the bandits.[29] The field guards were actually private *campieri* who in 1866 had been organized as municipal police. They were employed by the communes but received a salary that came from contributions by the landowners. From 1860 to 1875 they performed police functions in the countryside, where the official police and the *carabinieri* were often isolated and impotent. But this situation was certainly paradoxical, if we consider that as late as 1875 Franchetti maintained: "In the part of the island that is infested by malefactors it is certainly a rarity for the field guards not to be malefactors themselves. . . . Giving the field guards the authority of police agents cannot . . . favor anyone but the malefactors. . . . Far from investing them with authority, it would be helpful to have them closely watched by the police."[30]

The mounted militia drew their origins from the Armed Companies, an auxiliary group of the Royal Police who were set up in 1543 and composed of volunteer formations of armed men. Their task was to maintain public order in the countryside and in the farm clusters, by protecting "the manor and the farm cluster, but on condition of being defended and protected from the legal authority for all the abuses, crimes, and robberies that others committed. . . . Thus the most hardened scoundrels instead of a noose were given a uniform, pay, [and] sometimes a decoration and became the guarantors of public security."[31]

The Armed Companies were abolished in 1837 under the Bourbon government, and their members became enemies of the regime, which they fought during the rebellions of 1848. Subsequently they once again pledged their allegiance to the Bourbons, so that during Garibaldi's dictatorship in Sicily they were disbanded and replaced by the mounted militia, a corps made up of members of the disbanded companies. They brought with them their traditions, which included the so-called system of *componende* (or settlements). Since the recruitment of the mounted militia was entrusted to the private initiative of the corps members, and since they were often thugs and malefactors, the recruitment took place among the very people who committed such crimes as cattle rustling, thefts, and robberies. When a crime was committed, the intervention of the mounted militia, and of the armed companies before that, did not consist in charging and prosecuting the crime's perpetrator but in attempting to retrieve part of the stolen goods, so as to return part of it to its owner, while the remainder was shared by the perpetrator and those who had recovered it. In exchange, the person who had suffered the theft agreed not to go to the police with charges or to drop the charges that might have been brought. This sort of transaction, called, as we have said, a *componenda*, not only created a system of illegal complicity but also brought with it the territorial delimitation of the field of operation of the armed companies and the mounted militia. In fact each of these police forces had jurisdiction over its own territory, but its members acted as mediators in cases where the crime was committed by individuals belonging to other territories. These traditions lasted throughout the first years after unification, so much so that Villari was led to declare that "public safety was entrusted to the Mafia, thus handing society over to it.[32]

To make matters worse, during the first years of the Kingdom of Italy, the custom was to send to Sicily, especially for the police, the worst administrative personnel, who relied not only on local elements but chiefly on those of the Mafia. The prefect of Palermo himself declared in 1874: It is an opinion that in these provinces has . . . to this day the value of an axiom, namely, that without the Mafia it is impossible to do good police work in the city and countryside."[33]

Nor was the situation any better in regard to the administration of justice. And that was not all. Lawyers—by their skill in suborning juries, their ability to mediate through the use of patronage, their habit of finding their way into public offices so as to pick up secrets or influence clerks and magistrates—were among the worst scourges of the administration of justice in Sicily. And then there were the difficulties that derived from the perilous conditions of the courts, the justices of peace, and the people's juries.

In a social situation in which *omertà* ruled and the networks of instrumental friendship were widespread, juries were easily influenced and blackmailed. The large number of acquittals they handed down induced the government in 1874 to propose, in its special temporary provisions for a number of Sicilian provinces, that they be replaced by judicial groups composed only of magistrates.[34] But many magistrates were corrupt or simply mouthpieces of the local ruling class, which protected the Mafia chiefs. As for the justices of the peace, in whose hands rested the power to issue police warnings and to declare house arrests, their activity was made difficult by the isolation in which they found themselves and by their having to rely on the declarations of officials or of citizens above suspicion concerning the good conduct of those proposed for a police warning. (And this was important, since a warning, if ignored, often led to an arrest.) In Sicily it was not at all difficult for a malefactor to procure a certificate of good conduct from the mayor, even from the police commissioner or a respected citizen, because it was all to their interest to protect those who had committed illegal acts. According to Franchetti: "Some of the Mafia chiefs, the most notorious scoundrels in Palermo and its environs, who were about to be given a police warning, quite often were able to find people of considerable importance to speak on their behalf with the authorities, not only because of their wealth and their influence in the island, but also because of their official position."[35]

In short, the administrative and judicial system was organized in such a way that the laws of the new state, "have entrusted local interests to the wealthy population in all places. . . . They have confirmed and sanctioned the dependency of the poor classes on the rich, and they have added administrative to economic servitude."[36]

Land as the Source of Honor

In the South and in Sicily the forty years between 1860 and 1900 saw an expansion of bourgeois landownership. For Sicily it is calculated that bourgeois ownership almost tripled, rising from 250,000 to 650,000 hectares.[37] Two aspects of this expansion are noteworthy: the reinforcement of the economic power of the large landholding and attempts at development in a capitalistic sense of agricultural cultivation on the *latifondo*.

In Sicily the Italian state did not fulfill the fundamental task of responding to the hunger for land and promoting the emergence of a social class of small and medium peasant owners. This failure is revealed clearly in the manner in which the census of assets and properties of the church and the communes, and their leasing in perpetuity or their sale to private persons, was carried out. Even though in the ambit of the general process of the dismantling of the assets of ecclesiastic patrimony, which in Sicily constituted one-fourth of all cultivated land, medium-size landownership had risen here and there,[38] there is no doubt that the distribution and sale of the ecclesiastic mortmain favored the strengthening of the great landowners and the *latifondo*. No benefit, on the other hand, "fell . . . to the class that most needed to improve its condition, the very large class of poor and propertyless peasants. Church land passed entirely into the hands of bourgeois elements, of persons who were already economically strong, who possessed land and large estates."[39]

Indeed, the strengthening of large landholdings took place precisely in those parts of the island where property was least divided, and where the hunger for land and the need to form a class of medium and small peasants were greatest. The manner in which this took place was essentially due to the formation of *camorras* [intrigues] at the auctions of church properties:

> Only the rich could make friends with, and sometimes organize, the *camorras*, which absolutely dominated the auctions. The very fashion in which the auctions were held made it impossible to oppose those coalitions, which aimed at buying up the properties at a low price, or at speculating on the auction, forcing buyers to pay them large sums.[40]

To get some idea of land distribution in Sicily around the middle of the nineteenth century, we can refer to the data in the Bourbon land registry of 1853. According to these data, there existed in Sicily 506,628 registered properties, for a total of 2,400,000 hectares with an average area of 4.73 hectares per property. If the data are analyzed according to size, the following results are obtained:

- small properties (up to twenty hectares) constitute 96.7 percent of the total, with 37.4 percent of the surface; the average area for each of them is 1.83 hectares
- average properties (from twenty to two hundred hectares) constitute 3 percent of the total, with 33.9 percent of the surface; the average area for each is 53.29 hectares
- large properties (more than two hundred hectares) constitute 0.3 percent of the total, with 28.7 percent of the surface; the average dimension for each is 512.13 hectares

A look at the distribution of church assets sold or given in perpetual lease until 1882 reflects a clear imbalance favoring the large and medium properties.[41] Large properties obtained 52 percent of the surface distributed as a whole, whereas the medium-sized obtained 40.6 percent. Small properties obtained 7.4 percent. But this increase in large property is even more apparent in western as compared to eastern Sicily. In the provinces that make up central-western Sicily the distribution of Church lands allotted 55 percent to large property, 39 percent to medium property, and only 6 percent to smallholdings. It was precisely in the traditional areas of the megaestate and the power of the baronage and *gabelloti* that the completion of the process of land commercialization reinforced instead of weakening a traditional class—the local ruling class that represented interests that found in the Mafia one of its forms of expression.

Thus in Sicily, and especially in its central-western section, the development of bourgeois landownership came about through the disinvestment of church property rather than at the expense of an erosion of aristocratic property, which at any rate slowly began to take place toward the end of the century.

The persistence and strengthening of agrarian interests were combined with the incipient processes of capitalistic developments in agriculture. Despite the fact that the *gabelloto*'s profit had a usurious component, his position was potentially that of a capitalist who advanced capital, though, as we have seen, he tended to unload all risks onto the peasants and to nibble away at the owner's profit. Nevertheless, according to a contemporary observer:

> At the margins of the *latifondo,* especially in certain coastal zones, and in proximity to the large centers, there begins to form, at the expense of the *latifondo* itself, a medium and small bourgeois property. Even toward the end of the century this phenomenon does not yet spread as much as it will later on. . . . This new bourgeois property begins to differentiate itself, also externally, from aristocratic property: The new bourgeoisie—though remaining *landed* rather than *agrarian*—follows the cultivation of the land more closely, also adopting for this purpose particular forms of agrarian contracts; it invests a certain amount of capital in the land itself.[42]

The production method typical of the *latifondo* and the social relationships that marked it were so powerful that they also imparted their features to systems that had different bases.

In a situation of this sort the only classes that could act as protagonists in the processes of social transformation were those of the *gabelloti,* the landed bourgeoisie, and those groups that formed the constellation of its interests. Owing to an apparent paradox these classes and their constellations of interest were both subject and protagonist of the emergence of the Mafia as a form of social and land control and as the form assumed in relation with the local political power. There were indeed transformations, but in a framework in which the new classes became the proponents of old social relationships, combining these aspects in a hybrid with original characteristics.

Thus the Mafia sprang from the economic and political interests of the intermediaries who originated in the distant and recent past of preunification Sicily.

The State and the Genesis of the Mafia

Because the Italian state proved unable to guarantee continuous effective control and manipulation of the growing social tensions, this task was appropriated by the lords of the land.

Recourse to violence was certainly nothing new. Now, however, it had not only changed meaning, but in contrast to what had happened in the past, it occurred within the framework of the weak authority of a state that formally held, but failed to exercise, the legitimate monopoly over violence. It therefore compelled the state to come to terms with those who exercised de facto power at a local level and to delegate to them the functions of exercising that monopoly. Indeed, in practice, the state deferred to their authority, for although it officially prohibited private violence, it nevertheless granted the power to govern on behalf of the central government to that same local ruling class that made use of it. So when it became clear that state sovereignty existed only on paper, recourse to private violence became generalized.

The formation of the state did not create any historical ruptures in Sicilian tradition. On the contrary, there was a fortifying of the structural conditions that had given life to the cultural code, and of the cultural code itself. And the Italian state too, instead of breaking up the Kingdom of the Two Sicilies, effectively extended it. Indeed, as we shall see, the creation of a system of national and local representation after 1860 strengthened the tendencies toward structures based on patronage, especially in the "infected" regions—those based on local Mafia power. In the end the state granted the local groups much broader power than that granted by the Bourbon regime and thus "reinforced the conditions conducive to the existence of the cultural code and the social relationships that were at the origins of the Mafia phenomenon.

76

In this sense we may say that the economic basis of the mafiosi as power brokers* finds a correspondence in the rise of broker capitalism. Just as broker capitalism emerged to fill the gap between agricultural production and commercialization, so the mafioso emerged as the power broker who filled the gap between peasantry and the state, by taking over from the latter the management of physical violence. The Mafia thus became, for practical purposes, an extension of the state.[43]

This pragmatic dimension of the Mafia was effectively described by Franchetti and Sonnino:

> So in Sicily the state finds itself in this painful situation, that in fulfilling the prime duty of a modern state, that is, the maintenance of material order, it does not defend the law, but rather the abuses and harassments by one part of the citizenry at the expense of the others. In fact, while the government's action is most efficacious and prompt against popular disorders, it remains miserably impotent against those who, like bandits and the Mafia, are supported by the wealthy class, or at least by its ruling caste.
>
> . . . In Sicily with our institutions, often modeled on liberal formalism rather than imbued with a true spirit of liberty, we have supplied the oppressing class with a means to dress up in legal forms the de facto oppression that already existed before, by seizing all powers through the use of force that was and is entirely in its hands; and now we are giving this class our support to ensure that, no matter to what excess it may carry its oppression, we shall not allow any sort of illegal reaction, while there can be no legal reaction, since legality is in the hands of the class that rules.[44]

*In this paragraph the terms *power broker, broker capitalism,* and *gap* are English in the original text.

5

SOCIAL HYBRIDIZATION

The Mafia that exists in Sicily is not dangerous; it is not invincible per se, because it is a tool of local government.
—D. Tagani, speech at the Chamber of Deputies, June 11 and 12, 1875

Since its origins, the Mafia has been a phenomenon at once rural and urban. The social tensions that arose on the *latifondo* could only be controlled in Palermo. Even before the unification of Italy, Palermo was traditionally the decisive center of life in all of central-western Sicily, because it was the seat of the Parliament that constituted the chief center of the political power of the landed aristocracy and also because, with the great weight of its population and the consumption requirements of the barons, it was the main place of commerce in central-western Sicily.

The state's establishment enhanced Palermo's importance in respect to the countryside both near and far. Palermo continued to be the center in which a great deal of what was produced in the interior was gathered, for local consumption as well as for export. If control of social tensions had to be exercised with regard to the peasants in the countryside, the political instruments used to exercise this control were located in Palermo. In Palermo were concentrated the means responsible for public order, justice, and administration. It was home to those same agrarian landlords whose interests continued to determine the actual configuration of the state's presence.

In addition to economic considerations, social and political factors made Palermo the natural center of the Mafia. Although the landed bourgeoisie, consisting of the *gabelloti,* failed to fully develop capitalistic qualities, and had to rely on force to prevail so did their urban counterparts. Just as on the *latifondo* the *gabelloto* seized key positions in economic life, so in the city brokers skilled in the networks of instrumental friendship tried to monopolize market licenses, concessions for tolls and taxes, and permits for the export and import of goods. For the rest the citified bourgeoisie essentially had its origins in those professions that were typical of a capital city in a portion of the kingdom governed by a viceroy, such as the law, the clergy, and the myriad functions and professions linked to public offices. These included administrators, middlemen, and in general the liberal professions that revolved around the custody and protection of landed property.

Palermo stood out as a city that had very sharp social contrasts. While on the one hand there was the conspicuous consumption of the landowners, a sizable population lived in conditions bordering on starvation. In 1838 Cala Ulloa maintained that in Palermo there lived "forty thousand proletarians, whose subsistence is dependent on the luxury and whim of those in high places."[1]

The city lived on a class of profiteers and a large subproletariat and middle class composed of the free professions and a horde of intermediaries and clerks. The latter were especially numerous, as a result of the concentration of political and administrative functions in the city. The attorney general at the Court of Appeals described the city's situation in 1867 as follows:

> Palermo is a city that has a large population and lacks the means to support it. Palermo—singular phenomenon—is a sea town without commerce; it is a large population center without agriculture and without industry. Palermo is a big city that has lived for centuries on a huge, fictitious, and precarious movement of wealth: the bureaucracy and the courts.[2]

The formation of the Italian state in the 1860s exacerbated Palermo's social tensions. The increase of its political importance was occasioned by the role it assumed in the context of a state that, unlike the Bourbon regime declared itself to be one of law and a promoter of modernization. But precisely for this reason the city of Palermo was deprived of a series of privileges that it had enjoyed as the capital of Sicily under the Bourbon reign. First of all, after the elimination of a large number of political offices, there was an increase in unemployment.[3] The police commissioner of Palermo declared in 1869 that

> Palermo, unlike any other province in the kingdom, including Naples, because of national unification lost a great part of its resources on the basis of which it had collected such a large population, and this population, living a fictitious life of unproductive trades, or personal services, no longer finds the means of subsistence since it has lost those provided by the government administrations that are now dissolved and had been centered here, and also by the courts now scattered through the outskirts in the different jurisdictions.
>
> After a decade this fact is still . . . pulsating with actuality, because no new industry has developed and demanded laborers, nor have large public works given a livelihood to many workers, nor finally, has any part of these many inhabitants tried to find the means of sustenance by emigrating, because of that tenacious sentiment that binds the islander to his land. . . . The discontent is augmented considerably by the starving hordes of clerks who worked in the dissolved administrations and religious corporations and are now without salary and without resources.[4]

And a few months later General Giacomo Medici, prefect of Palermo and commander of the armed forces in Sicily, in a report to the Ministry of the Interior pointed out that administrative and judicial decentralization had deprived Palermo's clerks and legal class of a substantial part of their previous opportunities for earnings, and that to these specific hardships were added those common to the rest of Sicily.[5] Nor were these isolated opinions. The report by the junta regarding the inquiry into the conditions in Sicily in 1876 emphasized:

> The new decentralized institutions condemned numerous clerks whom the elimination of their offices left unemployed to take up new occupations and often a less comfortable life. The political life and the improvements brought to the provincial cities by administrative freedom caused a number of rich families to leave Palermo; the new taxes forced others to be less open-handed with their dependents; and finally the abolition of the convents and the seizure of the church's assets put an end not only to the employment of numerous parasites who lived off those administrations, but also to the infinite number of charities and free foodstuffs, to which the plebs of Palermo to a great extent owed its easy life.[6]

Becoming part of the national state therefore also brought about a worsening of living conditions. This is attested to by the disorders that took place in 1866 and the abysmal state of public order that existed during at least the first fifteen years of the new Kingdom of Italy. Thus a whole series of specific developments contributed to a greater maturing of the mafioso system more in the western than in the eastern section of the island, and more in Palermo than inland. In his inquiry into conditions in Sicily, Sonnino clearly described this relationship between Sicily's hinterland and Palermo:

> We believe that in the conditions of the hinterlands we can historically pinpoint the prime cause of the deplorable moral conditions in the ancient capital and its environs, as well as in the remainder of the island; that the Palerm[o] Mafia still draws support and sustenance from the conditions of nearby provinces of the interior; and that unless the ills in those provinces are cured, it will at the most be possible to suppress with an iron hand the Mafia's criminal excesses everywhere, but it will not be possible to extirpate the evil plant at its roots in or outside Palermo. The evil is general, and its symptoms are also present everywhere; *but the historical conditions peculiar to Palermo, as ancient capital, center of the government and all its administrations, and place of residence of the nobility and the great landowners, have contributed to ripening the boil, here rather than elsewhere, and to give it a specific form of suppuration.*[7]

The Mafia and Palermo

But what particular conditions determined the Mafia's emergence in Palermo? On the one hand they can be identified with the fact that in the city political and organizational conditions merged so that the industry of violence became autonomous. On the other they can be traced to the availability of individuals who, as a result of social dislocation, were ready to become the day laborers of violence.

There is no need to emphasize further the wretched conditions in which the people lived: The lack of work for the greater part of Palermo's population, living on alms or charity under the Bourbons, the effects of the decentralization policy, and the elimination of numerous administrative offices by the new state resulted in spectacular population displacements. A good part of the population became available to be hired by the violence industry whose principal organizational and management corps were located in Palermo. In fact, conspirators in Palermo arranged

> many of the acts of banditry to be committed in the hinterland. And it is in Palermo that a good part of the profit from these acts end up. . . .

It is also one of the centers for fences for stolen goods. . . . This can easily be explained by the fact that for the greater part of the year the city is the residence of many important proprietors of the land overrun and dominated by the bandits; it is a notable center of business and wealth; and finally [it is] the seat of important civilian, judicial, and military administrations, of whose procedures and intentions the male-factors need to be minutely informed, and with which they must be continuously in contact, and over which they must have influence.[8]

The reasons why Palermo became the central point of an autono-mous violence industry can be traced back to the diverse nature of its relationship with authority. On the *latifondo* the management of vio-lence, though still connected to ownership of land, rested de facto in the hands of the old and new proprietors. The former, mostly absentee, administered the land through the *gabelloti,* who in great part coin-cided with the latter, that is, with the newly emerging landed bour-geoisie and with the bourgeoisie of the free professions. This last group held title to the monopoly of private violence. Competition for title to the exercise of violence was at most an intramural one that took place among a few powerful families who exercised social control over the peasant masses.

The peasant masses could avail themselves of three choices: resign themselves to their fate, become the armed extension of the landown-ers, or, finally, rebel by becoming bandits. The last phenomenon was extremely rife in the Sicilian countryside, as it was indeed in the entire South for a relatively prolonged period after 1860.[9] The *gabelloti* effi-ciently managed power and authority relationships because the chief political and administrative functions of the local government came to be concentrated in their hands or in the hands of the small intellectual and professional bourgeoisie hitched to the cart of the landowners' interests. A further consequence of this state of affairs was the reduced dimensions of the market of violence, which was accepted more out of a necessity to submit to power than out of an awareness of the advan-tages to be derived from its exercise. Consequently *omertà* was also less widespread and socially less legitimized, as proved by the fact that it became possible to defeat the bandits who thrived in the countryside when the state, though with many doubts and uncertainties, decided to make it clear that its title to the monopoly of physical violence left no room for discussion. And in any case the presence of banditry pointed to the existence of a social fracture that somehow reflected the latent class conflict between peasants and lords, even though these conflicts were not fully expressed and the lords often used banditry against the peasants. As Franchetti underlines:

> in the provinces, the interests of the violent class are identified and merged with those of specific persons. Consequently these interests, which are predominant, and which are materially and morally imposed on the entire population, are those of specific individuals who have interests in common, or are divided into two, at the most three, adversary camps. The man who uses violence to react against those who are predominant will take their place if he proves to have greater strength; if he is weaker, he is defeated and destroyed. The man who makes use only of the law inevitably remains the weaker and is also destroyed, and, if the victors declare him to be despicable, that's just icing on the cake. Consequently each person, in his struggle, can if he wishes use not only his violence but the law's as well, without risking a collision with the fixed and immutable obstacle of custom and public opinion. Because there are no other violent persons who in the interest of a class will claim and sanction the application of the code of *omertà,* except for the members and followers of the opposing party. . . . Thus it is not certain that the code of *omertà* will be respected, except for the not very frequent instances of struggles between professional malefactors. . . . As a result in the provinces the rules of *omertà* have made an impact on public opinion only to the extent that they favor the strongest; they are only valid when in their favor and not [when] against them.[10]

In Palermo, however, power and authority relationships were in much greater disrepair than they were in the provinces. With the demise of the traditional subordination-solidarity relationship that bound the feudal lords to the urban populace and that manifested itself in the obligation of assistance; with the increase in the deterioration of the population's living conditions; and, finally, with the creation of a new class of speculators and intermediaries who did not feel a moral obligation to respond to any demand of solidarity toward the lower classes, a social situation was created in which no class was in a position to maintain the monopoly of power and authority relationships. Certainly the old class of the barons—which lacked the economic and social basis essential to exercise such a power, and which had been deprived of the basis of political power typical of the Sicilian baronage under the Bourbons—could not hold the monopoly. Nor could it be conquered by the new emerging middle class, which traditionally did not have an autonomous power base since it performed a role of mediation between barons and plebs, and which was gradually linking up with the new organs of the state and the functions performed by it. As a result no class in Palermo was in a position to affirm its economic interests absolutely, while the weapon of violence was within the reach of anyone who was able to demonstrate that he knew how to use it effectively. All this was accompanied by a greater "moral density" of the social conditions that favored the emergence of an autonomous industry of violence, and which consisted of the combination of the displacement* of a large part of the population and the absence of a class that could monopolistically control the exercise of private violence. Thus the prevailing interest— the interest that was in fact protected to the greatest extent—became in Palermo the interest of those who ran the industry of violence as an autonomous profession. And since a considerable percentage of the population was involved, the code of *omertà* became more widespread there than in the provinces and the *latifondi*. In this regard, too, Franchetti's analysis is illuminating:

> In Palermo . . . the single common interest that unites the lawless in a constant manner is the preservation of their class as such—in other words, impunity in the exercise of violence, whatever its purpose might be, against the forces meant in general to suppress it. The rules of conduct that prevailed in the lawless class and were imposed by them materially or morally on the rest of the population are rules that by the nature of things are effective in protecting the use of violence, and like all other rules that have a special character, set aside the momentary and immediate interests of individuals—indeed, are often in conflict with them. Hence the code of *omertà* in Palermo does not allow for exceptions, and in actuality suffers few of them. [11]

Only the state could have resolved this disruption of the relationships of authority by taking over title to it. But the political and administrative structures created by the Italian state both at the level of the peripheral branches of the central administration and that of local government, instead of defeating the Mafia, by their very nature sanctioned its propagation and its success.

The State's Difficulties in Gaining Administrative Control

From its very formation the Italian administrative system, especially in the South, was weak and ineffective. This was so, despite the fact that the new state badly needed to exercise control over the periphery with

*The word *displacement* is English in original.

very strong measures, in order to avoid the emergence of social problems. After all, the liberal and Cavourian elite with the loyalty of the local—in particular the southern—elites, joined forces in their attempt to unify the nation. And they also needed to bolster what they discovered throughout the South to be an anemic and disintegrating civil society. Local politics appeared there as "profoundly deprived of vitality and, if not undifferentiated, certainly resting on individual personalities rather then on clearly defined groups that might constitute even a potential embryo of modern political parties."[12]

However, the ability to overcome the structurelessness of civil society and the meager potential for autonomous political and social organizations, could not be entrusted to the spontaneous initiative of the local ruling class. This class was in no position to enforce a political-cultural hegemony over the masses. Since its power was based on the exercise of violence, it was substantially vulnerable.

Thus the central liberal elite opted for an administrative system patterned on the French model, in which the only form of decentralization was the bureaucratic one, accompanied by political and administrative centralization. The prefect was the guarantor of this centralization, and of control over local political life. Nonetheless he was not someone who could bring about the interministerial unity of the administration in the French manner, because—unlike what happened in France, where the prefect exercised control over the territorial activities of all the ministries—his control embraced only the courts and the local administration. The upshot was insufficient administrative integration between center and periphery, and insufficient control by the state at the local level.[13] But if there was a paucity of administrative penetration, it was accompanied by the government's strong political control over local political life. The prefect was in fact an agent of political control; his appointment was political, and so were the forms of control he exercised as emissary of the incumbent government. These functions took the concrete form of

a systematic work of supervision and suffocation of local political life, an assiduous and painstaking intervention that constantly and systematically transformed the representative of the state into a representative of the government, and the representative of the government, in his turn, into the executor of the will of the political party in power.[14]

The prefect maintained contacts with the provincial leaders, protected the interests of the government in various ways, selectively transmitted to Rome the applications he received after evaluating them politically, organized election campaigns on behalf of the incumbent party, and manipulated elections by the most varied means, from promises of help to threats and even assistance in the organization of alliances among the candidates.[15]

The sensitivity of administrative institutions to the political pressures of local interests—a general characteristic of the Italian administrative system in the South—assumed special characteristics in Palermo. Here the traditional dominance of landowners, even when compared to the rest of the South, and their connection to the groups that emerged with the rise of the industry of violence, played a decisive role in bringing about the infiltration of Mafia groups into organs of the state. The lack of administrative control resulted in the fact that "in 1860, these very same people who previously by the nature of things enjoyed de facto authority have now also been given legal authority within the judicial, administrative, and political order."[16]

"Those very same people," namely, the landowners, were closely tied to those who exercised violence as a profession. But the former were no longer in a position to exert any control over the latter. So in order to have at its disposal violent men who would protect its interests, the ruling class was forced to allow the entrepreneurs of violence to operate also on their own behalf and in their own name. Consequently, even when the entrepreneurs of violence acted autonomously and in defense of interests connected with perpetuation of the industry of violence itself, they were protected by the arms of the law and administration controlled by the ruling class:

> Whoever agrees with the Mafia is safe; whoever commands it is the master of an extremely large force and can maintain order or promote a revolt. . . . Public safety was entrusted to the Mafia, thus putting society in its hands, and this system, which unfortunately was adhered to for a long time, strengthened the organization whose destruction was desired.[17]

So Villari bitterly concluded his observations on the Mafia.

But the dispersed administrative system and its lack of penetration had the effect of favoring the affirmation of the Mafia not only directly but also indirectly, by contributing to a considerable extent to the formation of the patronage system in the local governments on the periphery. In fact, the dispersed character of the administration resulted in the bureaucracy being subject to the influence of pressures from local special interest groups. This had as its effect a distortion in the attempts to introduce an impartial and modern administrative system in the South. Therefore, from its very emergence the administration of the state remained subject to local interests and pressure groups and was unable to assume a national bureaucratic character— that is, impartial regarding special interests.

Patronage as an Instrument of Local Government

The patronage relationships of the time had features in common with mafioso-type relationships. It was in fact an ensemble of one-to-one relationships (similar in this to the structure of the Mafia *cosca*), each of them characterized by a client's subordination to a patron. This subordination was based on inequality. Between client and patron there existed a barter-exchange relationship because the patron possessed certain resources and guaranteed that he would use them to help the client, while the client in exchange pledged fidelity to the patron, abstention from acts that displeased him, and use of his vote as the patron indicated. In this sense the patronage relationship was reciprocal but not symmetrical. Furthermore, it was an all-encompassing kind of relationship since the obligations of protection and fidelity on the part of patron and client respectively were not restricted to certain spheres of individual behavior but tended to color all its aspects. Finally, the relationship was institutionalized, because precise social sanctions were applied for transgression of the obligations that derived from it. The patronage chain therefore endured through time and was reinforced by institutions meant to create a solidarity based on relationships of ephemeral equality: This explains the emergence of the godfather phenomenon. Thus the exchange relationship, besides being based on reciprocity, had an emotional component that served to compensate for the inequality between the individuals involved.

Traditionally it has been thought that patronage relationships were the result of economic and political backwardness. This explanation, however, revealed itself to be untenable when it was discovered that patronage relationships exist and characterize the political systems of countries that cannot be considered backward from either a political or an economic standpoint. A more acceptable thesis is the one that considers patronage not as a particular instance of political relationships but as the natural and spontaneous form of such relationships. Patronage is, in fact, the most "natural" form of association for both the voter and the political party. It is so for the voter for two reasons: first, because it is the easiest form of behavior, the one to which one most spontaneously has recourse; second, because voters are not autonomous actors but are largely conditioned by the parties that ask for their votes, and therefore are conditioned by their eventual patronage methods. But patronage is also a simpler and more profitable form of association from the political party's standpoint. In fact the patronage method is the one that entails the lowest cost and the greatest benefits: Material resources are much more easily manipulated than appeals to nonmaterial and symbolic motivations that constitute the basis on which are erected the ideological associations founded on alternative methods. Obviously the advantage of the patronage relationship depends on the availability of material resources. And in this regard, the question is not why patronage exists, but why there are situations in which this "spontaneous and natural" tendency does *not* arise. In fact, these situations exist when the parties cannot freely make use of resources and of the public administration. In order to understand the genesis of patronage it is therefore necessary to examine the historical period in which bureaucracy in the modern sense of the word came to be formed in the national state.[18]

According to this thesis, the structuring of the political system into patronage forms springs from the relationship between reform of the bureaucracy in a legal sense and the mobilization of the masses. For patronage not to arise, (1) there must be a reform of the bureaucracy in a legal direction; (2) this reform must be promoted and supported by a bloc of social forces in a position to oppose the propensity of politicians to make arbitrary and partisan use of the administration; and (3) the reform of the bureaucracy must have been completed when the political mobilization of the people takes place through universal suffrage and the formation of popular political parties.

In Italy these conditions arose only partially, and furthermore they were not uniform throughout the national territory. The dispersed character of the state's peripheral administration heightened its vulnerability when confronted by local political pressures. Wherever, as in the South, bureaucratic reform with a legal intent remained only on paper, due to the nonexistence of a bloc of forces able to oppose successfully the pressures to use the public administration for special-interest groups, the administrative system fell into the hands of local cliques. Despite the facts that popular political parties had not yet formed and the political mobilization of the people had not yet taken place, this fostered the emergence of the patronage system and, in areas where the local chiefs had strong ties to the industry of violence, it resulted in the orientation of the local political system in a mafioso-patronage direction.

This orientation was reinforced by the use of the communes as centers of autonomous power.[19] By concentrating all power in the mayor's hands, the creation of institutions of local autonomy intensified the struggle for the conquest of local power, thus strengthening the importance of clients, who were considered the sole effective instrument for the capture of the municipalities.

The installation of a patronage or mafioso-patronage system at the periphery had repercussions on popular political participation as well as reinforcing the public bureaucracy's tendency to resort to patronage. Patronage certainly did not favor political participation. As has been observed,[20] in the South the two parties that fought each other at the local level (both composed of the petty bourgeoisie) did so not on the basis of ideological or programmatic disagreements but simply because one was composed of people who had been able to obtain public employment and the other of those who were endeavoring to obtain it. The victory of one of the two parties meant the ousting from employment of members of the other. It was a sort of spoils* system that certainly did not favor the development of a conception of the bureaucracy as an impartial entity. On the contrary, the possibility of getting ahead in a career lay in tying oneself to a faction or party and in allowing the obligation of factional solidarity to prevail over one's duty to be impartial whenever a conflict arose between the two. As Alongi pointed out, members of the mayor's party

> are certain to obtain whatever they wish, while the opposition has reason to fear every sort of harassment. The former are immediately given certificates of good conduct, they are less heavily burdened by local taxes, they receive a seat at the great banquet of communal assets, charitable organizations and contracts. . . . While for the latter matters proceed quite simply in the opposite direction.[21]

Thus neither the peripheral administration system nor local-government administration was able to act as intermediary between local society and the state. The introduction of the institutions of local autonomy concentrated political resources in the hands of a few powerful local people or in the hands of those beholden to them, resulting in an intensification of competition for the conquest of

*English in original.

power at the local level. This competition could only unfold in a patronage and special-interest form, due to the characteristics of the groups that took over local government. Political life therefore assumed the aspect of a competition for power on the part of the clients. In fact attaching oneself to a group of clients was the only available way of protecting oneself from the consequences of an abusive, discriminatory exercise of power. And this obviously was all the more true in the case of the Mafia groups: "The Mafia group often hides behind political-administrative guises, so that the need to join, cordially or out of fear, a group of clients, or, as they say here, a party, becomes necessary—indeed, I should say, almost indispensable.[22]

Patronage, which arose as an instrument of social control in the absence of political participation, was certainly not the instrument best suited to promote that participation. The bulk of the population was therefore excluded from a relationship with the state, and their integration was entrusted not to political-administrative means, but to the patronage-inspired management of local power. In central-western Sicily this resulted in a powerful intertwining of Mafia and political power, at the local-government level as well as that of the peripheral branches of the central administration. And in any case the Mafia groups, trained by instrumental friendship to move skillfully through its networks, certainly did not feel uncomfortable navigating the meanders of state administration. In the brief span of Sicily's first fifteen years after unification the intertwining of the Mafia and the state powers had become so widespread that it could be documented in the course of investigations undertaken by the government and in parliamentary debates:

And so the government, in trying to gain the sympathy of local elements, sees its concessions turned against it, and where it tries to make the ruling class its instrument, it becomes instead its instrument; to the point that, if at times it seems to have any strength at all, it means that it has fallen into the hands of a local party. . . . Hence in Sicily, the state finds itself in this . . . situation, so that in fulfilling the first duty of a modern state—that is, the maintenance of material order—it does not protect the law, but rather the abuses and harassments by one part of the population at the expense of another. In fact, whereas the government's intervention is most efficacious and prompt against popular disorders, it remains wretchedly impotent when it comes to dealing with those disorders, such as banditry and the Mafia, which are based on the affluent class, or at least its dominant section.[23]

The Mafia thus found in the structures of the state a fertile ground from which it drew nourishment for its thriving existence. The picture that emerged less than ten years after unification was one of overwhelming desolation, at least if we are to judge from the reports that the military authorities forwarded to the Palermo prefecture. Corrupt and inefficient administrations, easy prey to the Mafia, were numerous. Most of the mayors and communal secretaries looked to their own affairs and made private use of the local administration.[24]

During the first forty years of life in Sicily after unification we can identify three stages in the genesis of the Mafia. The first stage covers the first fifteen years in the new state's life—that is, the period from 1860 to 1875—and it marks both the formation of an administrative system tied to local interests and the emergence of the Mafia as a phenomenon distinct from banditry and political opposition. The second stage has its turning points in 1876, with the coming to power of the left, which attached great weight to the deputies from the South, and 1882, with the first extension of suffrage. The third phase centers around 1894, when the first type of peasant-class organization, the Sicilian Fasci, brought to light what has since become one of the Mafia's typical traits and one of its traditional hallmarks; that is, not to remain indifferent to social transformations.

The Crystallization of Mafia Power

The opposition that the unified Italian state encountered in Sicily was neither of small account nor was it limited to certain political and social sectors. On the contrary, a multiplicity of forces closed ranks against the new state, organized in varied alignments that ran from pro-Bourbons to clericals to republicans, and the latter in turn comprised at least three different groups: the followers of Crispi, those of Mazzini, and the anarchists; and, later on, the first members of the Socialist International.[25] The opposition, at first complex and undifferentiated, was in any case widespread and public authority was morally isolated.

> The government's administration is similar to an encampment at the center of a society all of whose arrangements are founded on the presumption that public authority does not exist. . . . Lost at the center of a universal conspiracy of silence and deceptions . . . the authority casts about for some support and clings to the first it finds; it relies on the

abuses granted it by law, and it seeks its salvation only from these same abuses.[26]

In short, there was a situation of general dissatisfaction, as a magistrate stressed in 1867:

> As many times as the country has been afflicted by the grave catastrophe of a popular uprising, the restoration of order has been undertaken by persecuting a political party. But what is the point of fighting a consortium in which the revolutionary element has neither a banner nor a principle of faith but is simply the result of general dissatisfaction? Where the people in order to revolt wait not for a *program*, but for an *occasion?*[27]

Because it was based on a situation of general dissatisfaction that embraced all social classes, the opposition was particularly hard to fight. Dissatisfied, "were not only peasants and workers, whose iniquitous living conditions all the government functionaries on the island could not help but stress in their reports, but also the entire clerical class, damaged both in their professional interests and as pure and simple consumers; dissatisfied was a good part of the old ruling class, that would not adjust to the new mores and expressed through Bourbonism and clericalism its attachment to the ancien régime and its protest against the centralized and suffocating unified government."[28]

In about 1865 there appeared two further phenomena that helped to hasten the development of a socially autonomous group of entrepreneurs of violence—that is, the Mafia. These were differentiation among the parties of political opposition[29] and the deterioration of the general conditions of public order in western Sicily.

In 1875 the government confronted the problem of public order in Sicily by proposing special laws for the island. During the ensuing parliamentary debate the deputies on the left opposed the special laws, pointing out that the government of the right had governed the island by oppression and by offending its traditions and customs. It was further emphasized that the roots of the Mafia could be found in government offices, and that the system of permitting known malefactors and criminals to enter the police in order to control crime had opened the door to abuses and corruption in the public administration.[30] The rightist proposal of extraordinary measures for public safety in Sicily was approved, but was stillborn from the outset and in 1876 was definitively shelved.

Political Imprimatur

With the coming to power of the left, a process of political legalization of the Mafia began. This was one natural outcome of the progressive co-penetration and identification of mafioso and public power at both the peripheral and the local-government levels. While it continued to apply the methods of government typical of the right, on the other hand also the left stressed the patronage-oriented use of the administration and public good.

> The left . . . had contracted many political and moral debts during its sixteen years of struggle against the right. It could pay them only at the expense of the public weal, at the expense mainly of justice and legality. Favors and rewards therefore began to rain down on friends, clients, and creditors in the form of jobs, concessions of all kinds, honorific titles.[31]

The left's advent to power had the effect of increasing governmental interference and omnipotence as a system. The power of direct intervention by the minister of the interior in local affairs and control over the local government were extended by laws that authorized the minister to grant loans to the communes or placed in his hands the control of entrepreneurial and productive activities. In these circumstances "the role of the deputies as a conduit between the power of the government and that of the local patronage groups [became] more systematic, indeed it facilitated the economic and political ascent by groups formed on the basis of patronage in the ministerial and governmental system."[32]

The development of cliques and *cammorillas* (secret societies) in the communal and provincial councils had already been described by Francesco De Sanctis, the writer and critic, who remarked that

> [in them were formed] associations of people having the same interests, which—whatever sort of mask they hide behind—are true associations with criminal intent, or, if you prefer, [people] who will *eat with anyone*. They look upon those who are shocked by this with a certain characteristic smile, as though to say: Poor in spirit, they do not know the world.[33]

The partial expansion of suffrage in 1882 helped to strengthen this system. The fact that suffrage was expanded, though only to a limited degree, contributed to the institutionalization of the patronage-client links between deputies and voters.

> A few years after representational government was introduced into Sicily, the Mafia *cosche* immediately understood the great advantages they could draw from participating in political and administrative elections. Their participation became more effective and active after [promulgation of] the laws that expanded suffrage and gave the right to vote even to members of the *cosche* and to the classes in which they can exert the greatest influence and enjoy more prestige.[34]

So Mosca summed up the process that had brought the mafiosi personally to enter political competition. And while Colajanni declared that, after the coming to power of the left

> the Mafia spirit no longer sprang exclusively from the authoritative sources of the police, the prince, the big landowner, the *gabelloto,* the *campiere,* the *armed guards;* but onto these sources was grafted, and, over them often prevailed, the influence of the deputy and sometimes that of the mere candidate, who always set store on being (and calling himself) governmental.[35]

Mosca also maintained, however, that

> wherever the Mafia is strong it is impossible for a candidate to win a parliamentary or local election unless he promises [the constituency] his protection. The Mafia therefore has its patrons in the Senate and in Chamber of Deputies, and uses them for political ends and even worse; and the government entertains relationships that can easily be imagined with the great mafioso electors; the bands have full freedom of action; they have the authorization to carry arms, which is denied the most honest citizens; and they know that discreet extortions will not be hindered provided the opposition voters are intimidated at election time.[36]

The process of the Mafia's political legalization has consequences of great importance. According to Romano, "during this period . . . *the Mafia . . . evolves . . . in the sense that it becomes a system of real power groups* that influences and conditions political life, especially through the electoral system, the appointment of deputies, and the support given to government ministers."[37]

The first of these consequences was the growth and expansion of the Mafia groups' sphere of economic intervention. The Mafia's "normal" economic activities increased as a result of the opportunities offered by the state's formation. We have already seen how the action of Mafia groups at the auctions of church assets had powerfully contributed to the formation of bourgeois and Mafia landownership. Public works and government contracts also constituted a fertile terrain for their intervention.[38]

A second important consequence was the full-fledged entry of Mafia groups into political life as active protagonists rather than simple intermediaries or brokers. We only have to read N. Colajanni's charges to understand how the groups of Mafioso power had become an integral part of the political-administrative system:

> In order to judge this mechanism in its entirety one must see it in operation in political and administrative elections. . . . The communal councils are dissolved on the eve of political elections; the persons who make a commitment to support the *government* candidate are appointed royal commissioners.

The Mafia entered this mechanism as a protagonist. Mafiosi who had been arrested "were set free when they could be trusted to work for the government candidates." And Colajanni's conclusion was that "this degenerate political system not only generalizes and consolidates the spirit that gives birth to the Mafia; but it is often expressed directly through the Mafia and for the Mafia, which is in itself and for itself considered and recognized as a criminal association."[39]

The importance of the assumption of political and governmental functions by the mafiosi must be emphasized. In fact, inasmuch as they were brokers, the members of the Mafia were expected to avoid directly taking on political posts. Their mediatory functions could be better performed if they acted informally, without completely identifying with any of the interested parties. This informal status made it possible for them to make explicit the ambivalence that constituted the basic premise of their activity as social intermediaries. If the mafiosi took on public political functions, it meant that their power position was so secure that there was no fear of endangering the basis of their activity and the sources of legitimation of their power. In this sense we might say that by the end of the nineteenth century the Mafia firmly represented part of the civil and political society of central-western Sicily and of its links to the state.

The assumption in their own name of political-administrative functions by mafioso groups, together with their activities as power brokers, did not take place only on the local level. This is the period in which the Mafia expanded not only as a local power group but with national ramifications. The combination of economic activities with penetration of state agencies on the level of local political representation and in Parliament brought about the formation of a broad network of Mafia connections that reached beyond the confines of Sicily. Astuteness in the use of the law for partisan purposes tended in great part to replace violence as a means of exercising power. Violence tended to become a weapon of last resort.

In the Notarbartolo case of 1893[40] we find, in a condensed form, most of the ingredients that would constitute the leitmotiv of relationships between Mafia organizations, and economy, finance, and politics. In this case a group of highly placed people appropriated the administration of the Bank of Sicily and used it—something neither new nor particularly original in the climate of Italian bank scandals during those years—for purposes of speculation and fraudulent business deals. The Marchese Notarbartolo, a man of absolute integrity was prepared to denounce the scandal and embezzlement but a politician, a member of Parliament, and a communal and provincial councilman in Palermo, together ordered Notarbartolo's murder. They had a mob of accomplices and an even larger mob of people who acquiesced in the crime. Deputy Palizzolo, charged with the murder of Marchese Notarbartolo, was first found guilty by the Bologna Court of Assizes and subsequently acquitted for lack of evidence by the Florence Court of Assizes.[41]

But if at this point in its development the Mafia could be interpreted only in terms of economic and power relationships at the national level, it was also true that, as Mosca himself recognizes, the conditions for homicide ripened in Palermo because its moral climate was most suited to the carrying out of assassination—a climate in which a totalitarian and all-encompassing power competed with that of the state and at the same time represented one of its principal instruments of action. Competition and collaboration with the state coexist in the Mafia.

The Mafia and the State:
The Deceitful Game of the Parties

The problems that faced the state agencies in Sicily when it came to the control of public order were resolved by seeking the support of the local ruling class and by entrusting it with the power to maintain order. If this fact was already observed in 1875, when the political and parliamentary representatives of the Sicilian ruling elite were to a great extent in opposition, complicity in the state's identification with the Sicilian agrarian landowners and mafiosi would become even more apparent beginning in 1876, when they became part of the parliamentary majorities.

The episodes of banditry during the first sixteen years following unification, and their almost abrupt disappearance at the time the Sicilian elites became part of the government's majority—without any special measures having been adopted for public safety in Sicily, and precisely around 1875 when the conditions of public order had worsened due to the combining and intertwining of the problems posed by the Mafia, banditry, and political opposition—constitute exemplary proof of what has been stated above. According to Blok:

> Banditry flourished until 1877, shortly after the admission of the Sicilian elite to Parliament . . . [when] it lost a great part of its usefulness for the Sicilian upper classes. So that, deprived of the protection of the large estate owners and their numerous Mafia clients, the bandits were left out in the cold and easily fell prey to the army.[42]

The protection and cover granted the bandits by the landowners for orienting their activities in an antigovernment direction were in fact well known. However, the network of interests created around banditry was not confined to the landowners:

> Around the bandit springs up a network of interests: the rich proprietor and the powerful man who want to satisfy their arrogance and lust for power; the bourgeois who must lease estates at a modest price and destroy the competition; the speculators in the cities who organize the black-mailing of wealthy people; profiting from a lion's share of the extortions; and finally the shepherds and peasants, who as a reward for their faithful spying receive gifts in money or livestock.[43]

The left was a knowing supporter of these interests. Baron Giovanni Nicotera, minister of the interior in the first Agostino Depretis government in 1876, knew quite well and cynically admitted that an in-depth operation against the Mafia and banditry would have alienated a great part of the electoral support that the left enjoyed in the South and that was the basis of its national power.[44]

Thus the operation was aimed at striking low, safeguarding the upper reaches of society, and inflicting damage on banditry and not on the Mafia. Though the network of interests that had protected banditry lost its effectiveness beginning in 1877, it was not dissolved and moved on to protect the Mafia.

The result of this process was the emergence of Mafia groups that were put in charge of functions of social control. The control demanded by the latent conflict between landowners and peasants was taken over by Mafia groups for both their own purposes and those of the landowners.

The Mafia's functions of social control are not expressed only through violent repression. The control consists essentially in muffling the intensity of social conflict. In the performance of this function specific importance is assumed by the positioning of Mafia members as power brokers. This gave rise to the characteristic ambiguity of Mafia power, whose basis is to be found in the dualism between state and popular morality that is a particular feature of the ethics of the Sicilian population[45] and is expressed by the general conviction that state regulations are in reality formulated and utilized in favor of the interests of private individuals who, because of their strength and power, turn them to their own advantage. Consequently, whenever state and private norms come into conflict, the latter prevail because the former are not endowed with a higher moral validity.

Contempt for the state's laws and functionaries is typical of Mafia members, who are often able to corrupt the latter and with impunity defy the former. At the same time, however, the Mafia connives with the authorities and with the local ruling class on whose behalf it often exercises control.[46] Its contempt for the laws of a state considered alien and oppressive characterizes it symbolically as an expression of the resistance and needs of the local society, and supplies social legitimation of its activities as the guardian of order. But the pragmatic relationship that the mafiosi have with state authority qualifies them in the eyes of the latter as authoritative exponents of local society. In this manner the activities of mafiosi groups that manipulate norms and values typical of two different spheres legitimizes their existence in the eyes of both and facilitates their establishment and deep roots in Sicilian society.

This ambivalence is matched by an analogous ambivalence on the part of the state, which sees the members of the Mafia as enemies since they represent a competing power and as allies since they contribute to the maintenance of order.

The Process of Social Hybridization

The Mafia emerged as the periphery's answer to the impact of the center; but it would not have been able to succeed without the latter's support. The utilization of mafioso power by the state authorities points to the fact that the mafioso phenomenon must be set within the framework of the system of alliances between social classes and political interests realized at a local level, but in order to survive and succeed it must go beyond the local political system and set itself in a medium composed of national political balances. In Sicily the regional alliance of the agrarian bourgeoisie, the intellectual petty bourgeoisie and the aristocratic estate owners can be based only on the Mafia's repression of the peasants. But for this repression to take place with impunity, it is necessary for a national alliance to be formed between the various regional elites that contribute to the formation of the national state. So the Mafia, born of the state's inability to exercise legitimately the monopoly of violence, struck social roots for reasons broader than those that have defined its origin. The causes of the persistence of the Mafia phenomenon are not identical with those of its genesis. The phenomenon acquired its own autonomy, which guaranteed its reproduction and impeded its uprooting.

What are the reasons for this ability of the Mafia to endure, to adjust by changing shape while often succeeding in becoming more pervasive? It has been pointed out that one of the fundamental behavioral models of the Mafia groups is initial resistance to the introduction of social change and then, when this change appears inevitable, exploitation of it for their own ends.[47] This, too, can be considered a matter of ambivalence and perhaps the emblematic example is the attitude of the Mafia groups vis-à-vis the movement of the Sicilian Fasci.

It has long since been documented how together with the police, and perhaps to an even greater and more ferocious extent than the former, the Mafia carried out the suppression of workers involved with the Fasci. According to Romano:

A certain number of riots and killings that took place between the end of 1893 and the beginning of 1894 were the work of mafioso groups in the communes that defended their hegemony and indeed their despotic power in the local administrations. . . . If in fact some of the deaths in those disorders were caused by the intervention of the troops, who used firearms, the others were caused by groups of guards in the service of

99

the Mafia chiefs in the communes. . . . In certain places the victims had been caught in a crossfire . . . the bullets shot by the troops . . . and [those] shot by the field guards.[48]

But while suppression was within the customary mode of Mafia group behavior, more interesting, though less documented and perhaps less widespread, was the attempt by Mafia groups to become part of the organization of the Fasci. Despite the fact that police reports tend to exaggerate the presence of ex-convicts in the ranks of the Fasci movement in order to discredit the organizations and justify their suppression, there is no doubt that in certain places Mafia Fasci were formed. Romano discovered:

> Several workers' societies that had been founded during the period in which Crispi was minister of the interior . . . were nothing else but electoral organisms run by the mafiosi, having changed their names to workers' Fasci. . . . In the province of Agrigento the mafiosi leaders of several organizations of existing political societies had put themselves at the head of new associations that were called Fasci.

Romano concluded that "a number of mafiosi had entered the Fasci or had organized some for purposes of local struggle, above all for the conquest of the communal administration, to a degree in all provinces."[49] To this we must add that Blok in his work on Contessa Entellina [renowned fief-holder] found that some of the local Fasci were in fact ruled by mafiosi, such as the organization in Bisacquino, famous as the birthplace of Vita Cascio Ferro and his friend Nunzio Giaimo.[50]

Certainly Mafia groups have always run into difficulties at moments of intense class struggle. Their recourse to open repression proved their inability to manipulate open class conflict. But this is indicative of the extremes to which the Mafia groups will go in their work of social control. The example of the Mafia Fasci is not only further proof of the Mafia's capacity for pragmatic opportunism but also of its being the expression and emerging tip of a social class: "the new rural bourgeoisie, [which] made use of the legal or illegal methods of feudal landlords and at the same time of the most modern commercial systems of agricultural capitalism."[51] In other words, it was a social class capable of blending old and the new when it was impossible to resist social change.

Another of the many examples of this mode of behavior is resistance to the introduction of the cooperative movement among the peasants and, subsequently, to the organization of cooperatives by the Mafia itself. Don Calò Vizzini, one of the principal "big guns" of the Sicilian Mafia during the first half of the century, began to organize agricultural cooperatives among veterans of World War I. He was also intent on this activity after World War II, in the fiery climate of the class struggle of Sicilian peasants and farm laborers,[52] and he succeeded in disrupting the peasant movement by using a typical organizational tool of the traditional Socialist type.

One of the consequences of this behavioral pattern was the utilization of new institutions for the realization of traditional values. On the one hand, modern institutions were modified and instrumentalized for different purposes from those for which they originally arose. On the other, traditional values did not disappear; they were not replaced by new values but adjusted to the traditional use of new institutions. This process of social hybridization, in which the Mafia was perhaps emblematically both agent and result, constituted the basis of Mafia power and its extraordinary capacity for persistence and reproduction. To better understand this process we should dwell on the example of the cooperative organization promoted by the Mafia chief. He succeeded in blocking a cooperative founded by the peasant movement, establishing his own. The peasants who saw their initiative fail depended on him for their survival. Those who would be admitted into the cooperative perceived their admission not in terms of a normal economic transaction but as a form of the unconditional concession of benefits. The person who felt thus benefited was described as one who "becomes his protector's man in the feudal sense of the word; he has somehow received from him a life in a fief and, from then on, is readily at his service."[53]

What are the consequences of the persistence of this precontractual conception[54] of economic transactions and their blending with relationships typical of a market economy? The characteristic of the unconditional concession of benefits is that no specific counterservices are asked of the recipients of the benefits. But in a social environment like that of central-western Sicily, which is based on personal relationships and on the power of private force, the vagueness of return service is translated into a perennial ability to demand proofs of ethical obligation—that is, symbols and guarantees of fidelity and loyalty. From the individual who has received a benefit one can therefore obtain an unspecified series of services, ranging from a vote for a candidate to the murder of an enemy.

Thus economic functions and functions of social control and political power fuse together in the mafioso obligation. As a social entrepreneur the mafioso combines old and new values by continuously converting the resources available to him in the circuit of kinships and friendships into economic and political activities. He converts resources of one kind into resources of another, and by so doing acquires control over other individuals, those he has benefited, with the result of multiplying the resources at his disposal. In fact, counterservices based on fidelity are a perennial credit, a sort of IOU with an indefinite due date, but the sort that can be called in repeatedly and at any time.

Paradoxically, the inability of Mafia groups to institutionalize their power beyond a single person and his charismatic qualities became the foundation on which the strength of the Mafia power system rests, since it allows for adjustment to new situations.

The inability to become institutionalized in the form of a bureaucratic or traditional enterprise is in fact the condition that allows for the constant self-renewal of the Mafia universe in terms of new groups and emerging individuals, who push aside those who are no longer able to understand the reality of the times. The continual change of the Mafia groups is a condition of the survival of the Mafia system as such.

These characteristics explain why members of the Mafia were able, even from the beginning of their establishment in central-western Sicily, to adjust to processes of social change and economic transformation in a society that, even though it did not develop in an industrial direction was far from being static and showed instead a certain dynamism in economic enterprises.[55] The constant adjustment of this behavioral model to the changing historical conditions has been the Mafia's strength. This strength had already struck root in Sicilian society at the end of the last century. It is not by chance that the practice of kidnappings for extortionist purposes was never much used in Sicily by Mafia groups, whereas it has been one of the main characteristics of the *camorra* and of the *'ndrangheta*. Unlike the latter, the Sicilian Mafia was not only an expression of the regional ruling classes but had also deeply penetrated and become a part of society. The historical demonstration of the difficulty of eradicating the Mafia is given by its quiescence during the twenty years of fascism and its sudden reemergence in new forms after World War II.

III
EVOLUTION

6

HIBERNATION AND REAWAKENING: FROM FASCISM TO THE POSTWAR PERIOD

To defeat the Mafia in its men but above all in its mentality, prestige, intimidating strength, and economy, . . . to eliminate . . . the system of necessary mediation due to which the citizens could not or did not know how to approach the authorities except through intermediaries . . . then to receive, as a favor, also that which was their right.
—Cesare Mori, *Con la Mafia ai Ferri Corti*

The Integration of the Periphery

During the first twenty years of this century, the Mafia power system had already been fully established. It was the periphery's twofold answer to the principle of the land's marketability—that is, to the introduction of the market system—and at the same time to the formation of the national state.

The resistance of the Sicilian landowners—which first became apparent during the long process of the abolition of feudalism, and subsequently in the survival of their power and their integration with the leadership of the new state—testifies to the traumatic effect that the principle of commercial use of the land and the regulatory policies of the national state had upon them. The emergence of Mafia groups was the result of the attempt by the Sicilian ruling class, which consisted of the new landed bourgeoisie and the absentee landlords, to introduce into the market a principle of heteroregulation based on violence. But at the same time they are the result of the attempt to avoid a direct relationship between the peasant masses and the new state, by setting up gate-keeping* functions vis-à-vis the peasants. These answers permit the emergence of entrepreneurs who accumulate a capital of violence on which their legitimation in terms of honor is based, and of resources that consist in the network of instrumental friendships on which rests their legitimation as power brokers.

The full introduction of the principle of market self-regulation would deliver a decisive blow to the power of the Sicilian landlords, which historically was founded on the sovereignty deriving from possession of title to the land. The resistance to the introduction of the principle of the marketability of the land by methods of usurpation, fixed auctions, and so on, helped maintain the power of landownership as the chief axis of Sicilian society, especially in the central-western section. At the same time it contributed to the strengthening of a class of intermediaries that came from among the *gabelloti* and the overseers in charge of the large estates, who exploited the absenteeism of the proprietors and the state agencies to assume mediatory functions. This class, the new landed middle class, was not in a position to propose and promote a different type of development for Sicilian society. Though it was autonomous enough to impose itself as the pivot around which center and periphery revolved, its interests were nevertheless linked to the persistence and reproduction of the system that, by sustaining the individuals among whom it mediated, favored the continuance of the conditions essential for its existence.

Incapable of realizing directly the integration of the peasant masses and of assuming the monopoly of legitimate violence, the Italian state de facto delegated both these functions to the local ruling class and the Mafia. This meant the intensification of those aspects of ambivalence in the social system that had been typical of Sicilian society since the time of the Spanish domination—that is to say, the combination in an absolutely singular manner of the principles typical of a market economy and society and of the principles that—on the contrary—are rooted in a feudal conception of the relations between individuals. This combination in turn became fertile ground for the growth of the Mafia groups, which were in their element since they were the chief protagonists of the processes of social hybridization. The coexistence of different principles regulating social action was brought to light in the most acutely contradictory forms in the conflicts between aspects of economic

*English in original.

106

and political action and aspects of social action, tied to the solidarity system. While the former seemed to be inspired by more modern concepts, the latter remained anchored to archaic views and modes of behavior. In particular, a system of solidarity that stood outside the family, kinship, artificial kinship (godfather relations), or instrumental friendship had difficulty in asserting itself. The persistence of solidarities centering essentially on these types of relationships shackled the peasants when it came to the formation of collective associations that went beyond the "natural" limits of primary relationships, thus severing the bonds of subordination/devotion toward the landowners and their Mafia intermediaries. The basic homogeneity of the solidarity structures that inspired both peasant culture and the Mafia groups determined their substantial similarity and facilitated Mafia activity. At the same time this coexistence of different principles of action—while it was a crucial factor in the inability of Mafia groups to become rooted in institutionalized forms and therefore to pass stably to legitimate economic activities stripped of forms of power alien to the marketplace—was also the basis for the reproduction of the Mafia power system and the ability of Mafia Groups to adjust to social change.

Eloquent proof of this facility for social hybridization was seen in the wake of World War I, when social upheaval was caused by contact at the front between southern peasants and the northern working class, by the return of the veterans, by the exacerbation of the land problem, and by the emergence of political and trade-union organizations typical of the workers' movement. From this upheaval there emerged new Mafia chiefs, among whom the most prominent was Don Calò Vizzini, who introduced new methods in the maintenance of Mafia power, employing the weapon of cooperative organizations usually associated with the peasant and farm laborers' movement. Thus was amplified the gamut of the Mafia's activities—already fully involved in economic operations on a large scale—while its process of expansion on a supranational level had begun more than thirty years before. Through overseas immigration, bonds had long since been formed between the Sicilian Mafia and American organized crime,[1] which would later stamp the Mafia as a multinational crime organization and which today constitute one of the chief conduits for international drug traffic.

The increase in activities and the emergence of new Mafia groups were accompanied by a situation of profound social upheaval and a reshuffling of Mafia groups. The emergence of young pretenders to the Mafia's well-established thrones in general led to the increase of internecine struggles between Mafia groups and the resultant bloodshed.[2]

Despite these events, however, which strikingly returned the Mafia phenomenon to the forefront of national attention, the Mafia power groups were so deeply rooted in society as to have taken on directly, and in the first person, positions of political responsibility at the local and national levels, as had already been demonstrated by the Notarbartolo case and as Mussolini himself was able to see during his visit to Sicily in 1924.[3]

The Politics of Suppression

At the time of the advent of the Fascist regime, the Mafia was going through one of its characteristic cyclical phases of transition between old and new groups whose consequence was an increase in crime. But besides this, more general reasons induced the totalitarian organization of the Fascist state to fight the Mafia. The first of these was the need to gain the support of the Sicilian landowners who, after a few years of suspicion toward the regime, soon decided to support it, at first obliquely and later openly.[4] The reasons for this support could be found in the guarantees that Fascism offered with regard to the maintenance of order and the suppression and prevention of any "Red perils" of the kind that had erupted in northern Italy in 1919–20 and that, though only skin-deep in Sicily, represented a considerable danger to the Sicilian landlords. To assure this support it was necessary to undertake open suppression of the Mafia, something in keeping with the principles of the Fascist organization of the state. To begin with, the regime could not tolerate competition for the control of violence; besides, the state had to maintain a reputation of strength by guaranteeing order and by preventing private groups from controlling violence in the name, and on behalf, of the state. To these two reasons was added a third, which sprang not so much from the necessity to affirm state authority as from the need to ensure that the Fascist party was the sole intermediary between the population and the state—a requirement that was, of course, incompatible with the mafiosis' traditional mediatory role.

The suppression of Mafia and bandit activities that took place from 1925 to 1928 had its antecedents in actions conducted from 1916 to 1922 by squads of provincial police that, originally set up to fight cattle thieves, were used with considerable success against the Mafia in the Madonie and Caronie areas. The programmatic objectives enunciated by Prefect Cesare Mori—the regime's executive in the 1925–28 operation, who, together with Police Chief Battoni and Commissioner Francesco Spanò, had previously coordinated the operation in Madonie—therefore had their basis in that experience. The Fascists had to prove that they were stronger than the Mafia on its own terrain—that is, in terms of the concepts of honor and the use of force; they also had to use to the state's advantage whatever was positive in the idea of *omertà;* and last they had to shatter the mediation system in which the mafiosi specialized.[5] All this induced the regime not to hesitate even at the prospect of attacking precisely those groups of new, young mafiosi who had emerged after World War I and had been the most eager to support Fascism.

These new Mafia groups, whose leaders and representatives to a large extent belonged to the rural middle and small bourgeoisie, had at first put themselves at the head of soldiers' and veterans' cooperatives and then, faced by the decline of the popular movement, had become supporters of nationalism and the Fascist squads.[6]

The suppressive actions against the Mafia began in 1925 with Prefect Mori's well-known ordinance, which established measures meant to strike at all forms of Mafia mediation, doing away with cattle rustling and clandestine slaughtering and subjecting to strict control and rigorous regulation those activities from which Mafia members could emerge.[7]

This preventive campaign was accompanied by forthright suppression, carried out by a series of roundups. On the grounds that the Mafia was an association conspiring to commit crimes (a definition not provided for at the time in the penal code dealing with Mafia activities), it followed that mafiosi were in a perennial state of flagrante delicto; hence the judicial justification for the roundups, technically motivated by the urgent need not to allow reported criminals to be able to escape. Often the roundups were conducted with methods worthy of a siege, encircling entire communes and arousing the hostility of the population. In the course of one of these episodes, during which a number of fugitives were sought, their families' houses were surrounded, with instructions to allow entry to everyone and to follow anyone who came out. Communication between the fugitives and their families thus severed, three days later the fugitives had not yet given themselves up. This was "a sort of minisiege," reported by Mori himself, who—realizing that the fugitives were not turning themselves in—forcibly transferred their families to Palermo, where they were quartered in charitable institutions. In the end the fugitives did give themselves up. "Their families—the prefect concluded—after a very short vacation in the city, quietly returned to their homes."[8]

The result of this huge police action was a notable decrease in crime in the province of Palermo. The criminal statistics, some of which were quoted by Mussolini in praise of the operation, emphasized the fact that in the province of Palermo between 1922 and 1928, homicides had dropped from 223 to 25, robberies from 246 to 14, extortions from 53 to 16, and thefts of livestock from 51 to 6. For the same area during the same period, there had been a decrease in the number of permits issued to carry firearms.[9] Even if the regime was able to claim victory by proving more mafioso than the mafiosi, defeating them on the terrain of honor and violence, Mori himself was probably aware that the struggle against the Mafia could not stop with the suppression of the low echelons of the Mafia groups. However, the policeman's logic clashed with the political logic of the regime. Mori was able to strike at several important names of the high Mafia, such as Don Vito Cascio Ferro, who was in 1909 suspected of having killed Joe Petrosino, the New York policeman pursuing him, and was sentenced for the crime of smuggling; also sentenced were a provincial councillor at Caltanissetta and a well-known Palermo eye doctor, Deputy Alfredo Cucco, a Fascist official accused of having ties with the Mafia.[10] But when the prefect began to target sectors, individuals, and groups that could not be touched, with the chance of spoiling the balance established between the regime and the local Sicilian potentates, his actions were judged dangerous and the regime dismissed him.

The Mafia Goes into Hiding

Like all the operations of Mafia suppression conducted on a pure police basis, the one carried out by the Fascist regime—though characterized by its amplitude, generous deployment of means, and long duration—was fated to eliminate the phenomenon's outward manifestations while leaving its social roots intact. Fascism monopolized the use of violence and deprived the mafiosi of the conditions of their existence as mediators, replacing the electoral system by the single-party system. Thus the political foundations of Mafia power disappeared but its social foundations remained untouched. Indeed, the reinforcement of the economic position of the large landowners accentuated the social imbalances whose existence, at the end of World War II, gave rise to the most intense expressions of class conflict in Sicily since the unification of Italy.

The first and perhaps most important outcome of Mori's repressive campaign in Sicily was the pegging of agrarian income at levels greatly higher than those that existed before. By means of a system of ordinances following the verification of tenancy contracts that were extorted or at least based on rates greatly below the value of the properties, Mori rescinded and renewed the contracts, which, together with the police action against the mafiosi, freed the landowners from the burden of Mafia mediation. Their economic position was strengthened, thus they applauded the action undertaken by the prefect.[11]

The police suppression of the Mafia was essentially aimed at protecting large estate ownership, that is to say the members of the class whose dominance in Sicilian economy and society had given the Mafia its first impulse. It is obvious that, the totalitarian state and Fascist party having guaranteed the repression of the peasants, the landowners were more than happy to free themselves of the Mafia burden; they did in fact achieve the same guaranteed agrarian income that they obtained under the Mafia system, but without having to pay the heavy price of mediation.

The police operation also brought with it protection of the high Mafia of the landowners, while the new Mafia that had gradually emerged between the end of World War I and the early twenties was in part eliminated, some of its members finding places within the system by entering the ranks of the Fascist party and the regime's various organizations. These, by their political control, replaced the market of violence that was one of the principal means of social mobility in central-western Sicily. As a result, during the Fascist period the Mafia became latent. The Mafia groups operated in the guise of a landownership that no longer needed to have recourse to private violence since the direct protection of its interests had been taken over by the state and by many important and petty party officials who pulled the strings of political life on the local level.

If one considers the Mafia simply in terms of rural crime, then Fascism took its place as a less costly form of defense of the *latifondo,* which was not only left intact but even fortified.[12] This fortification took place not only through pegging agrarian income at higher levels but by leaving intact the social power of the local potentates and allowing them to acquire political power at a local level. In fact, the abolition of the electoral system removed the political basis of the system, on which was founded one of the essential functions performed by the power brokers, but it also permitted a new form of undisturbed monopolization of local political power—the system of appointments controlled by the Fascist party organizations. Whereas electoral competition allowed for renewal, albeit in the form of a succession of Mafia groups, the new system produced a concentration of political power in the hands of the most powerful family or families at the communal level, which of course included the landowners, the rural bourgeoisie, and the intellectual petty bourgeoisie. As Pantaleone reports, "we only have to glance at the roster of Fascist officials in Sicily to see how many leading groups in western Sicily were almost exclusively composed of the surviving landed aristocracy, Mafiosi, or well-known Mafia lawyers."[13]

Since the main political positions were in the hands of the local potentates, the power of the great families—the very same families that had always given fodder to the Mafia in order to defend their own interests—was not even touched, a game that was to be partially repeated for the nth time upon the collapse of the Fascist regime.

So Fascism shattered the Mafia's front, because it protected its top leaders and destroyed or integrated its rank and file. But for the destruction-integration of the Mafia to endure not just for the brief span of Fascism's twenty years, what was needed was a radical solution of the land problem and thus of the social conflict between peasants and owners. But when the conditions arose for this to be possible, during the struggle for land after World War II, the Mafia groups had resumed their freedom of action precisely when the conflict between peasants and owners had become more intense. The Mafia had been given the opportunity to emerge from its latent state and to reorganize, before the traditional foundations of its power were eliminated.

Sicily After the War

The Allied occupation of Sicily began on July 9 and 10, 1943, after overcoming fierce resistance from Italian and German troops. Sicily was therefore peripheral to that complex series of events that—between the fall of the Fascist regime on July 25 until the liberation of Italy on April 25, 1945—led to the emergence of the social forces and political alignments that would become the framework of the Italian republic. However, two characteristics of Sicilian liberation had an impact on the subsequent social and political struggles and the reemergence of the Mafia. First, the liberation of Sicily took the form of occupation by Allied troops. Sicily was liberated without the active contribution of its population, save for cases of passive resistance, sabotage due to dislike of the Fascist regime, or support given to the American landing and occupation.

Second, Sicily's liberation occurred when the Italian government was still officially at war with the Allies, which meant that—until the government of Marshal Pietro Badoglio negotiated an armistice with the Allies—for a time Sicily had no government with which the Allies could work. The occupation commanders solved the problem of governing Sicily by turning to the most authoritative local forces—those who were willing to cooperate, who expressed anti-Fascist sentiments, and with whom it had been able to communicate even before the landing, through Sicilian-American connections in the United States and Sicily. The speed of the Allied occupation of Sicily, the lack of the political and social forces that in Italy would organize the Resistance, and finally the support that the Allies gave to the dominant social classes, helped to strengthen those very classes, who dominated the early years of political life in Sicily after World War II. [14]

Among these social forces the *latifondisti,* the Sicilian agrarian class, were once again the dominant organized group. The period between 1943 and 1950 marks the last attempt by the Sicilian agrarian and *latifondista* class to affirm its political predominance, first through the separatist movement and later with its entry into the Christian Democratic and right-wing parties.

At the time of the Allied occupation, the landowners were strong locally but weak at the national level. Fascism—with such measures as reclamation of the swamplands, the "battle of the wheat," the agricultural contracts that unloaded all risks onto the peasants, and finally with its struggle against the Mafia—had bolstered the landowners' power base as the ruling political class at the local level. The Sicilian agrarians, who—as early as the first years of the unified state and then subsequently, starting with the advent to power of the left—had played an important part in the political direction of the state (when they did not have its actual leadership), had completely lost this function during the twenty years of Fascism. This was essentially due to two factors: the totalitarian principle of political representation exclusively through the national Fascist party made it necessary for those who wanted to assume leadership positions to go through party channels, thus it became impossible for the landowners to be represented by the liberal-conservative current that had traditionally expressed their political interests. Moreover, the favor with which the Fascist regime was viewed by the Sicilian agrarians had severed the bonds between them and other southern intellectuals of a liberal-conservative tendency, who traditionally had been the cultural proponents of the southern agrarian class.

To these causes of weakness were added preoccupations concerning the possible collapse of the agrarian bloc's power bases. Even though Fascist agricultural policy had substantially supported the large estate, in 1940 the final measure concerning the Sicilian *latifondo*—that is, the collective agricultural tenancy—had aroused considerable apprehension among the Sicilian agrarians. In fact, it did not constitute an immediate danger for the large estate owners, for it did not undermine the ownership of the land; furthermore, even though it introduced the sharecropping principle, it entailed heavy burdens for the peasant tenant.[15] The owners showed, however, that they were not pleased by the measure. They feared that the peasant and his family might settle on the shared-out land, thus introducing the principle of dividing the land among the tenants for long periods of time.[16]

In this situation once again, as in the aftermath of 1860, the Sicilian ruling class chose to take a position opposing the state. The Sicilianist tendency reemerged in an acute form, as a separatist political movement demanding that Sicily become an autonomous state in the most varied guises: first as the forty-ninth state of the United States, then later as a personal union of the crowns of Italy and Sicily. Contrary to what had happened during the years after 1860, opposition to the reconstitution of a unified state was strong, and the separatist movement gained considerable political importance. Popular dislike of the Italian state induced part of the population to identify with separatism and its illusory slogans, which promised that Sicily's separation from Italy would bring the island wealth and prosperity.

Finally, the Allied military government, needing local support in order to govern, was forced to find it among agrarians, separatists, and mafiosi. The Mafia groups' renewed autonomy of action was an additional element contributing to the intensification of political and social conflicts in Sicily. Against this background the Mafia would in its turn find ample room for its powerful reestablishment.

With the Agrarians for Separatism

In various ways the Allied occupation of Sicily favored the reemergence of the men of respect out of the forced inactivity in which the Fascist regime had constrained them.[17] True enough, the "big guns," such as Don Calogero Vizzini, had had troubles during Fascism, but they had never been harassed very much; Don Calò himself had been placed under police supervision in 1925, but after that he had lived undisturbed.[18]

When the political-military situation in Sicily changed as a result of the Allied occupation, the mafiosi were able to come forward and take over again the positions they had lost during the previous twenty years. The Allies were eager to appoint to local-government positions those who were believed to have opposed the national government and at the same time enjoyed authority in the community. As a result many mafiosi became town mayors in occupied Sicily. Don Calogero Vizzini himself was appointed mayor of Villalba only twenty days after the landing and a few days after American troops had taken his village. [19]

As mayors the mafiosi resumed their time-honored functions as brokers between the Allied government and the population. But it was not only this position through which the mafiosi once again began to exercise their traditional function. They acted as interpreters at the military command posts; they held (as Vito Genovese did at Nola) important jobs and performed important tasks that once again gave them the opportunity to place themselves at critical junctures of the relations between political authorities and the population. "Mafia elements had infiltrated all [levels] of the new administration; they held public posts and found themselves in the most favorable situations to control the movement of goods and the means of transport."[20]

As a result the mafiosi were enabled to perform once more a mediatory function that extended from the political to the economic sector. The war economy had opened up incredible opportunities for rackets and black marketeering, into which the Mafia element plunged head-first, taking advantage of their privileged position vis-à-vis the Allied occupation government.

The extent of the impunity and protection enjoyed by the mafiosi is reflected in the investigation conducted by an agent of the American army in regard to Vito Genovese, who had returned to Italy to escape charges brought against him in the United States, and who had become one of the undisputed chiefs of the underworld during Fascism and up until 1944, when he was arrested. After his arrest a series of pressures and murky episodes came into play, which proved that Genovese—despite being responsible for thefts from Army warehouses and being accused of receiving and transmitting information damaging to the American army—still enjoyed considerable support in high places. For more than six months after his arrest, Genovese was not formally charged, and the agent who had arrested him was unable "to find anyone willing to help him bring this man into court. . . . There is no doubt that everything began to move more easily only after the death of the principal witness against Genovese."[21] The episode came to an end nine months after his arrest with his leaving for the United States, where he would end up reacquiring his freedom.

To these opportunities, offered by the black market and by the important positions in which they had been placed by the Allies, was added a third for the mafiosi—that is, the emergence of separatism. In its development a number of points must be stressed that can contribute greatly to a comprehension of how the Mafia reemerged during the period following World War II.

In the separatism episode, the differences between eastern and western Sicily once again leapt to the eye. In eastern Sicily the separatist movement at the first assumed, under the leadership of Antonio Canepa, populist and leftist traits, and it is not by chance that contacts were made with the Italian Communist Party in order to agree on common actions, that is, until Canepa was killed. In western Sicily the movement's leadership was from the start in the hands of the large landowners, who will later on constitute its actual political backbone.[22] With the defeat of its left wing the separatist movement increasingly became a manifestation of the agrarians, whose basic weakness it exposed.

In fact the Sicilian landlords had never been in a position to oppose the state's central elite with the support of the peasants. And this is the fundamental reason why in Sicily, despite the recurrent stirrings of an independence movement and the strong Sicilianist ideology, there have never arisen the conditions necessary for the formation of a party of the agrarian right or a party of territorial defense with national functions and representation. The agrarians have always chosen to enter the state through executive positions, and because of this they have always needed a class of mediators that could guarantee the peasants' political fidelity and lack of insubordination. At the end of the Fascist regime, and as soon as the war was over (in Sicily but not on mainland Italy), they had lost their positions of national representation and had not gained hegemony over the peasant masses, which in any case they had never had. Thus, with the separatist movement, too, in order to insure their presence in the civil society, they were forced to resort to the use of the Mafia and banditry. Only with the help of the Mafia and bandits would they be in a position to organize a form of guerrilla warfare or at any rate a sort of military counterpower to the state. The Mafia groups, Don Calogero Vizzini first among them, seized the opportunity offered by separatism; once again a central, mediatory, role was given them through the performance of liaison activities in which they had historically specialized and that they had temporarily lost during the twenty years of Fascism. In any event, the separatist movement was the only banner under which they could freely circulate despite the prohibition of all forms of political activity decreed by the Allied military government. And Vizzini, though he did not represent the province of Caltanissetta, where there was no branch of the independence movement, became part of the movement because of his importance as a Mafia chief.[23]

The position of the mafiosi groups, however, was not confined to simple support of the separatist movement; as usual, they again began playing on more than one table while maintaining a certain autonomy vis-à-vis their allies, an autonomy that guaranteed the amplest possibilities for maneuvering among the different forces and permitted them to switch from one alliance to another. Thus Don Calogero Vizzini, while part of the independence movement, was already an informer for Police Inspector Ettore Messana, who later on would play such an important role in the episode involving the bandit Salvatore Giuliano. Calogero's nephew, who succeeded him as mayor of Villalba in 1944, was a member of the Christian Democratic Party, and Don Calogero himself went so far as to offer exponents of the Italian Communist party "permission" to open a branch at Villalba,[24] in an attempt to apply to the Communist party the old but effective and tested method of instrumental friendship and of swallowing mass movements and organizations in the patronage and mafioso networks. But meanwhile there arose the peasant movement for land, which would force the Mafia to use not only the weapon of mediation but also that of violent repression.

The turning point would be marked by the shoot-out that occurred on September 16, 1944, when the Senator Calogero Li Causi, a prominent member of the Italian Communist party in Sicily, during an election rally at Villalba, became the target of a Mafia attack with pistol, rifle, and even hand grenades. Li Causi continued to speak, even though wounded, until he fell down unconscious.[25] For the Mafia the Villalba episode meant its entrance into the thick of the peasant struggle, forcing it to play a complex role among the disparate forces of separatism, banditry, emerging mass movements, and the new political parties being formed in Sicily during those years.

The Struggles for the Land

As late as the mid-forties, the distribution of landownership in Sicily did not substantially differ from what it had been for years. Also unchanged were three basic traits: the predominance of the *latifondo,* the meager distribution of medium-size landownership, and the increased fragmentation of small property.

The data published by the National Institute of Agrarian Economy (INEA) in 1947[26] showed that ownership in Sicily exceeding fifty hectares amounted to 39.3 percent of the entire agricultural and forest surface of the island. The true and proper *latifondi*—that is, properties measuring more than two hundred hectares—made up 26.5 percent of the total surface. The medium-size property, measuring between five and fifty hectares, amounted to 27 percent.

These figures were consistently below (by six to seven percentage points) the national average. But the simple average statistical data cannot give an adequate picture of a reality in which the weight of the *latifondo* was overpowering. In Sicily, at that time, "282 proprietors with more than five hundred hectares of land owned . . . 249,581 hectares, that is, 10.6 percent of the entire land and forest surface,"[27] with an average area of 885 hectares each. In 1947, in the commune of Contessa Entellina, bordering on the provinces of Agrigento, Caltanissetta, and Palermo, properties measuring more than one hundred hectares, which in 1900 amounted to two-thirds of the entire agricultural and forest land of the commune, still measured 47 percent, whereas the *latifondi* measuring more than two hundred hectares amounted to one-third of the entire surface. In 1946 the largest fief (and one of the largest in Sicily) measured 2,078 hectares, equivalent to 16 percent of the entire surface, and was the property of a single family.[28]

In contrast to this continued concentration of *latifondo* property, an increased breakup of small landed property took place. Properties of up to five hectares composed exactly one-third of the entire agricultural and forest surface, but "it was pulverized into 1,184,588 separate lots with an average surface per lot of 0.66 hectares."[29] According to calculations based on the 1936 census, four-fifths of agricultural workers did not possess even a handbreadth of land—that is, they were impoverished peasants.

It is therefore not surprising that the principal problem after the Allied occupation of Sicily was that of land distribution. The hunger for land was spurred by the large number of poor peasants and by the relatively low number of day laborers that from the very beginning characterized the Sicilian movement for land reform, unlike what happened in other regions of the South, where day laborers were in the majority.[30] This resulted in a greater frequency of peasant revolts, which, though present throughout the South, appeared in Sicily in an exacerbated and recurrent form starting in the second half of 1943, and then again in October 1944, December 1947, and thereafter.[31]

To better understand the role of Mafia groups in the struggle for the land in Sicily—a role that as always included the twofold roles of repression and mediation—we should examine the first phases of the struggle, which revolved around the three decrees issued in 1944 by the then Minister of Agriculture, Fausto Gullo, a Communist. By the same token we should consider the overall results of the struggle.

Of the three Gullo decrees, the third, which covered the procedure for elimination of the civic use of land and the division of public lands in favor of the peasants, had no impact whatsoever in Sicily because the problem of public lands did not exist there. More important was the decree concerning the sharing of the products from improperly supervised sharecropping, from tenancy, and from coparticipation (that dealt also with modification of these agreements). But most relevant was the decree that mandated the concession of uncultivated or badly cultivated land to the peasants' cooperatives. The effects of these two decrees in Sicily were quantitatively and qualitatively broader and deeper than in other regions of the South. Because of this the peasant movement in Sicily assumed, as early as the period 1944–47, greater scope and importance than in other southern regions.[32] The consequences of the implementation of these decrees were manifold. Even though the nature of the tenancy contracts did not change, there was a substantial diminution of income from the land, which decreased from 30–35 percent to 20–25 percent.[33] What is more, the interests of affluent peasants came into conflict with those of the landowners.

By favoring the concessionaire in the division of the product, the Gullo decree set the large estate and the medium-size farm at loggerheads, helping to align the latter with the well-off and average peasants.[34] Thus the economic foundations of traditional Mafia power were under attack. At the same time that it weakened the position of the large landowners, the decree struck at those functions of mediation and protection of the fief on which Mafia power rested.

But the movement that had the greatest impact in Sicily from the point of view of its potential threat to the Mafia system on the *latifondo* was the struggle of poor peasants for the occupation, and concessionary distribution to cooperatives, of uncultivated or badly cultivated land. The size of the movement and the massive participation of the peasants made this aspect of the struggle for the land a symbol of the entire Sicilian situation.

With the exception of some areas in the eastern part of the island, the entire vast zone of central-western Sicily, the traditional realm of the *latifondo,* was swept by this movement, whose protagonists were poor peasants and day laborers but which also involved other agricultural classes, such as the medium and rich peasants, who saw an opportunity to increase their properties.

The occupation of the large estates, with its ups and downs, characterized the entire period from 1944 to 1950—the year of agrarian reform. A great upsurge took place in autumn 1945, a second in autumn 1947, and finally a third (in which, unlike the first two, the occupation was more than merely symbolic) in autumn 1949. One year later, in December 1950, the Sicilian agrarian reform law was promulgated.

Despite its size, the movement was nevertheless characterized by several basic weaknesses that influenced its results. The first came from its confinement to the large estates, even in areas where it was strongest. The movement was thus unable to deal with the more general aspects of agrarian reform; moreover, it came to grips with only marginal matters, due to the scant importance that the problem of the *latifondo* would have in the South and in Sicily shortly thereafter. A second element of weakness was the fact that more than one force inspired the movement—that of the poor peasants and day laborers and that of the medium peasants and independent farmers. All this produced a phenomenon of social fragmentation that translated into the organization of a plurality of cooperatives.

Sometimes in the same commune one cooperative represented the poorest strata of the peasant world, and one represented the more affluent. Often these cooperatives belonged to the same political alliance, that of the Socialist-Communist left. To this was added a further element of fragmentation, caused by political-ideological divisions. The cooperatives were more often organized on the basis of political and party loyalties than on the unified momentum of a mass movement. There were also instances of communes in which three cooperatives competed for land allotment—a Communist, a Socialist, and a Christian Democratic cooperative. This produced an excessive number of allotment applications, many of which were turned down. All in all, during the course of the eight years between the Gullo decrees and 1952, 4,809 applications for the allotment of 904,743 hectares were submitted in Sicily. The 987 applications that were accepted involved an overall surface area of 86,420 hectares, with an average of 88 hectares per concession; however, the rejected applications numbered 3,822, and land surface applied for and not granted amounted to 820,323 hectares, with an average area of 214 hectares per application.

120

The applications that had not been accepted involved tracts of land whose average size was much higher than that of those that had been granted. This is an indication of the ferocious resistance the Sicilian large landowners put up when confronted by attempts to alter property and production relationships. But another, perhaps more significant, indicator is furnished by an analysis of the manner in which the land was allotted. Of the 86,420 hectares assigned over all, little more than 20 percent (16,350 hectares) were obtained through friendly settlement with the owners, whereas almost 80 percent (70,070 hectares) had to be forcibly seized by law, by means of a special decree of the prefect. This percentage was much higher than the average in the South,[35] and bore witness to the adamant resistance of the Sicilian large landowners to peasant demands—a resistance that would cost a not inconsiderable price in blood.

The Attack on the Union Movement

Starting with the Allied occupation of Sicily in 1943, the agitation and dissatisfaction of Sicilian citizens grew apace with the emergence of the separatist movement. But despite the simultaneous development of these phenomena, the peasant movement never joined up with the separatist movement. To the traditional inability of the agrarians to act as an independent ruling class vis-à-vis the peasants without Mafia mediation were added the effects of the Gullo decrees, which by giving a concrete outlet and legislative support to peasant demands removed them from the influence of separatism, which had counted on the movement's strategic weakness and makeshift organization.[36]

Despite some temporary electoral successes, the separatist movement was unable to create, much less consolidate, a mass base, so that "the attempt to prevent the end of the agrarian system . . . is carried on jointly by separatism, the Mafia, and banditry: in a first phase (1943–45), through political struggle and, during a subsequent phase (1945–47), through the attempt at armed insurrection."[37]

The separatist movement's attempt at political contacts with the British and Americans having failed, the separatist barons tried to win support from the Savoy monarchy, but above all they formed an alliance of the separatist agrarian front with the armed bands that during the period roamed all over Sicily. In particular, in May 1945 Baron Stefano La Motta and a number of young aristocrats, members of the youth league of the separatist movement, asked for and were granted a meeting with the bandit Salvatore Giuliano. During that meeting Giuliano declared that he was ready to act in concert with the Esercito Volontario Indipendentista Siciliano, the Sicilian Voluntary Army for Independence (EVIS). Thus began the collaboration between the barons and bandits which during that year and throughout 1946 would result in the political utilization of Sicilian banditry to oppose the state.

During the same period of time there also came into existence an alliance between the EVIS army led by Concetto Gallo in eastern Sicily and a band of outlaws in the area of Niscemi: Together they would engage in a series of skirmishes with the Italian Army that would end with the defeat of the separatists. In the areas of activity of the band of Salvatore Giuliano, who in the meantime had been appointed commander of EVIS in western Sicily, the military operation against the state, such as the attacks on the carabinieri barracks at Bellolampo and Montelepre, were more successful. While in eastern Sicily separatist guerrilla activity was petering out, and the last fires would be definitively doused in 1946, in the western part of the island Giuliano's band acquired ever-greater importance until the turning point in May 1946.[38] Meanwhile the threat of the peasant movement kept growing.

The first wave of mass occupation of the feudal estates, which took place in the autumn of 1945, was for the conservative forces a clear harbinger of danger. On the other hand the policy of the Italian Communist party, which aimed mainly at protecting the position of the poor peasants, opened up spaces for the Christian Democratic Party, especially among the independent farmers.

Meanwhile the Christian Democratic party, but also the parties on the right, the monarchists and liberals, launched a salvage operation of the separatists, due to which the Mafia groups began to become full-fledged members of these parties. At any rate, after the armed attack on Li Causi, Bernardo Mattarella, who would subsequently become one of the most discussed men in the Sicilian Christian Democratic party, because of his presumed friendship with noted mafiosi, published an article in *Il Popolo* inviting the separatists to enter the ranks of the Christian Democratic party, which, with its prompt choice in favor of regional autonomy, had adeptly played the card that tried to salvage them. Beginning in May 1946 and through 1947 there began a wide-ranging operation for the integration of separatists, mafiosi, and bandits. While Salvatore Aldisio, the high commissioner for Sicily, following Alcide de Gasperi's instructions, continued a policy of mild sanctions in regard to ex-separatists who entered the Christian Democratic party, the Mafia groups began to shift to the side of the newly constituted order, once again defending the interests of the agrarians, by doing away with the armed bands, organizing the repression of the nascent peasant and union movement, and becoming members of the parties with national representation. Don Calogero Vizzini also became a member of the Christian Democratic party, officially welcomed by Deputy Giuseppe Alessi (later president of the regional government).[39] With the end of all prospects of success for the separatist movement, local interests and national interests again came to terms. In the cautious words of the Anti-Mafia Commission,

[in 1946–48] The Mafia decides . . . to support the positions of those forces of the reactionary and agrarian right that, like the liberals and above all the monarchists, most brazenly ensure representation of the interests of the agrarian-feudal structure. . . . Finally, and precisely in the span of the three years that run from April 18, 1949, to the second regional elections of 1951, the Mafia changes its orientation, directing it toward the political side that the interests of moderate restoration in the island have chosen as the central element for stabilizing the system (that is, the Christian Democratic party).[40]

Clear indications and documentation exist of these two shifts in alignment of mafioso groups and agrarian interests. In May 1946 there was a meeting between Giuliano, Santo Fleres, the recognized chief of the Mafia in Partinico, and local leaders of the Liberal party.[41] Not altogether coincidentally, this period saw the beginning of a rapid elimination of banditry at the hands of the state's agents or of unknown assassins, or as a result of internecine struggles among the bands. In addition to two hundred minor criminal associations, the large bands were eliminated, all this in the space of a few months. The only one who was left undisturbed was Salvatore Giuliano, whose band, as a result of these events, no longer had as its target the forces of the carabinieri and police.[42]

It certainly was not by chance that this was happening on June 22, 1946, when those who had been implicated in crimes related to separatism had just been granted amnesty. Paradoxically, however, it was precisely this date that marked the transition from common to political banditry; while the other bands were being eliminated, Salvatore Giuliano's began its activity against peasants, union members, and the headquarters of the Communist party. The first three murders in the long list of assassinations of union members that characterized mafioso repression of the struggles for land took place in May and June 1946. Salvatore Giuliano's band operated in spectacular style, as was apparent from their attacks on various Communist party headquarters and the massacre at Portella della Ginestra, when eight people were killed and thirty-three wounded during a May Day celebration, in which the police were accomplices and bore heavy responsibility.

The massacre at Portella della Ginestra took place on May 1, 1947,[43] the year in which the political struggle in Sicily became radicalized and in which, two weeks earlier, the coalition of the left had won an unexpected victory in the elections to the Sicilian Regional Assembly. The Giuliano episode testified to the existence and reproduction of traditional modes of behavior in the relations among Mafia, politicians, members of the government and the authorities in charge of public order. The Anti-Mafia Commission concluded its reconstruction of the entire episode with the following judgment:

> The phenomenon of banditry in Sicily, above all as it regards the Giuliano band, continued to rage in the western region of the island until 1950, chiefly with the help and protection of the Mafia; . . . in obedience to this clear design, the Mafia abandoned banditry when it realized that it might certainly damage it. . . ; so it put itself at the disposal of the police to hunt down the individual bandits in their hideouts. . . . In this game, and in difficult conditions of time and environment, the state apparatus, still under reconstruction after the war, ended up by not performing, objectively, an autonomous and decisive role in the elaboration of a general plan aimed at definitively destroying banditry; at the same time the police forces, . . . have occasionally failed to fulfill their principal duties, such as those of opportunely enforcing the various arrest warrants issued for the bandits; nor unfortunately did they refuse to help create, . . . immediately after the event, an untrue account of Giuliano's death.[44]

Both the Viterbo sentence and the Anti-Mafia Commission's Report accused the police inspectors, the carabinieri colonels, and other functionaries involved in the Giuliano case of grave omissions and connivances, while they cleared of all charges those who were repeatedly indicated as the persons responsible for the crime at Portella della Ginestra: the Deputies Mario Scelba, Giacomo Cusumano, Tommaso Marchesano, Piersanto Mattarella, and Prince Alliata. Though nothing indictable emerged against these men, it is inconceivable that Giuliano could have acted on his own and without some sort of cover and, moreover, that in a situation such as the one that existed in Sicily at the time a number of public officials could have acted on their own, evading all control by their superiors and by responsible politicians.

In fact, the radicalization of the political and trade union struggle in Sicily had produced a serious situation for the Mafia. Confronted by a growing movement, the crisis of the agrarian bloc, and from the point of view of political alliances a fluid prospect that could have guaranteed the preservation of established interests, the Mafia's recourse to direct repression not only assured it an effective defense but allowed it to reemerge by fully assuming its old function as a mediator.

The Reemergence of the Mafiosi as Brokers

Between 1945 and 1955 the Mafia killed at least forty-five union and political leaders, the greater part of whom belonged to opposition parties on the left (Communists and Socialists) but who also included a few Christian Democratic leaders,[45] not to mention the murder of peasants, day laborers, and shepherds, together with the habitual murders among Mafia *cosche*. In the years between 1943 and 1947, the Mafia groups had progressively reacquired weight and power; at first through the good offices and support of the Allied government, then later due to the role played in the separatist episode, and finally from resuming their function of mediators among the state, large landowners and peasants.

The definitive reconquest of the old functions of political and social mediation took place through the role played in the struggle for the land, which led to the agrarian reform of 1950. The Gullo decrees not only had the effect of mobilizing the peasants, they also contributed powerfully to the intimidation of the large landowners and induced them to respond to the growing peasant movement. One of these responses was Mafia repression; the other was the utilization of legal and bureaucratic weapons. The applications submitted by the farm laborers' cooperatives that had been formed to request that uncultivated land be leased to them were not considered for several months, thus giving the owners an opportunity to simulate cultivations. If this did not happen, the agencies charged with the implementation of the law granted the owner more time, arranging for an inspection of the area; and if, even with this, the land remained uncultivated, a few hectares were granted to the applicants. The land at stake was almost always rocky, unsuited for cultivation, and with its concession the owner certainly made a

greater profit than he could have through regular leasing. If the applicants, during the delay, proceeded to symbolic occupation of the land,
they were usually denounced to the judicial authorities and given heavy
penalties. Obstructionist procedures of this kind were also employed in
the distribution of agricultural products based on the new norms established by the Gullo decrees. In fact, the general opinion was that whenever an owner or his representative disputed a tenant's right to apportion
the product in accordance with the new criteria, litigation would be
initiated so that police and carabinieri would sequester the disputed
share, which would be deposited in a government warehouse until, six
months or a year later, the matter was resolved in court.

In many cases the landowners went so far as to regard as arbitrary the
tenant's right to divide the product in accordance with the criteria of the
law, without having first turned to the magistrate.[46] This interpretation, on whose basis occupation of the land represented a serious distur-
bance of public order, was used by the regional government headed by
Alessi, who, in September 1947, after the breakup of the unity agreement between Christian Democratic and Socialist-Communist forces,
issued the order requiring the police forcibly to evict from the fiefs the
peasants who had occupied them. On September 16 the national government had promulgated a decree that established the rules for the maximum employment of agricultural labor—a decree that to some extent
fulfilled the expectations of agricultural laborers. During that same
September there had been a great upsurge of land occupation, and it was
not by chance that the regional government's ordinance followed by a
few days the occupation of the Polizzello fief, in whose management the
foremost Mafia family of Mussomeli, headed by Giuseppe Genco Russo,
had an interest. The roster of names indicating Mafia presence in the
latifondo was extensive. In fact:

> At Villalba, Calogero Vizzini was the manager of the Miccichè
> fief. . . . Salvatore Malta took on the lease of the Vicarietto fief, Vanni
> Sacco had the Parrino, Barbaccoa held the lands of Ficuzza in the
> Godrano zone, and Joe Profaci the Galardo fief. At Corleone, . . . the
> hometown of Michele Navarra and Luciano Leggio,* the Donna Be-
> atrice fief was held in lease by the noted Mafia chief Carmelo Lo Bue,
> while Mafia ex-convicts Michele Pennino, Mariano Sabella, and Biagio
> Leggio were leaseholders of three estates no less important, while Fran-
> cesco Leggio, another mafioso, was for his part in charge of the

*Here, as elsewhere, the name Liggio is spelled in an alternative form.

Sant'Ippolito fief of 415 hectares. Even in those years, when he was sought by the police after being accused of serious crimes, Luciano Leggio became the leaseholder of the Strasatto fief. At Roccamena dangerous mafiosi, such as the brothers Raimondi; Cirrincione; Leonardo, Giordamo and Gioacchino Casato; Vincenzo Collura; Michele Bellomo, and Antonio Cianci were all *gabelloti* of fiefs in the area, and similar situations were repeated at S. Giuseppe Jato, Marineo, Contessa Entellina, Belmonte Mezzagno, and in practically all the agricultural communes of the hinterlands of western Sicily.[47]

The events connected with the crisis of the *latifondo* and land reform in Sicily during the period after World War II once again testified to the Mafia's ability to introduce itself as a protagonist into processes of change. The perception that the end of an epoch was approaching was inescapable, and the Sicilian agrarians set in motion a series of strategies aimed at avoiding agrarian reform and the institution of peasant ownership. These strategies consisted mainly of the real or fictitious fragmentation of the large estates in order to avoid the laws that they feared would sooner or later introduce expropriation of large estate ownership. To get some idea of what this strategy meant we need only cite the example reported by Blok of the fragmentation of more than two thousand hectares that made up the great estate of Contessa Entellina. Between 1945 and 1950 (when the agrarian reform law in Sicily was promulgated), no less than seven hundred hectares were distributed among the owners' heirs, more than nine hundred were sold, and little more than four hundred—that is to say, 25 percent of the entire holding—remained available to land reform. But this was land of the worst quality, rocky and hard to cultivate. Besides, division of the land did not involve a division of the estate: Even though the plots belonged to different owners, estate management remained in the hands of one person, proving the fictitious nature of the operation, whose purpose was not a technical improvement of production but the avoidance of expropriation.[48] In this operation the estate owners formed an alliance with the mafiosi, to whom they found it necessary to turn for help. Thus it happened that well-known mafiosi were appointed managers, as *gabelloti* or overseers, on many estates, and in this guise were later able to acquire portions of land by keeping them from land reform and so from the peasants. This is the context that surrounds the examples reported by the Anti-Mafia Commission, testifying to the progressive reemergence of mafiosi as brokers among landowners, peasants, and the state.

This was linked with the resumption of a tradition of mafioso behavior whose first expressions, after World War I, were abruptly interrupted by the Fascist repression. The example of Don Calò Vizzini and the estates located in Villalba fits to a T. With the help of the cooperative system, Vizzini had succeeded in obtaining the concession of the Micciché and Vicarietto estates in the early 1920s, and he took them over again in 1945, when the Princess of Trabia and Butera appointed him "acting manager" of the estate. The application submitted by the peasants organized in a cooperative to obtain concession of these lands was shelved by the high commissioner for Sicily, the Christian Democrat Aldisio. Don Calò formed his own cooperative, La Combattenti, at the head of which he placed his nephew Beniamino Farina. In the end the cooperative obtained a lease in perpetuity of the Micciché estate, and the best plots were assigned to those who had participated in the Villalba massacre.[49]

The End of the Peasant Problem

The agrarian reform law approved at the end of 1950 sanctioned with legislative authority a situation that had evolved in the South beginning in 1943–44 and that brought to an end a long historical phase. The disintegration of the economic and social fabric of the *latifondo*, presaged during the final years of the Fascist regime, aggravated by the peasant and farm laborers' struggles, and long since rendered inevitable by the political and social crisis of the agrarian bloc, was being proclaimed officially by a law that had been preceded in 1948 by a legislative measure that, by allowing allotment of land to single applicants rather than cooperative associations, shattered peasant unity.[50] The reform law stated that properties exceeding two hundred hectares must be subject to expropriation, whereas those between one hundred and two hundred hectares had to be cultivated intensively. The expropriation indemnity amounted to approximately 40 percent of the land's market value. This prompted the owner to sell the land, with the result that landownership passed through many hands:

> From a political point of view the agricultural reform played the main role in the peasants' conquest of the land. . . . In fact, besides the seven hundred thousand hectares expropriated under the 1950 laws, at least another million and a half hectares were purchased by the peasants on the free market during the twenty years between 1948 and 1968.[51]

The sales were not only the result of fear of the reform; they continued after the law's promulgation, fueled by the possibility of making large amounts of money—a situation created by hunger for land and the sudden availability of large tracts that could be cultivated. As a historian who was himself involved in the struggles during that period observed:

> The availability on the market of a large quantity of land, and the financial, credit, and tax incentives granted by the state and region, created a sort of gold rush. Thousands and tens of thousands of peasants plunged headfirst into the frenetic search for a piece of land to buy or to obtain by lifetime lease, no matter what the price. Therefore it happened that estates sold by their owners at 150,000 to 200,000 lire per hectare were resold a few weeks later by Mafia middlemen at 300,000 lire. . . . Mafia intrusion was a generalized phenomenon, above all in the provinces with the strongest Mafia tradition, such as those in western Sicily. The sales racket [English in original] brought in many billions, partly in kind—that is, substantial slices of the sold estates—and partly in cash, later transferred to building and other nonagricultural activities.[52]

The consequences of Mafia intrusion were considerable. One of the most important was the reduction of expropriated land and the increase of land sold, accompanied by a great deal of speculation. Whereas in the mainland South during the years immediately preceding and following the agrarian reform, 33.3 percent of the land changed hands as the result of expropriation and 66.6 percent was sold on the free market, in Sicily the proportion between these two figures showed an even smaller amount of expropriated land in respect to land sold. Furthermore, of the 625,000 hectares composed of properties measuring more than 200 hectares, only 93,000 hectares were in fact assigned to peasants, barely 15 percent. If we compare the data of the mainland South with those of Sicily we see that in the former 59.4 percent of the land that changed hands was sold on the free market, while in Sicily the percentage was 67.6.

Moreover, in Sicily the average area of the land alloted on the basis of the reform law measured 4 hectares, whereas in the mainland South it measured 5.5 hectares. Conversely, the average area of a tract of land changing ownership on the free market as a result of purchase was higher in Sicily (2.3 hectares) than in the mainland South (1.3 hectares).[53]

But still another consequence was the fact that implementation of the land-reform law required a serious struggle against the legal obstructionism interposed by the Sicilian regional government and by the office of agrarian reform itself. As documented in the minority report of the parliamentary Anti-Mafia Commission, the land-reform law was "openly sabotaged" and remained

> unimplemented for five years. The Sicilian agrarians unleashed an offensive of legal papers to block implementation of the law. But that offensive was able to succeed only because the regional government headed by Franco Restivo was more than happy to abet the maneuvers of the agrarians and their lawyers.[54]

Thus at the beginning of the fifties the Mafia had again taken full possession of its mediatory political and social functions. It had become legitimized as an instrument for the maintenance of social order, albeit vis-à-vis a state that claimed it possessed the monopoly of legitimate violence under republican legality. The episode of the bandit Giuliano had created an inextricable nexus between a state that had already proved its structural identification with the Christian Democratic party and the organization of a de facto power with which it not only had had to come to terms but had also created an organic alliance. While the state could insist that it had eliminated banditry from the Sicilian countryside, it was well known that without the support of the Mafia groups the operation's success would have been less rapid and less certain. The Mafia groups had once again been given an IOU with periodic and perpetually valid due dates, as long as the political groups in power remained the same.

By their management of the complex series of events involving land reform and the peasant struggle, the Mafia groups had proved that they were once again the necessary point of reference for action on the part of the agrarians and the Christian Democratic party, which emerged as the organic expression of the power bloc that was gradually being reconstituted on new foundations in Sicily. But the mafiosi's reconquest of positions as power brokers had occurred during the course of a historical process that, while it allowed them to regain a position in the society, established the premises for the rapid mitigation of the social conditions that had historically been the basis of its genesis and its existence. The end of the *latifondo* and the solution (through disappearance) of the peasant problem rendered obsolete the two pivots on which Mafia action had revolved for almost a century. However, new conditions for the reproduction of the *cosche* were surfacing and beginning to stabilize, within a new social framework, with which the Mafia would have to reckon. In the course of the fifties these conditions would not appear without some damage to the equilibrium of Mafia power and profound alterations in the relations among the Mafia, politics, and the economy. Confronted by the challenge that sprang from the elimination of traditional opportunities for enrichment through mediation among peasants, landowners, and the state, the Mafia power groups became involved in the tumultuous transformation that Sicilian society soon underwent.

Changes in spheres of activity—the relationship with politics, the state, and the parties—would initiate an extremely bloody decade because of conflicts among the Mafia *cosche* themselves. The new role played by the Mafia groups would see the emergence of new personalities, not to mention a leap ahead in organizational dimensions and widespread business deals—a leap that would be manifested in its full potential for danger from the end of the seventies through the first half of the eighties.

7

SURVIVORS, PISTOLEROS,
AND INNOVATORS

ANTONIO: Don Artu', the greatest invention of all was paper. . . .
There was a fellow, certainly a man of genius, who knows who it
was . . . who cut a square piece of paper, folded over the four corners,
glued together three of them, and left one of them open. On this open
side, with a brush he applied two small strips of glue that dries immediately and becomes sticky again only when you spread saliva on it with
your tongue.

ARTURO: The envelope!

ANTONIO: It becomes an envelope if before closing it you put bank notes
inside it that are also made of paper.
—Eduardo De Filippo, *Il Sindaco del rione Sanita'*

Social Transformations and Assistance
Programs for the South

The reemergence of the Mafia at the end of World War II, and Italian
history as it unfolded during the last forty years, cannot be understood
unless one takes into account the social transformations that occurred
in Sicilian society and the new functions assumed by the state in
pushing programs for the economic development of the South. This
policy was the result of the confluence of two orientations: on one
hand, the promotion of economic development in an underdeveloped

area; on the other, the redistribution of resources, that is, the institutionalization of the rights of citizenship.[1]

World War II was characterized by an expansion and transformation of the integration of southern society into the national society. Once again the leaders of this process were the market and the state, though a larger segment of the population than before became involved.[2]

The war had had negative consequences for the South. The concentration of industrial resources, located essentially in the North, had hurt southern economy; in addition, the war had blocked the migratory flow that had represented a small outlet for the overabundant southern labor force. A general indication of this destructive effect is given by the trajectory of the per capita income during the period 1928–52: In the South this income decreased to 12 percent, whereas in the North it increased to 27 percent. Hence the Fascist period and the war had exacerbated the differences between North and South.

At the end of World War II the problem of the South evinced potentially explosive aspects. The structural characteristics of southern economy were those typical of a backward economy:

- a particularly low per capita income (in 1959, 63 percent of the Italian average)
- low amounts of capital (in 1959, 98.9 percent of the entire internal gross product of the South went for consumption, so that investments could be financed only by imports from the North)
- the prevalent agricultural structure of employment (in 1951, 56 percent of those employed worked in agriculture)
- the limited role of industry

The solution of the South's problems clashed with decisions on economic policy adopted by the Italian government after the end of the policy of national unity, which essentially meant gaining for the Italian economy entry into international competition and encouraging specialization in the production of goods salable on the markets of advanced capitalistic economies. In order to be competitive, the production of such goods had necessarily to be concentrated where an industrial tradition existed, while it was thought that the promotion of new industries was not advisable. Furthermore, the first priority in reconstruction was the rehabilitation of the productive bases of the country that had been transferred to the North. Of course, the combination of these elements meant ruling out the possibility of industrializing the South.

The South's integration into a national market in which much-more-developed regions operated, and its participation in an economic system based on the growth of exports and internal consumption, gave severe shocks to a southern economy characterized by an overabundant agricultural labor force and general low productivity. With its insertion into a market economy, the overabundance of agricultural labor was transformed into excess population. The result was the expulsion from the countryside of the agricultural labor force and its frantic rush toward the cities and the country's industrialized areas. However, these excessively rapid population shifts created problems that were difficult to solve and produced tensions that were difficult to control. A particularly high state of tension would pervade the labor market, since the growth rates of employment in the nonagricultural sectors would not be able to balance the increase in available labor, which derived from population growth and the large labor force expelled from agriculture. The state then assumed the functions of regulating and controlling population movements from one area to another and among the various production sectors.

In the South, meager agricultural productivity and an overabundant labor force combined with the tensions that arose from the distribution and use of the land. It was impossible to maintain the old property relationships, and it became mandatory to find a solution in order to avoid a massive expulsion from the countryside.

In this situation, recourse to the old method—delegating the functions of social control to the local ruling class—would have proved of scant usefulness. In the immediate postwar period the local ruling class had entered a deep crisis. Large numbers of peasants and farm laborers became active in determining their own lives and no longer submitted to their traditional fate of being excluded from political participation. It was precisely this exclusion (not only the fact of not having the right to vote, but that of being *objects* of the patronage-oriented system on the political market, and not active participating *subjects*) that had been the basis of the agrarians' power. The peasant and labor mobilization for land occupation, the agrarian reform, the entry of peasants and laborers into democratic life as active subjects and as citizens who have all political and electoral rights swept away the forms of vertical solidarity and constituted one of the decisive elements of the crisis and the disappearance of the ruling bloc, which took place definitively with the end of the agrarians as a social force. This disappearance was sanctioned by the land reform which brought about the capitalistic restructuring of southern agriculture and the emergence of the small land holding.

This did not result in efficiently cultivated properties, but it helped impede excessively rapid migrations from the agricultural sector; it was therefore a way of keeping the excess segment of the population tied to the land. In this context there appeared the need to reinforce the ideological appeal of the family farm enterprise and also that of intervening with forms of assistance and subsidies in order to render their fate of low productivity and low income acceptable to the peasant family.[3]

The New Structures of Mediation

The disappearance of the agrarians as the ruling class in the South created the conditions for a new balance of power, while it eliminated one of the conditions for the existence of the traditional mafiosi as brokers. The other conditions were the formation of political parties, of the political–trade-union mass organizations, and of the massive expansion of the state's intervention with the resultant penetration of the apparatus of the party in power—that is, the Christian Democratic party—and the public apparatuses. These transformations caused a very important transition from the patronage of the notables to the modern mass clienteles. The new clientele system was characterized by its horizontal and bureaucratic features. The horizontal character of the new clienteles was due to the fact that they no longer revolved around the local notables but around the secondary organizations rotating in the orbit of the Christian Democratic party, which captured these organizations, transforming them into electoral and clientele recruitment centers. In the South the most important of these organizations that arose after World War II was the Coldiretti (direct cultivators or family farmers). However, the bureaucratic aspect of the new patronage system consisted in the replacement of local notables by party bureaucrats in the public offices. In this way the distribution of favors that previously took place on the basis of personal and direct relationships is now chiefly mediated by the party organization. This, among other things, had brought with it the tendency to eliminate relations of an affective type between patron and client, now replaced by an instrumental exchange relationship. Changed also is the nature of the favors that, to an increasing extent, consist in the distribution of assistance on a mass scale (public works, development programs for entire areas, subsidies for enterprises in distress). All this was carried out within the framework of the economic development programs promoted by the state but was rarely presented as a public initiative. Because of this, the interventions continued to have the character of favors. They take place and are presented, always or almost always, through the intervention of a politician in favor of an area, a population, or a category. This requires the development of a relationship of continued and progressive compenetration of the public bureaucracy and the bureaucracy of the party in power. In this fashion there is created, between the Christian Democratic party and the organs of the state, a "kinship" relationship determined by the frequent exchange of personnel between party and state.[4] Such a relationship puts at the disposal of the party in power a considerable mass of resources it can distribute at the periphery, and through which it can exercise social control.[5]

This in turn has profound effects on the constellation of secondary organizations (unions, workers' organizations, producer groups, voluntary associations of various types) that become incorporated in the patronage system and exercise mediatory functions between its own members and the organs of the public bureaucracy in charge of the distribution of resources. In this manner in the parties and in the secondary organizations there are again established dyadic relationships of a vertical type between leaders and card carriers. They become a privileged site in which the mediatory functions are concentrated. The Italian state, while it promoted the penetration of market principles, assumed, through the agrarian reform policy, the distribution of subsidies to persons, families, and enterprises, the protective functions of traditional southern society against the threats of disintegration that would have followed a too-abrupt penetration. Thus were laid the foundations for the parties that control public resources, first among them the Christian Democratic party, which enabled them to take over in their own name the functions of the mafiosi as brokers.

This policy of intervention entailed a change in the individuals who performed the mediation; from notables and traditional patrons we go to the new political brokers who manage to have access to the places where decisions are made concerning the release of resources to the periphery. With the passage from resources that were in the main the property of the traditional notables to public resources, to which the mediator had access, the new broker is forced to assume an active role as an agent of social change.[6] He in fact continues to manipulate social norms, as in the past, but the relationship with his clients is less stable, since it is founded on his ability to produce resources that are not directly at his disposal. This transforms mediatory functions into activities that are formally more open and accessible to a larger number of individuals.

The introduction of public resources into the economic system represents an enormous incentive to the formation of a category of mediators. But for the mediation to be effectively performed within the new framework of the public promotion of economic activities it must be based on institutions that serve as agencies of political credit guaranteeing continuity and stability in the performance of those functions, and that assure the uninterrupted success of the mediatory activity.

The formation of agencies specialized in the functions of mediation within which single individuals act as agents or concessionaires of mediation, results in a crisis of the mafiosi as brokers. It becomes difficult for the men of respect to act as single mediators in a social environment in which access to resources is possible only through a connection with the political parties and secondary organizations. New client-patronage relations and mass parties therefore enter into competition with the traditional structures of social mediation, since they tend to gather within themselves the totality of mediatory functions. Thus the monopoly of the mafiosi as brokers failed just at the moment of its reaffirmation. The Mafia groups were forced to come to terms with the new structures and the agencies specialized in mediation. This was a completely new task for the mafiosi, who traditionally had exerted a role of continuous balance among the different political parties. But it is a task whose performance was facilitated by the characteristics of the mass patronage party.

The conquest of the public apparatus was a central instrument in the construction of the Christian Democratic party as a mass-patronage party. Hospital administrations, municipal enterprises, agencies controlling public housing and the implementation of development plans, banking and credit institutes for the financing and support of business, regional, provincial, and communal assessorships—all these were the sites in which financial resources were concentrated and the men of the party were entrenched. Thus the mass-patronage party brought together the most disparate interests, ranging from speculators, professionals, subsidized entrepreneurs, and the public bureaucracy to sections of the working class, the marginal population, people with precarious employment, and the underemployed and unemployed who depend on the subsidies issued by the public assistance agencies. Its structure has a pragmatic and not an ideological character, for it takes in different individuals gathered together by a leadership whose task it is to distribute resources to the clients.

The nonideological character of the mass-patronage party, together with the fact that it essentially performs mediatory functions, presents an ideal condition for the rebirth within it of Mafia groups in a new form.

Reconstruction of the Mafia Humus

The establishment of the Sicilian region as a region under a special statute took place in 1947, shortly after the war, and on the not-yet-becalmed tide of separatist disorders. The first elections for the establishment of the Sicilian Regional Assembly take place on April 20, 1947, and show a considerable success for the left, carried on the tide of the struggles for land occupation and the agrarian reform. The massacre of Portella della Ginestra took place on the following May 1. Until the middle of the fifties the problem of land reform and the assassinations of union men and militants of the left characterized Sicily's political life and social climate. So the region was established when the crucible of transformations that had overwhelmed Sicily after World War II was still seething. The establishment of the region was premature in two respects: First of all, it was too hastily put through as compared with other regions under special statute, and, secondly, it was premature in regard to the relations between the state's central administration, with its insensitivity to new forms of local autonomy, and the Sicilian political world.

Generally speaking, therefore, the times were not quite right for the establishment of an organ of regional self-government. Moreover, regional autonomy had been granted on the heels of the separatist episode, which had proved once again the existence of those signs of discontent with the unified Italian government that had troubled relations with the central government from 1860 on. In Sicily the granting of autonomy was considered a victory brought about by the separatist disorders and the struggles for occupation of the land. The political forces and the central administrative apparatus saw this as a concession obtained by extortionist methods, and this first experiment with an autonomous regional government was regarded with suspicion. The most widespread opinion was this:

that regional autonomy was the price the state [had been] forced to pay in order to bring the dangerous separatist protest back into the channel of legality. It seemed . . . that without separatism the state would never have granted autonomy and that therefore it was not a legitimate aspiration of the Sicilian people but rather an unjustified claim that had to be contained and redrawn if one did not want it to compromise and undermine national unity.[7]

Furthermore, from a functional point of view, the Sicilian regional government was granted a range of powers much broader than that given to the regions under ordinary statute and to the other regions under special statute. Among them are the following:

• political-administrative powers, which had previously been within the competence of the national government at its central seat or through its peripheral organs: the appointment of ex-officio members of the provincial control commissions, members of the regional council of administrative justice, and commissioners of local agencies or commissioners *ad acta;*

• economic powers. It is within the competence of the regional organs to appoint the administrators of institutions of great economic importance: the Bank of Sicily, the Sicilian Provincial Savings Bank, the Regional Financial Institute for Sicilian Industry, the Committees for Industrial, Land and Monetary Credit, the Fund for Industrial Promotion, the Sicilian Financial Society, the Sicilian Agency for Industrial Promotion, the Sicilian Energy Agency, the Sicilian Sulfur Agency, the Sicilian Transportation Enterprise, the Agency for Agrarian Reform in Sicily, later named Agency for Agricultural Development, and the Sicilian Agency for Workers' Housing. The region furthermore has the power to make inquiries into and to authorize the opening and closing of banks, to give loans and arrange for financing of the communes, to convert nominal registered securities into bearer securities, to grant contributions in the capital account and privileged loans to building cooperatives and funds for regional employees, as well as the acquisition of rural property for the agrarian reform and reforestation;

• fiscal powers, consisting mainly of the concession of tax collection powers and the determination of the rate to which the collectors are entitled.[8]

In the government and the bureaucratic structure of the region are therefore concentrated such powers as to render the conquest of the administrative apparatus particularly desirable. The phenomenon was analogous to the one that had marked the introduction of communes as autonomous power centers just after the unification of Italy. The sudden appearance of a large number of political resources resulted in the creation of enormous opportunities for the ruling groups; at the same time it intensified the competition for power, since it increased the number of potential competitors. Nonetheless, the forms in which this competition manifested itself did not cause any basic changes in the traditional party-switching strategies, at least until the mid-fifties. Immediately after the 1947 regional elections, the process of incorporation of the agrarian and separatist forces in government ranks led by the Christian-Democratic party was not yet complete, and for almost ten years the region was governed by the center-right majority with the Christian Democratic party at the head of an alliance that once again included Liberals and monarchists—that is, the parties that traditionally had represented the interests of the agrarian classes.

In the formation of the region a decisive role was played by the policy affecting the personnel of the regional administration and the regional public agencies as well as the guidelines that determined how they were hired. As regards the recruiting guidelines, a 1950 regional law had decreed that the permanent personnel working in the branches of the state's central administration who were transferred to the region would be included in the roster of the corresponding regional administration. In 1953 this measure was modified, and the employees' right to opt for or against the regional administration was established. Therefore, a series of incentives were offered, such as the possibility of being included in a higher grade or of being given a grade even without having earned the necessary degrees required for that grade.

There were also some economic incentives, for instance, the granting of special indemnities that could not be voided by career changes. In addition, beginning in 1947, the region had employed temporary personnel whose numbers soon got completely out of control. These temporaries were included in the rosters, while further and more conspicuous favorable treatment was decreed for the staff attached to the cabinets of the assessors, especially the secretaries. A 1959 regional law provided for an increase in the employment rolls established in 1953. In only six years, and just for the rolls of the region's central administration, the number of employees rose from the 1,486 of 1953 to 3,529 in 1959, with an average increase of 137 percent, which attained 183 percent for executive positions and 207 percent for auxiliary positions. All this took place despite the fact that during the years from 1947 to 1949 there had not been a single competitive examination. The first positions were put up for competition in 1955. By the end of 1958, of the 3,529 available positions on the rolls only 262 had been awarded through competition, a percentage of 7.4 percent, while all other positions had been assigned through direct hiring.[9] In the period ending in 1963, 8,233 employees of the region (belonging to both central and peripheral administrations) out of 8,887 had been hired without competitive examination, a percentage of 92.7 percent.[10] Perhaps even more significant than these data is what was discovered at the Agency for Agrarian Reform, which had 1,884 employees:

> People with degrees in agriculture received symbolic salaries, totally inferior to those received by technically unqualified personnel, [hordes of whom] stood in line every morning in front of the agency's offices only to sign in and then leave, as they had neither tasks to perform nor a desk to work at. Entire families were on the lists here, just to receive an unspecified cash assistance; a mob of university students received from the ERAS agency (Agrarian Reform Agency of Sicily), either as salary or indemnity, what they needed to pay their room and board and attend the university; a swarm of technical consultants, legal assistants (approximately one hundred!), teachers, and so on complete the picture.[11]

The consequences of this personnel policy had a great impact on the new relations between the Mafia and politics, and had a disastrous effect on the Sicilian economy's ability to take off, even though it had been supplied with the necessary political means and massive resources. The control of the region's powers of intervention was put in the hands of a bureaucracy that, because of its recruitment methods, proved to be technically incompetent and politically corrupt.

Hence, no barrier could be erected against party control of regional expenditures, the definition of methods and sectors of intervention, or the amount of expenditures; there was neither the curb of technical competence on corrupt bureaucracy nor the curb of integrity on a technically incompetent one. The recruitment of administrators and politicians from the same class applicants imparted a louche character to the management of regional politics and resulted in the formation of a social coalition that has always been the hard core with which any innovative proposals have always collided in Sicily, in economic, social, and cultural progress.

This situation not only permitted but promoted the infiltration of mafiosi in the vital ganglia of the regional administration. The clients favored by these massive hirings were those who were closest to the operation—that is, those in places centered around Palermo, which meant that during the first ten years of the regional government, all the protagonists came from western Sicily. Not by chance did three-quarters of the personnel hired by the regional administration come from the provinces of western Sicily, while among the employees of the central administration alone 54 percent came from the province of Palermo, even though at that time it contained only 23 percent of the Sicilian population. Mafia families and groups in serried ranks entered the region's administrations, assessorships, and regional public agencies placed at the head of the various economic development branches. The rather cautious majority report of the Anti-Mafia Commission testifies to this fact, asserting that "it has happened . . . that people were hired who had been sentenced for crimes of all sorts, relatives of mafiosi, or even individuals themselves suspected of belonging to the Mafia."[12]

But perhaps one of the cases that best exemplifies how the regional public agencies were run, and the ease with which notorious Mafia members could enter them as employees, is the episode in which are implicated the regional agencies of the Sicilian Mining Agency; the Sicilian Mining and Chemical Corporation; the well-known Mafia boss Giuseppe di Cristina, the president of the Sicilian Mining Agency; Senator Graziano Verzotto, an important figure in the regional Christian Democratic party; and Deputy Aristide Gunnella, chairman of the board of the Sicilian Chemical and Mining Corporation, who would later become national vice-secretary of the Italian Republican party. In 1963 the Sicilian region established the Sicilian Mining Agency, in order to promote the commercial exploitation of the mineral resources existing in the territory. For many years sulfur mining had been one of Sicily's few industrial resources, but for some time it had been in difficulty due to foreign competition. But the mines had also been a privileged focus of mafioso activity, both through mediation and accessory services (transport) and direct participation of mafiosi in companies that had been given a franchise. The most prominent Sicilian Mafia member until the fifties, Don Calogero Vizzini, was a shareholder in the Gessolungo Mine in Caltanissetta province, and so was his nephew Beniamino Farina. In the mines run by Montecatini-Edison the transportation contracts were in the hands of well-known mafiosi, though their prices were higher than those of their competitors. In the Trabia-Tallarita Mine the hiring monopoly was held by a group of mafiosi connected with the Di Cristina family, which demanded a 150,000-lire toll on all hirings, and neither the employment office nor the police authorities had ever intervened.[13]

According to the institutional law, the activities of the Sicilian

Mining Agency had the purpose of forming corporations with public stock, with the agency reserving the rights to a capital share of not less than 51 percent. These corporations were supposed to promote the research, development, processing, and marketing of Sicily's mineral resources. Among corporations of this kind, a prominent position was occupied by the Sicilian Chemical and Mining Corporation, founded in 1964, which had about five thousand employees and hired the notorious mafioso Giuseppe Di Cristina as an employee in the Trabia-Tallarita Mine in Caltanissetta province, transferring him later to the Palermo office as assistant cashier. The hiring had been warmly recommended by Di Cristina's father-in-law, Di Ligami, a former employee of the Sicilian Chemical and Mining Corporation, with two letters, the first dated February 1 and the second February 22, 1968. On the same date, with a regularly postmarked letter, Aristide Gunnella, who was not yet a deputy and held the post of managing director and acting vice president with the same powers as the president, as well as the post of director of the Sicilian Mining Agency, informed Di Cristina that the Sicilian Chemical and Mining Corporation had hired him.[14] Graziano Verzotto was a member of the board of directors of the Sicilian Chemical and Mining Corporation, and was also the president of the Sicilian Mining Agency.

When he was hired, Di Cristina was subject to police measures imposed on him by the Catania courts, consisting of four years' special surveillance, with the prohibition from residing in the provinces of Caltanissetta, Trapani, Agrigento, and Palermo. Because of this measure he had been dismissed by the savings bank for the Sicilian provinces (previously he had also been employed by the Bank of Sicily). During the sessions of the Anti-Mafia Commission, Gunnella stated that the hiring had taken place because of the recommendation of his father-in-law, a former employee of the corporation; that this was current practice, since the Sicilian Chemical and Mining Corporation's main purpose was to remedy the severe unemployment in the provinces where it operated, and that pressure to hire was the order of the day; that the penal certificate submitted by Di Cristina was in order, while afterward it became known that it had been falsified; and that most probably approval of the hiring had been asked of the president's office of the Sicilian Mining Agency (that is, Verzotto's office). Moreover he declared that, although he knew of the question raised by the Communist group in the Sicilian Regional Assembly regarding the Di Cristina case, it was not in his power to dismiss an employee whose hiring had taken place according to regulations and not for political reasons. He did not exclude—while not admitting explicitly—that there might have been a verbal suggestion regarding the hiring from the office of the president of the Sicilian Mining Agency.[15] Verzotto, summoned in his turn to make explanations to the Anti-Mafia Commission, stated that usually the Sicilian Chemical and Mining Corporation did not ask the Sicilian Mining Agency for authorization to hire personnel and maintained that he had been informed of the Di Cristina hiring after the query from the Communists in the Sicilian Regional Assembly. After another request for clarification resulting from his interrogation, he sent a letter to the office of the region's president and to the assessors of industrial and economic development. In this letter, a masterpiece of hypocrisy and feigned naïveté, Verzotto wrote that the Sicilian Chemical and Mining Corporation had hired Di Cristina

> to replace his father-in-law Signor Di Ligami, *founder of the Communist Party in Riesi, former Communist mayor of that town, father of the local secretary of the Communist party, veteran of the workers' struggles, sentenced to political internal exile by Fascism,* an employee of the Trabia group. Signor Di Ligami's application was accepted by the Sicilian Chemical and Mining Corporation also because of humane and personal considerations, presented by the same verbally and in writing to the corporation's offices, which wished to show their appreciation of Signor Di Ligami in his *twofold quality as former employee and veteran of the trade union struggles.*[16]

It is incredible how to these justifications were later added those according to which it was normal practice to give economic support to a nuclear family, one of whose members was retired. In the course of his declaration, Verzotto stated that the president of the Sicilian Chemical and Mining Corporation had no knowledge of Di Cristina's hiring, but he was forced to admit that he had knowledge of his Mafia activities even as early as 1964, and that he had been a witness at his wedding, which took place on September 2, 1968, in Catania. His excuse was that he did not know Sicily well, or the differences between western and eastern Sicily, and that he had agreed to act as witness at the request of Di Cristina's brother, who from time to time would come to Catania, where Di Cristina was a bank employee (Verzotto had been secretary of the Christian Democratic party in Siracusa and in 1960 he was its regional undersecretary). Verzotto further maintained that, after an uninterrupted five-year sojourn in Sicily while holding important posts (from 1955 to 1960, and before that he had lived there for two years immediately after the end of the war), he did not know exactly what the Mafia was.[17]

Confirming the implausibility of these declarations, it should be borne in mind that another of the witnesses at Di Cristina's wedding was Giuseppe Calderone of Catania, who in 1970 would be denounced to the Palermo carabinieri together with several other mafiosi, among whom were Gerlando Alberti, Natali Rimi, the Teresis, the Gambinos, and the Spatolas (the latter were implicated in Michele Sindona's fake kidnapping in Sicily), as members of a conspiracy with criminal intent for the kidnapping of Mauro De Mauro and international drug trafficking.[18] The De Mauro case is still unsolved. As a journalist for a Palermo newspaper he had uncovered certain facts regarding the mysterious death in a plane crash of Enrico Mattei, the president of the Italian National Hydrocarbon Agency, that led directly to the Mafia. His body has never been found.

The destinies of the protagonists of this case would be very different. Verzotto, who was elected senator in 1968 but resigned due to a conflict with his position as president of the Sicilian Mining Agency, would subsequently be involved in the agency's scandal, be incriminated because of his relations with Sindona's banks, and become a fugitive from the law.[19] And the circle of relationships with Di Cristina, Calderone, and the Spatolas, who were also connected with Sindona, would thus close. Di Cristina (sentenced in 1970 for ordering the murder of Candido Ciuni, who was killed in a Palermo hospital), the moving spirit behind the reconstitution of the Mafia organization in the seventies, was implicated—although indirectly, through the participation of men from his *cosca*—in the massacre at Viale Lazio in Palermo in 1969, when mafiosi disguised as police killed two men and badly wounded two others. Together with his patron Verzotto, Di Cristina would be involved in the defeat of the Spatolas, Bontate, and Inzerillo mafiosi groups, tied to Sindona, and in April 1978 he decided to talk, furnishing the Palermo carabinieri with information about the Mafia organization. On May 30 he was killed, bringing to an end—until 1981—a war between Mafia bands.[20] As for Gunnella, who had also become a representative of the people in 1968 (the same year in which Di Cristina was hired and in the same electoral area) in the Chamber of Deputies, he will have a better fate than the other two. Despite the fact that at the 1975 congress in Genoa the ombudsmen of the Republican party had presented an extremely serious report on the corruption of the Republican party in Sicily in which Gunnella was directly involved, the leadership of the party and first of all Deputy

Ugo La Malfa ended by expelling the ombudsmen from the party, that is, the investigators and not the person being investigated, while the latter rose to the position of national vice secretary of the Italian Republican party.

These events prove that the Mafia's infiltration of the regional administration and agencies was not an isolated episode. Beyond this single instance what emerges is a series of complicities—among politicians, administrators, adventurers of every kind, and Mafia groups—which took on an organic character and put their mark on Sicilian life in the period after World War II.

> Instead of taking a position antithetical to the methods and mentality of the Mafia, the region created new and more conspicuous spaces and opportunities for the practice of illegality, for the protection racket, for intrigue—that is, for everything that is ordinarily fertile soil for mafioso practices.[21]

How had this process of mutual penetration between the Mafia and the new public apparatuses taken place? The Verzotto-Di Cristina-Gunnella case is exemplary because of the status of the political representatives involved in it—one of them the spokesman of the party of moral improvement, correct administrative mores, and economic and political rigor, the other a leading figure of the left wing of the Christian Democratic party, who at a very young age had been in the Resistance, commander of a partisan brigade in the Veneto, had worked with Enrico Mattei at the National Hydrocarbon Agency and seemed to represent the new face of the Christian Democratic party. This last point bears some reflection. If in fact it is true that the Sicilian region was set up by means of an alliance between the right wing of the Christian Democratic party and the monarchist and liberal forces representing the Sicilian agrarians and Mafia groups, it is just as true that from 1947 to the end of the fifties many things would change in the systems of alliances and in the configurations of Sicilian political groups. These changes, of which we can see some examples in the events in the commune of Palermo, would lead to the establishment of an organic relationship between the Mafia and the politicians.

The Sites of Mafia Activity

In June 1964 the Regional Council of Administrative Justice, charged with the task of investigating the Communal Council and the Communal Junta in Palermo, issued an opinion in which it affirmed that in the sectors of housing, contracts, city planning, and building permits, the Palermo Communal Administration

> certainly offer[ed] an alarming picture in which the objective ascertainment of frequent violations of the law, of ordinances and of good and correct administrations encounters . . . the survival of abuses, favoritism, or corruption that go beyond simple negligence and administrative disorganization.[22]

The conclusions arrived at by the Anti-Mafia Commission leave not a shadow of a doubt concerning the fact that the Communal Administration in Palermo was the privileged center of relations among politicians, administrators, and mafiosi. In fact, it points out that:

> (1) building activities and the acquisition of building sites, *with the decisive assistance of the administrative irregularity observed in the city planning sector and in the granting of building permits,* have proved to be fertile ground for the flourishing of illicit activities and extralegal power . . . , (2) in the development of building activities in the span of just a few years individuals of unknown background have emerged who have rapidly enriched themselves in the most suspect manner; (3) not a few among the irregular applications, especially in the field of building permits, benefited individuals declared to be mafiosi in police reports and in subsequent criminal and judicial proceedings; [and] (4) some of the protagonists of the most spectacular criminal cases in the province of Palermo figure in the changes of ownership of building sites and are reported to be capable of bringing considerable influence to bear on the city's administrative organs.[23]

Mafia activity concentrated mainly in three sectors: wholesale markets, construction, and credit. But these activities could not have become the realm of Mafia practices without the organic mutal penetration between the new mafiosi and the new wielders of political power. The latter engineered the reconstruction of the Christian Democratic party, and in Palermo, as in other Italian cities, they were tied to the group headed nationally by Premier Amintore Fanfani. These individuals rapidly seized control of power in the city and, due to their presence at decisive places in the local government, could bring about the working together of the Mafia groups and politicians. From a political perspective the chief figures in this process were three men: Giuseppe Gioia, Salvo Lima, and Vito Ciancimino.

In the early fifties in Sicily, political alignments, were characterized by great fragmentation. The parties on the regional scene, both in the Sicilian Regional Assembly and in the island's various communes, especially in Palermo, were very numerous, and each had considerable power. This fragmentation was extremely high on the right-wing of the political spectrum, where alongside Liberals, the various monarchist groups, and the neofascists, proliferated the Qualunquisti (or man-in-the-street party), leftovers from the separatist movement. Until shortly before the mid-Fifties the policy of the Christian-Democratic party was in the hands of the traditional notables (professionals, lawyers, and landowners), personified by Restivo, and was based on a laborious patching together of alliances with various groups in order to prop up the center-right coalitions. Proponents of the right, an expression of *cosche* and Mafia groups, had in part joined the Christian Democratic party immediately after the defeat of separatism, but the right still had a considerable power of its own, which the Christian Democratic Party had not yet tried to absorb.[24] In the mid-fifties the strategy of the Christian Democratic party toward these groups changed, owing to a change in the party leadership. If a turning point can be pinpointed, it is definitely the year 1954. In fact, during that year three important events took place, the first within the dynamics of the Christian Democratic party on the national level, the other two in the commune of Palermo.

The 1954 congress of the Christian Democratic party was held in Naples, and the victory of Fanfani's position set in motion the transformation of the party.[25] This produced a series of consequences, of which the most important were the prevalence of party functionaries over the traditional notables and the taking over of the state, the public agencies, and the public administration by the new Christian Democratic clienteles. For the party functionary the multiplication of posts, subsidies, and possibilities for legal or illegal gain were the conditions essential for the maintenance and broadening of power. In order to do this it was first of all necessary to have control of the party and insure that it will, almost physically, merge with the government at its various levels, central, regional, and local. In Palermo these conditions were realized starting in 1954. Following the victory of Fanfani's group, Giuseppe Gioia assumed a prominent position in the leadership of the Palermo Christian Democratic party at the provincial level. One of the upcoming young men, a follower of Gioia's and the Fanfani alignment, was Vito Ciancimino, who in 1954 was appointed communal commissioner of the Christian Democratic Party in Palermo. During that same year another personality in the Christian Democratic "renewal," Salvatore Lima, took over the public works assessorship of the Palermo commune, a position that he held until 1959, when he became mayor and Ciancimino succeeded him as assessor of public works.[26]

The concern with the multiplication of resources available to the Christian Democratic party in order to broaden its electoral base and thus maintain a substantial monopoly in the management of Sicilian public affairs lasted for almost twenty years. But it also brought about the entry into the Christian Democratic party, in Palermo as well as the other areas of Sicily characterized by the presence of *cosche* and Mafia groups, of the political forces that traditionally represented those groups. In 1963 there were no less than 18 communal councilors who had moved to the Christian Democratic party, coming from the most varied political alignments:

> The "foreign legion" today can count eighteen councilmen in the communal council, partly elected on the Christian Democratic list in 1960, while in 1956 they had been elected from other lists and before that from still other lists. Among these is the present Mayor Di Liberto, who, going back to the first legislature, was a *Qualunquista*.
>
> Among the eighteen legionnaires, Cerami, Di Fresco, Ardizzone, Pergolizzi, Maggiore, Amoroso, and Di Liberto were "enrolled" in the first category, in the sense that, coming from other groups, in 1960 they were elected on the Christian Democratic list. The case of Di Fresco is particularly scandalous; elected in 1956 on the monarchist list, five days after entering the communal council he went over to the Christian Democratic group!
>
> The other "legionnaires" are registered in the second category, that is, absorbed in the course of this legislature by other political groupings, running from right to left, as was the case with Councilman Volpe, "recruited" by the Communist group in the council on the occasion of the vote for the renewal of the contract for highway maintenance for Baron Cassina, which was also approved by Arcoleo, who came from the Socialist party; and Seminara, formerly a Christian Socialist, and Guttadauro, Giganti, Arcudi, Sorgi, Spagnuolo, Adamo, Di Lorenzo, Ballomare, all recruited by the Right . . . The Mafia *cosche*, the power behind the electoral success of these personages, had all flowed into the Christian Democratic party led by the Mafia bosses* of the various zones of Palermo: Paolino Bontà, Vincenzo Nicoletti, Pietro Torretta, Salvatore La Barbera, Michele Greco, John Gambino, Leonardo Vitale.[27]

One of the principal changes in the management of Christian Democratic power in the Palermo commune was the "styles" of relationship

*English in original

with the clients, and in particular in the place that for many years was the nerve center of power: the assessorship of public works. The revolution in the system of alliances carried through by the Fanfani current had its most obvious manifestation in the actions of Salvatore Lima. When he became the assessor of public works in 1956, Lima centralized all decisions, forcing the clients to submit all their requests directly to the assessor or his personal secretary. In this way he deprived the old patronage systems of the Christian Democratic notables of space and freedom of maneuver; he succeeded in absorbing the old clienteles into his personal following; and by eliminating the previously widespread practice of small departmental deals with those in charge of the various offices he tied to himself personnel who could no longer hand out favors directly:

> Lima transformed the fundamentally episodic favoritism of the notables, which lacked a broad vision of the overall situation and was confined to a restricted social elite, into an articulated strategy of the urban expansion of Christian Democratic power, managed personally from positions of power that controlled the city's administration.[28]

The centralization of operations also meant a centralization in favor of the groups that were granted building permits. In 1964 the commission of inquiry appointed by the region to investigate the administrative situation in the Palermo commune found that 2,500 of the 4,000 building permits granted by the commune's office of public works in the 1956–63 period (the two assessors had been Lima and Ciancimino) had been given to three persons, who were acting as fronts for the various interested construction companies.[29] The system devised by Lima and Ciancimino was extremely ingenious. By interpreting in a broad and distorted manner an 1889 regulation, never abrogated, under which building permits required the intervention of a master builder or a capable and skillful contractor, there was set up with the help of the assessor:

> a roster of builders "for third parties . . ." in which . . . were listed persons who have no clear professional merits or titles and who, in recent years, have almost completely monopolized the sector of building permits, evidently acting as fronts for the actual contractors who remained in the shadows.[30]

The aims of this system were many. To begin with it was possible for the Mafia contractors to remain in the shadows.

The Mafia builder never has a permit in his own name; typical is the case of Michele Cavatajo, one of the most ferocious criminals in Palermo, who calls himself a building contractor but has no permit in his own name. His wife obtains the permit and then Cavatajo uses it.[31]

With this method certain companies were formed, in which it was possible for politicians and administrators to participate, using fronts to whom they issued the permits and concealing the fact that the public administrator was issuing permits to himself, his clients, relatives, and Mafia associates with whom he had formed the company.

An example is the case of Francesco Vassallo, a building contractor who popped up out of nowhere to become, in a few years, one of the biggest building contractors in Palermo. Of humble origins, Vassallo obtained the license of building contractor on the basis of a declaration from Engineer Ferruzza, whose son would become Vassallo's partner in a company that would launch a large-scale building speculation, in conjunction with the construction of the Palermo airport. Having won the first contract in 1950, when Palermo's mayor was Professor Gaspare Cusenza, Vassallo obtained unguaranteed loans for more than 700 million lire later on. Cusenza became president of the Savings and Loan Bank for the Sicilian province. One of Professor Cusenza's daughters married the politically prominent Giuseppe Gioia and bought several apartments from Vassallo, as did her other brothers and sisters. Moreover, Vassallo not only built in defiance of city regulations but with the prior guarantee that a majority of his buildings would be bought or rented by the commune or by other public agencies to be used as schools. Because of his relationship with Vassallo and his position as administrator, Lima was indicted and subsequently acquitted of a series of crimes:

- personal gain in the performance of his public duties, having permitted Vassallo to put up buildings in violation of the city plan
- having induced functionaries of the communal technical department to certify adherence to housing regulations and the consequent fitness for habitation of the buildings constructed by Vassallo in violation of the building code
- having corrupted functionaries of the technical department, paying them for work within the competency of the department
- having given employment in the Palermo commune to relatives of functionaries active in the Provincial Control Commission in order

to obtain their goodwill.[32] Despite all this, Lima was never summoned before the Anti-Mafia Commission!

These episodes are exemplary, since they bear witness to a number of mechanisms essential for the operation that the group of young Fanfani followers performed in Palermo in the fifties. On one hand we have centralized control of power at the city level and control of what in Palermo, as in all of the South, was the most important instrument of local power after World War II: building expansion and the furtherance of large-scale speculation in building sites. On the other we have control of the central institutions distributing credits, indispensable in carrying the operations to a conclusion. Thus, while on the administrative level the technical aspects were covered, at the financial level the necessary guarantees were issued. A third element essential for centralized power management at the city level was represented by support and backing at a national level, through the presence of protectors and godfathers in the government. In this manner there was formed a group of operators who ran Palermo's administrative life for more than fifteen years, a group composed of politicians, party men, administrators, and public functionaries, entrepreneurs, and mafiosi, prominent figures in the banking and loan system and mediators of all types, old clienteles and new emerging groups that revolved around the granting of contracts, building permits, loans without collateral, handouts of all sorts, and the exchange of favors. And in all this the administration of public affairs was chiefly concerned with personal enrichment.

Another story that exemplifies the benefits to be derived from connections is that of Vito Ciancimino. Ciancimino began his career by working for a short time in the Roman political office of the Honorable Bernardo Mattarella. Upon returning to Palermo he became involved with the local Christian Democratic party and at the same time utilized his relationship with Bernardo Mattarella, then undersecretary at the Ministry of Transportation, to obtain the concession for the transportation of railroad cars, despite the fact that the company set up by him a few days before the agreement with the state railroad went into effect did not have adequate requisites to obtain the concession. In the performance of this activity, which lasted until 1971, Ciancimino had as his de facto partner the brother of a notorious mafioso. During the twenty years of the franchise, the company committed several fiscal crimes, such as partial or total tax evasion and the failure to issue invoices.

The focal periods of Ciancimino's activity were 1959–64, when he held the position of public works assessor, and a brief period in the seventies, when he was mayor. The five years during which Cianci-mino was public works assessor in the Palermo commune were the years of the most rampant building speculation. In the same period, with his relatives and his wife, Ciancimino participated in the estab-lishment of companies active in the real estate sector that were favored by his activity as assessor, and in which the presence of well-known mafiosi was conspicuous. In one of the companies in particular, in which his wife was the chief shareholder (she was an elementary school teacher with no declared assets, who nevertheless in 1962 held a participating share worth more than eleven million lire of a total capital of two hundred million lire) the Anti-Mafia Commission re-ported that:

> two persons who were part of the company are well known in the Mafia world: Angelo Di Carlo . . . who was one of the most authoritative mafiosi in Corleone [Ciancimino's birthplace], ex-convict and under police surveillance, and Antonino Sorci, a member of the Palermo Mafia, an ex-convict also under police surveillance.

And of other partners the commission said:

> Vincenzo Perrino is the nephew of Angelo Di Carlo, and has business connections with the known mafiosi Giovanni and Francesco Sorci and Antonino Collura; the Moncadas are all relatives of Girolamo Moncada, the owner of the office in which the Viale Lazio shoot-out took place; Antonina Di Gregorio is the wife of Francesco Sorci and belongs to a Mafia family; Antonino Collura is co-owner of an entrepreneurial com-pany that is considered to be of Mafia extraction.

Furthermore:

> ISEP [the company in which Ciancimino's wife was a shareholder] received a sum of money from Francesco Garofalo, a U.S. citizen, a well-known member of an international criminal network.[33]

In April 1971, when the new mayor had been elected but the office had not yet been handed over, Ciancimino signed two payment vouch-ers in favor of the Cassina company for greater expenses incurred in connection with the maintenance of the Palermo sewer system. Just as the Vassallo enterprise operated in the buildings and public works sector, so in the Palermo of the fifties and sixties the Cassina company was the main link among entrepreneurs, politicians, and Mafia *cosche*, controlling for more than thirty-six years the maintenance of roads and sewers in the Palermo commune at an exorbitant cost.

> In Palermo an annual expense of 4.4 billion is budgeted for the mainte-
> nance of streets and piazzas, while in Bologna the total cost amounts to
> 498 million. For the maintenance of the Palermo sewers an annual
> expense is budgeted in the amount of 5.9 billion, while in Bologna the
> total cost is about 200 million.[34]

The system of Mafia profitability in this case was obvious; the enterprise would obtain the contract at an exorbitant price and under monopoly conditions; then it would subcontract the work to smaller companies and to mafiosi. And that both Vassallo and Cassina were an organic part of the politicoeconomic mafioso power is demonstrated by the fact that in 1971 in Palermo Vassallo's son was kidnapped and a year later, Cassina's. In fact, the Anti-Mafia Commission observes,

> These kidnappings present us with homogeneous data and characteristics
> that render them suspect regarding their intent, which could not be a
> financial one; indeed, kidnapping is not unknown to the Mafia, but
> whenever it has been used it has had ambiguous aspects that have dimin-
> ished its economic importance, in order probably to assume the signifi-
> cance of a "warning" or a "lack of respect," so that it *always centered on the
> sticky area of relationships between the Mafia and the local power.*[35]

Together with building contracts and loans, a fourth sector appears to have had great importance for Mafia activities in the fifties and the intertwining of Mafia and politics: wholesale markets. In the report of the subcommission appointed to investigate the wholesale markets in the Palermo commune it was pointed out that between 1963 and 1965 there operated in this sector: eighteen Mafia ex-convicts denounced for conspiracy with intent to commit a crime, who were active in the fruit and vegetable market; sixty-four producers, retailers, and merchants in the same sector who had been the object of preventive police measures; fifty-one butchers, also the object of preventive measures; thirty-eight franchise holders, and five wholesalers of fruit and vegetable produce who had criminal records.

> From these inquiries it appeared that the meat market was seriously
> polluted by the presence, among the merchants and butchers of
> Palermo, of numerous persons who had been convicted of crimes and by

obvious and confirmed connections with Mafia *cosche* that were still involved in cattle rustling. What is more, a series of episodes confirmed the existence of an actual Mafia monopoly of the meat market and of control of the largest centers of product utilization, such as hotels and generally all types of communities. In the wholesale fish market, too, Mafia presence was made clear by the absolute monopoly enjoyed . . . by a relatively small number of concessionaires.[36]

Control of the wholesale markets had always been a reason for conflict among the Mafia *cosche* and a favorite area for their activities. When in 1955 the general market was moved from the Ziza to the Acquasanta quarter, numerous murders took place as a result of the Mafia war between the two *cosche* controlling those quarters. In the 1961–62 period no fewer than twelve murders of livestock, fodder, and produce merchants occurred in Palermo. In this sector, too, the responsibilities of the Palermo commune proved obvious, because the licenses had been granted without checking the good-conduct certificates.[37]

In the fifties in Palermo, therefore, new conditions arose in the relations between the Mafia *cosche* and political groups. The establishment of an efficient vote-getting machine in the Christian Democratic party, the conquest of the nerve centers of the city government by the "Young Turks" who had seized the party, produce further mutual penetration among Mafia groups and the party men who worked as public administrators. In this environment the Mafia maintained its control of its old activities (meat, fish, and produce markets), and spread to other areas: credit, construction, public contracts, and the administration of local and regional public agencies. As the traditional foundations of Mafia power disintegrated, new and much more remunerative possibilities for Mafia activity were created. Together with these developments, new Mafia groups also emerged, and the old groups were changed. The Mafia universe of the fifties was characterized by the simultaneous presence of the old and the new, such as never had occurred in the past. Still in action were the traditional mafiosi, the men of respect tied to the large landownership circles; but there also began to emerge the so-called gangster-mafiosi, prepared to use their weapons without scruple, who had replaced the traditional shotgun with the automatic pistol. New Mafia careers developed, exploiting real estate speculations, public works contracts, and the links with the credit and banking system in Palermo, Trapani, and Agrigento or the opportunities offered by the traffic in narcotics and the smuggling of tobacco.

The Survivors

In 1954 Don Calò Vizzini died in Villalba. The most famous figure in the Sicilian Mafia at the time was Giuseppe Genco Russo of Mussomeli in Caltanissetta province. But other mafiosi linked to traditional activities were active, often pervasively so: Vincenzo Di Carlo in Raffadali (Agrigento province), Mariano Licari in Marsala, Michele Navarra in Corleone (Palermo province). Some managed to end their lives by dying a natural death; others, like Navarra, were murdered by other more skilled pretenders to the scepter of command. Some were closer to the *latifondo* economy, others had begun to move away from it so as to undertake new activities. Some had direct links to the Christian Democratic party as card-carrying members or leaders; others remained relatively independent in political alignment. All of them had in common several traits of the traditional mafioso: They were individuals who specialized in functions of social mediation, who aspired to hold the monopoly of violence in a specific territory. But despite their qualifications as traditional mafiosi they had a further element in common: They lived in fluid societies and possessed a conspicuous dynamism when it came to business deals and maneuvers. They were certainly not innovators, like Liggio, Greco, and others, who moved beginning in the mid-fifties in the far-reaching circles of the narcotics ring. Their activities were mainly tied to the world of the land, but in some of them developments were already discernible that, though not unknown in the Mafia world, nevertheless became more prevalent due to the links with political power that were established in the Sicily of the fifties; for example, the connections with credit and banking.

Typical in this regard was the case of Mariano Licari of Marsala. His career was that of the traditional mafioso, involved in such activities as cattle rustling (1913), murder, and a sentence of house arrest (1929). But his career was not linear; Licari accumulated the greater part of his indictments during the final part of his life, starting in 1958. His real Mafia activity began after World War II, at a relatively advanced age, and only in the fifties did he make appearances as the head of his *cosca*. Yet, from the point of view of his battles with the judiciary, Licari almost always proved to be the winner. With a total of thirty-one indictments in the course of his career—twenty of them for murder—he was acquitted thirty times, thirteen times in the investigative phase, and seventeen times because of insufficient evidence, and was sentenced only once for conspiracy with intent to commit a crime. Even on this last occasion (1969) he was pardoned and freed. In the final upshot in 1970, he was subjected to measures of special surveillance and obligated to maintain a fixed residence.

Licari's activities were a combination of commercial and mediatory functions and of demands for payoffs and protection money. He managed a diesel oil depot, obtaining his supplies from the quotas issued to owners of fishing boats and selling it at prices lower than the competition. As a middleman he handled the sale and purchase of land, speculating on his position as mediator and imposing his mafiosi as *campieri* and administrators. He held the concession of various beverage companies, which preferred to entrust their representation to him rather than to possibly weaker competitors. He was the silent partner of a company handling the distribution of fuel, not to mention other companies. He imposed his protection and his control on all the criminal groups active in the area, forcing them to pay a tax on the profits they derived from cattle rustling, thefts, break-ins, and other crimes against property. He imposed tributes on moonshiners. His activities offer a prime example of the "normality" of Mafia operations, particularly when they involve his relations with the local banking system.

In the culminating phase of his activities, throughout the sixties, Licari had connections with seven banks, both in his own name and as partner of the many companies in which he participated. In all these banks—six of which were local, while the seventh was the Bank of Sicily—he obtained loans of rather large sums of money. In some of these banks he was also a shareholder. In the years between 1960 and 1962 the amount of these loans increased dizzyingly, and the overdrafts at times exceed the loan by more than 200 percent. In March 1963 his accounts were overdrawn by more than two hundred million lire. It must be pointed out that the banks continued to grant Licari credit during a period in which he was already known to be a mafioso, for in 1958 he had been under a police injunction. The technique used by Licari to avoid paying the debt was based on his being a shareholder in the bank whose customer he was, as well as on his personal relations with bank officials and on the fear inspired in his partners by his reputation as a mafioso. The negative accounts would be closed and the balances owed would be transferred from the company's accounts to the accounts of the other partners. By this method Licari exploited bank financing and unloaded on his partners the obligation to pay the outstanding balances.[38]

If Licari represented the attempt to impart respectability to his Mafia activities, and his sphere of action is essentially oriented to utilizing his acquaintances in economic circles, Di Carlo put his respectable position to use from the very beginning, and his career essentially developed through political channels and the performance of public functions. In fact he came from a relatively well-off family; the son of small landowners, he held the lease to a fifty-hectare tract of land; furthermore, he owned a small flock of sheep and a small herd of cattle (Licari, on the other hand, had started out as a *campiere*). Besides, he obtained a teacher's diploma and for a number of years taught in the elementary school at Raffadali (Agrigento). This position of social respectability was accompanied by an interest in politics that led to his becoming vice commandant of the Italian Fascist Youth in Raffadali and a member of the Fascist party from 1928 to 1943. In 1944 he joined the Christian Democratic party, and in 1957 he became a section secretary, a position he held until 1963. After the Allied landing in Sicily he had been put in charge of the office for the requisition of grain; previously he had been employed by the rationing office in the Raffadali commune. His activity in this field allowed him to enrich himself and come into contact with Mafia circles among the landowners. From 1950 to 1963 he held the position of arbitration judge in the Raffadali commune.

Di Carlo's position in public life was so secure that he even obtained a letter of recommendation from the carabinieri in which he was described as a reliable collaborator! And he was in no way hindered in his activities despite the fact that the commune's administration was always in the hands of the Communist party. In 1963, however, he was accused of various crimes, and his career came to an end.[39]

But the men who in the fifties epitomized the traditional Mafia were Giuseppe Genco Russo and Michele Navarra. The first was a winner, the second a loser.

Genco Russo, born in 1893 at Mussomeli in Caltanissetta province, was considered by everyone, at the death of Don Calò Vizzini, the undisputed head of the Sicilian Mafia. His career had begun in 1921, when for lack of evidence he had been acquitted of the crimes of cattle rustling and conspiracy. From then until 1946 his life was marked by an uninterrupted sequence of indictments that always ended in dismissal of charges or acquittal for lack of evidence. The only exception was a complex court case in 1932, when Genco Russo was sentenced to six years in jail for conspiracy with intent to commit a crime. He actually served only three years, for he obtained a pardon. What is more, he was rehabilitated in 1944 by a decree of the Caltanissetta Court of Appeals issued on the basis of information supplied by the commandant of the

Mussomeli carabinieri station. Eight years later that same commandant, as his proper recompense, received a three-and-a-half-hectare
share of the Polizzello estate, managed by a cooperative whose undisputed head was Genco Russo. And since the commandant was not
entitled to this allotment, it was carried out in the name of another
shareholder.

This rehabilitation put the official seal on Genco Russo's "honor-
ableness." From then to 1963 there were no more denunciations or
indictments against him. His economic position was reinforced, his
power expanded, and he also succeeded in taking on official functions.
In 1960 he was elected communal councilman for the Christian Democratic party, which he had joined immediately after the end of the war,
having been active in the Popular party and having been a separatist
and then a monarchist (in 1946 he was awarded the title Knight of the
Crown of Italy). Since he was a councilman he also managed to become
an assessor until 1962, when he was forced to resign as the result of a
press campaign.

Genco Russo is the typical figure of the mediator and social entrepreneur who made use of a combination of infiltrations of public agencies
and privileged relationships with important individuals in order to
build his position of power.

His points of reference were the large estate owners, the agrarian
reform agencies, the banks, and the politicians. Typical in this sense
was the episode of the Polizzello estate, in the Mussomeli area. This
estate of approximately 1,918 hectares had been the subject of an
expropriation request submitted as early as 1920 by the Combattenti
(veterans) cooperative in Mussomeli. However, the owner was able to
convince the members of the cooperative to withdraw the request and
accept a twenty-nine-year land improvement lease, renewable for another nine years, for a tract of 850 hectares on the same estate. In
September 1940 another cooperative, La Pastorizia (sheepherding),
made a bid for a *gabella* contract for another tract of approximately 850
hectares on the same estate. Almost the entire estate was therefore
leased by the two cooperatives, one of which, La Combattenti, was
presided over by Genco Russo and had among its board members his
compare, or godfather, Giuseppe Sorci and Calogero Castiglione, Genco
Russo's brother-in-law and a *compare* of Calogero Volpe, a deputy in
parliament for the Christian Democratic party; the other, La Pastorizia, was headed by Giuseppe Sorce and had Genco Russo among its
board members. The cooperatives prevented the distribution of the
land to the peasants, and permitted the appropriation of tracts of land

by mafiosi and individuals who had no legal title to the allotment. In fact, at the moment of expropriation the Mussomeli Veterans' Association would have had to pay the estate owners an indemnity of forty million lire; since it did not have such a sum it turned to the Combattenti and Pastorizia cooperatives, which collected among their members a sum of thirty-three million lire in payments of eighty-thousand lire each. The remaining seven million lire were obtained as a loan from San Giuseppe, the rural savings bank in Mussomeli, whose president was Vincenzo Noto, Volpe's chief elector. In this way Genco Russo's *cosca*, with the connivance of the local veterans' association, obtained monopoly control of the estate's expropriation. It was in fact thought that the payment of eighty-thousand lire was an indispensable requirement for participation in the land distribution, and therefore the veterans' association could not help but distribute shares of land to the cultivators designated by the two cooperatives, which in the meantime had set up a distribution committee in which, alongside the mafiosi, the Mayor and the Mussomeli parish priest participated.

The result of this operation was that peasants who had rights but did not have eighty-thousand lire were excluded; that shares of land were assigned to people who did not cultivate the land; and that 176 hectares of land were assigned to the Pastorizia cooperative, the majority of whose members were neither peasants nor veterans but well-known bosses of the local Mafia. Many shares were assigned to tailors, shoemakers, shopkeepers, and pharmacists, as well as to communal councilors and assessors and to the president of the commune's welfare agency. Among these assignees was the carabinieri marshal who had made it possible for Genco Russo to obtain his judicial rehabilitation. Genco Russo received seven shares in addition to an unspecified number of shares assigned to his front man.

This irregular situation was not remedied by the intervention of the Agency for Agricultural Development in Sicily, which bought the entire farm, paying 450 million lire—that is to say three times more than the price set by the law for agrarian reform in Sicily—and also taking on the burden of paying the outstanding fiscal and tax obligations that encumbered it. On the basis of a regional law issued in 1960, land owned by the Agency for Agricultural Development in Sicily was supposed to be assigned to farming families. Despite all the difficulties deriving from Mafia threats, from the position taken by the Christian Democratic party in Mussomeli, and from the pressure exerted by Volpe, the Agency for Agricultural Development in Sicily was in the end able to allot 104 shares to peasants who were entitled to them, first by taking them away from assignees who had no right to them. But the strength of the Mafia organization was such that the peasants, even though they were legitimate assignees, for some time continued to pay rent to the old mafioso assignees, to whom they were furthermore forced to give half of the crops they raised.[40]

But Genco Russo's activity was not confined to the local level. He played an important role when, in the mid-fifties, possibilities appeared for the development of drug trafficking. In fact, in October 1957 he took part in a summit meeting at the Hotel delle Palme in Palermo, together with notorious chiefs of the Sicilian and U.S. Mafia. Though Genco Russo was reluctant to embark on drug trafficking (younger men able to sense the potential of this new business were eager to do so), his presence, with his indisputable prestige as the biggest top banana in the Sicilian Mafia, validated and assured the formation of a group that through the Bonanno and Genovese clans in the United States, and the emerging mafiosi in Palermo, opened the way to the total involvement of the Sicilian Mafia in drug traffic. But he was not the mastermind behind this process of transformation, because he was still too closely linked to *latifondo* circles. Instead, one of the protagonists was the heir of Michele Navarra who, unlike Genco Russo, was to die at the hands of the very forces he had helped to unleash.

Michele Navarra was found murdered on August 2, 1958, while he was returning to Corleone from a nearby town. Killed with him was a colleague who sometimes accompanied him. Two months earlier he had been awarded the title of Meritorious Knight of the Italian Republic (which he did not receive until after his death); it set a sort of seal of approval on his Mafia career, which in exacerbated forms had made the obsession with power his life's aim. This honorific title could be set side by side with the title Knight of the Italian Crown, which he received in 1941—both of them testifying to the Mafia's ability to adjust to successive regimes, regardless of their ideological and political characteristics.

Navarra is different from the mafiosi described until now. First, he came in from the well-off middle class (his father—a surveyor, a teacher in the agricultural school, and a small landowner—hobnobbed with the local aristocrats), which, in a town like Corleone, represented a typical social and political elite.

Navarra, who had a degree in medicine and surgery and during his military service attained the rank of sublieutenant in the medical corps, after his discharge became the communal doctor. His practice covered a large section of Ficuzza forest, a perfect place to hide and butcher stolen livestock and from there take it to the Palermo whole-sale market. While his father's family did not have Mafia antecedents, his mother's family included his uncle Angelo Gagliano, indicted for, and subsequently acquitted of, the murder of the Socialist Bernardino Verro, the historical leader of the Sicilian Fasci killed in 1915, whose assassins were never identified. Furthermore, Navarra was related by marriage to the Riela family, some of whose members were part of the *cosca* led by Calogero Lo Bue, who was succeeded by Navarra himself.

Navarra's career proceeded, exploiting not only the opportunities offered him by his social position and his degrees, but also those connected with the social transition fostered by the Allied occupation of Sicily and the events that followed. From the Allies Navarra ob-tained authorization to collect the military vehicles abandoned by the army. As a result, he set up a trucking company, the International Transport Company, which was later regionalized and taken over by the Sicilian Transport Company, whose general manager was one of Navarra's brothers. The Allied occupation also led to the presence in Sicily of several Sicilians—many of whom were mafiosi—who had emigrated to America. Among these in Corleone were two members of the Di Carlo family, Navarra's cousins. Contacts with these individuals resulted in a greater range of opportunities for the Mafia *cosche*. Navarra, who in 1946 held the posts of municipal doctor, fiduciary doctor of the National Institution of Health Insurance, and head of the medical department at the Corleone Hospital, replaced one Dr. Nicolosi, who was found mysteriously killed and whose murderer or murderers were never identified. Navarra's *cosca*, which was already very well organized (see Figure 1), had the monopoly of a series of illegal activities, in particular:

> control over the hiring of unskilled laborers and of workers; payment in cash for presumed protection organized by mafiosi; crimes against prop-erty; crimes against individuals (and not only against personal or *cosca* opponents); crimes, finally, of all kinds, provided they resulted in profit or intimidation (abusive use of pastures, damages, theft of live-stock, fires).[41]

Meanwhile Navarra, who had joined the ranks of the separatist movement, thus consolidating his links with people like Vizzini and Genco Russo, and later, when MIS, the neo-Fascist party was defeated, turned to the Liberal party, becoming its main elector. Indeed, in the

Fig. 1. The Cosca of Michele Navarra

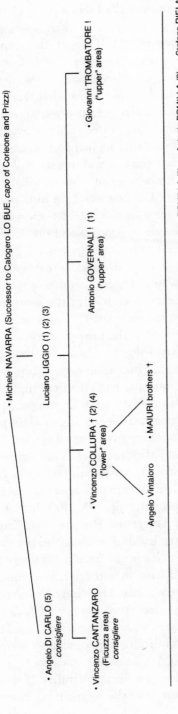

• Michele NAVARRA (Successor to Calogero LO BUE, *capo* of Corleone and Prizzi)

• Angelo DI CARLO (5)
consigliere

Luciano LIGGIO (1) (2) (3)

• Vincenzo CANTANZARO
(Ficuzza area)
consigliere

Antonio GOVERNALI ! (1)
("upper" area)

• Giovanni TROMBATORE !
("upper" area)

• Vincenzo COLLURA † (2) (4)
("lower" area)

Angelo Vintaloro   • MAIURI brothers †

• Michelangelo GENNARO Leonardo LA TORRE • Pasquale LO BUE • Giovanni LO BUE • Carmelo LO BUE † • Leoluca POMILLA (3) • Antonio POMILLA (3) • Stefano RIELA

• Andrea RIELA • Filippo GENNARO (1) • Rosario RIELA • Giuliano RIELA • Carmelo PENNINO (2) • A. MANCUSO MARCELLO • G. MANCUSO MARCELLO Fernando TROMBADORI !

Giovanni DELO ! Vincenzo LISTì ! Marco MARINO † Giovanni MARINO † Paolo RIINA † Vincenzo CORTIMIGLIA † • Innocenzo FERRARA • Giovanni FERRARA • F. P. STREVA

• Arcangelo STREVA • Antonio STREVA • Vincenzo RAIA • Luciano RAIA • Giulio RAIA • Biagio LIGGIO † Giovanni LIGGIO † Giovanni PASQUA

Giuseppe CANNELLA Antonio COMPARETTO Filippo MARRETTA Giuseppe LOMBARDO Carmelo PECORARO
(Prizzi *capo*) (Prizzi) (Prizzi) (Prizzi) (Prizzi)

LEGEND

Activity

(1) Assassin
(2) Field guard
(3) Meat trafficking
(4) Kidnapping for ransom
(5) Race course racketeering, prostitution, gambling

† = Died in fight with Liggiani's men
• = Family ties
! = "Missing"

SOURCE: Parliamentary Commission of Inquiry into the Sicilian Mafia, Report on Particular Mafiosi (Rome, 1971), author's adaptation.

1948 political elections the two deputies of the Liberal party elected in the Palermo constituency, got the greater part of their votes in the district of Corleone and nearby communes. One of the deputies, Geralamo Bellavista, was Navarra's personal attorney. But in Corleone, as in other areas of the Sicilian *latifondo,* the peasant movement for agrarian reform had grown, and its leader was the Socialist secretary of the Chamber of Labor, Placido Rizzoto. His presence was an inconvenient one for the Mafia and so Rizzoto disappeared. On the evening of his disappearance a young shepherd said that he had seen a man being killed, and he indicated the spot. Since the boy was in a state of mental excitation and it was impossible to make sense of what he said, he was taken to the Corleone hospital, where Dr. Navarra gave him an injection: shortly thereafter the young man died.[42] Held responsible by public opinion for Rizzoto's disappearance, Navarra and his lieutenant Luciano Liggio (also known as Leggio) were never sentenced, but they were considered socially dangerous by the police and were proposed for *confino*—that is, internal exile. While Liggio became a fugitive, Navarra was arrested and sent into internal exile. But the measure was revoked, and in a few months Navarra returned to Corleone. Meanwhile, this episode had convinced him that the Liberal party was not a winner. Not only had his personal attorney, to whose election he had greatly contributed, been unable to save him from *confino,* but during the 1948 elections the Christian Democratic party had triumphed.

So Navarra shifted his preference to the Christian Democratic party, as did his friends and teachers Vizzini and Genco Russo. His power reached its peak when he succeeded in taking over control of the Consortium for the Reclamation of Upper and Middle Belice. This consortium had been set up in 1933 for the construction of a dam across the Belice River to permit the irrigation of the land within the area of the reclamation project, which measured approximately 106,000 hectares in twenty communes of the provinces of Agrigento, Palermo, and Trapani. The consortium had always been in the hands of mafiosi and the owners of large estates, and until the mid-forties it had been completely inactive. The availability of water would have inflicted serious damage to the truck-garden Mafia, whose power was based precisely on its control of water irrigation. Opposed to the project, too, were the *gabelloti* who saw in the availability of water a way in which the peasants could free themselves from their dependent condition. Opposed also were the livestock thieves, that is, a not negligible part of Navarra's *cosca,* because irrigated cultivation would mean there was less possibility of stealing livestock. Instead, in favor of the dam were the segments of Navarra's *cosca* headed by Liggio, who had formed a trucking company and saw an excellent opportunity for his company in the increase of production.

The conflict came to an end with the victory of Michele Navarra, who stole the majority from Prince Giardinelli, who wanted the dam, and arranged for the election as president of Attorney Alberto Gensardi, son-in-law of the famous Mafia chief of Camporeale, Vanni Sacco.[43] But this was his last victory. He tried in fact to have Liggio murdered, but Liggio escaped the attempt and on August 2 Navarra himself fell under the killer's bullets. At the moment of his death his police record was immaculate. He did not leave his wife and children much. He had had a boundless thirst for power, but despite his great ability, he did not know how to keep pace with the times. Instead his successor Luciano Liggio would be one of the chief movers in the transformation of the Mafia during the fifties.

The Innovators: Continuity and Splits

In the fifties the old Mafia was composed of men characterized by considerable dynamism who were capable of dealing with the changed economic, political, and social conditions of a rapidly changing postwar Sicily. This was proved by their ability to adapt to the changing relationships of power among the political parties, their joining the party that seized power, and their skill in penetrating the new reform and economic development agencies and the public administration. But their stable interests were still linked to the situation in which landownership prevailed and were articulated through power groups that did not allow them to go too far in adjusting. Therefore not they but new individuals were to be the protagonists of the Mafia's transformation in the fifties. Among these a decisive role was played by Luciano Liggio and the Palermo clan of the Greco family.

Liggio, unlike Navarra, was the son of peasants and was raised in straitened conditions. He began his career very young; in 1914, when he was just nineteen, he was denounced for illegal possession of firearms and shortly after was arrested when caught stealing stacks of wheat. Six months after his arrest a sworn guard in Corleone who had collaborated in his capture was killed. Liggio, indicted at first for the murder, was acquitted due to lack of evidence, despite the fact that an accomplice of his during the preparatory phase of the trial had confessed, and then retracted his confession during the trial. At the age of twenty he became *campiere* on a large farm in the Corleone area, taking the place of a *campiere* who was found murdered. And it was by relying on his activities as *campiere* that he built his fortune and his reputation as a skillful, bold criminal. But he was not only a violent, bloodthirsty criminal; he did in fact have undeniable talents as a leader and organizer. Having attached himself to Navarra's *cosca,* Liggio quickly became one of its most prestigious lieutenants by organizing livestock thefts and clandestine slaughtering in the Ficuzza Forest. His career proceeded unhindered, puncutated by more murders and criminal exploits until, accused of having kidnapped the union organizer Placido Rizzoto and of being his murderer, Liggio became a fugitive in 1948. He remained a fugitive from November 1948 until May 1964 and in fact was deservedly awarded the nickname "the Corleone Pimpernel." When he was captured it was discovered that he had spent a great part of his fugitive years "in the Palermo Maritime Hotel under the assumed name of Gaspare Centineo, lodging in a comfortable, quiet room under the care of the medical doctor Gaetano LaMantia, evidently a good friend of his."[44]

It was precisely his experience as a fugitive that aided Liggio's acclimatization to the special traits of the Palermo Mafia, for he understood the possibilities for profit that had opened up to Mafia activities. Born and raised in the agricultural area of Corleone, he had understood even when he led livestock into the Ficuzza Forest that the true opportunities for enrichment lay elsewhere, in the markets of Palermo. But if he hadn't frequented the groups he did thanks to his being a fugitive, he would not have had the means, the organizational ideas and initiatives that in the mid-fifties would allow him to take the great leap from traditional activities to new and more profitable enterprises. It was precisely during the time spent as a fugitive that he built his fortune. The turning points are marked by the creation in 1956 of a company for the breeding of sheep and cattle, with its headquarters in the district of Piano della Scala, where Liggio owned land acquired with the fruits of his previous criminal activity. This company, in which Liggio did not formally participate but which he actually owned, had the aim of bringing together the two activities in cattle theft that, under the management of Navarra's *cosca,* were separated and performed by different organizations: the clandestine slaughtering of the stolen livestock and its transportation to the Palermo markets. Thus Liggio concentrated in his hands the two sources of profit; he eluded Navarra's control and challenged his monopoly; he realized his aim of entering the Palermo markets directly. Also connected with the formation of the cattle company was the creation of a trucking company; he

bought two trucks with which he transported the clandestinely slaugh-
tered livestock to Palermo. In this way the entire sequence of cattle
theft was in his hands: the theft of the cattle, its slaughtering, its
transportation to Palermo, and its sale to the wholesalers. This was an
important innovation that broke the chain of middlemen, made it
possible for Liggio to compete successfully with Navarra's *cosca,* and to
strengthen his ties with the circles of the Palermo Mafia. Furthermore,
the trucking company also performed another task; with it he planned
to make money out of the transportation of construction materials for
the Belice dam. However, in this fashion he was making enemies not
only with the *cosca* headed by Navarra, and with all the interests that
supported him, but also with persons among the old Palermo Mafia.
This became one of the factors in the collision that marked the hot years
of the struggle for supremacy in Palermo. But meanwhile, Liggio
had to reckon with Navarra, whom he defeated. Nevertheless, Dr.
Navarra's death did not put an end to the feud between his followers
and the followers of Liggio. In Corleone the armed struggle continued:
During the years between 1958 and 1963, ten people were murdered,
while six disappeared. Almost all of them belonged to the Navarra
group. From his hideout Liggio once again conquered the territory that
had been under Navarra's unchallenged domination. Having moved
into Corleone and made it the territorial base of his power, he could
now operate in Palermo from a position of strength and conquer new
territory in the capital.[45]

In Palermo, Liggio reinforced the ranks of the new emerging Mafia
which, beginning with the fifties, would put its stamp on all of Sicily,
going beyond the island's borders both in the direction of other Italian
regions and in that of the international narcotics traffic. Liggio,

> having left the feudal fortress of Corleone, descends upon Palermo and
> there becomes associated with the fearful Angelo La Barbera; Tommaso
> Buscetta; Rosario Mancino; Salvatore Greco, known as "the half-pint";
> the other Salvatore Greco, known as "the engineer"; Vincenzo Rimi,
> and Filippo Rimi . . . . He is also associated with the notorious
> Giuseppe Panzeca, Michele Cavatajo . . . ; Pietro Torretta; Francesco
> Paolo Bontade; Giovanni di Peri; becoming himself one of the chiefs of
> the association.[46]

All of these men became, in various roles, the chief figures in the
Palermo Mafia and its internecine struggles from the mid-fifties to the
eighties. And, among them, the most significant personages belonged

Fig. 2. The Greco Family

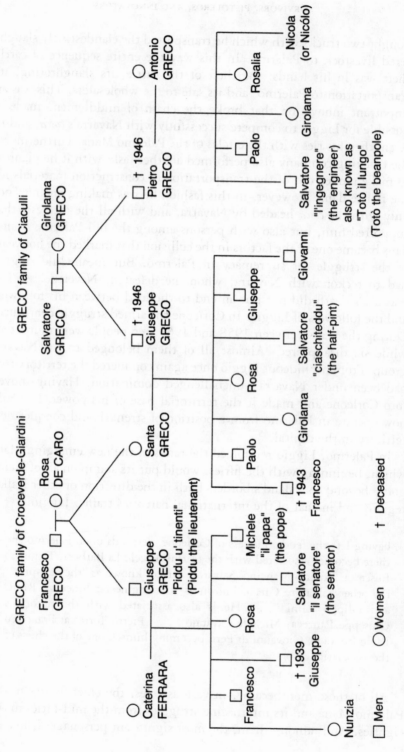

SOURCE: Parliamentary Commission of Inquiry into the Sicilian Mafia, Report on Particular Mafiosi (Rome, 1971), author's adaptation.

168

to the Greco family. While Liggio was an innovator who broke the tradition with violence, the Grecos represented a different sort of innovation. In fact, they took up a position inside a *cosca* that in its central nucleus identified with an extended family and evolved, through a few violent traumas, from the citrus fruit Mafia of the Conca d'Oro to the narcotics Mafia. And this evolution was continual, since the changes were channeled into the family tradition.

The Greco clan was composed of two families, one of them from the Croceverde Giardini area, the other from the Ciaculli area, both on the southwestern periphery of Palermo, where the intensive citrus cultivation of the Conca d'Oro begins. The two families were related; a daughter of the Grecos from Giardini was married to a son of the Grecos from Ciaculli (see Figure 2), whose major representative was Giuseppe Greco of Croceverde Giardini, nicknamed Piddu u' Tinenti (Piddu the lieutenant), *gabelloto* of a three-hundred-hectare estate that raised tangerines. Don Piddu u' Tinenti, even though there were no charges or police measures against him (only in 1966, at the age of seventy-two, was he sentenced to special police surveillance, but nevertheless left free to circulate in his place of residence), was unanimously recognized as the chief of the Mafia *cosca* of Croceverde Giardini. But the chief of the Ciaculli *cosca* was his brother-in-law Giuseppe Greco. The harmonious relationship between the two families was seriously disrupted in 1939, when due to a matter of who sat where on a bench during the Feast of the Crucifixion that took place at Ciaculli, several members of the two families had a quarrel. On that same evening there was a shoot-out, during which Giuseppe Greco, the son of Piddu u' Tinenti, was killed. Thus began a bloody feud between the two families that lasted until 1947 and in the course of which were killed (supposedly) the brother-in-law of Piddu u' Tinenti—that is, his namesake Giuseppe Greco—and also his brother-in-law's brother Pietro Greco. A year later one of Piddu u' Tinenti's most faithful men was killed, and at this point he decided it would be convenient to enter into an alliance with the powerful boss of Villabate, Antonino Cottone, the relative of well-known American gangsters. The alliance was sanctioned by the marriage of one of his sons with one of Cottone's daughters. This alliance constituted the premise for the peaceful solution of the feud. In fact Cottone and the two Profaci brothers, who were originally from Villabate and lived in New York but who at the end of the war had temporarily returned to their birthplace, pressured Piddu u' Tinenti to bring about a rapprochement, partly in view of the "patriarchal" responsibilities the latter had with regard to orphaned children in the family. The peace was ratified with the appropriate forms of economic alliance between the two branches of the family. The children of those men who had been killed became associated with the management of the tangerine groves and the administration of a company that exported the fruit; furthermore, they became partners in a trucking company. Thus began the career of the three most important criminal figures of the Greco family, whose exploits ran from the fifties to the eighties: Salvatore Greco, known as "l'ingegnere" or "Totò il lungo" (the engineer or Totò the beanpole); his identically named cousin Salvatore Greco, called "ciaschiteddu" or "cicchiteddu" (the half-pint); Michele Greco, called "il papa" (the pope), the son of Don Piddu u' Tinenti.

Certain traits found in the biographies of the three cousins confirm a typical aspect of the new mafiosi who emerged during the fifties. Unlike the old mafiosi, whose careers unfolded through a series of transitions from illegality to the attempt to conquer respectability, often ending, for those who rose to the position of Mafia chief, in a quiet life in their original community, the new mafiosi lived a great part of their lives, and particularly the stages of maturity and old age, as fugitives from justice. A prime example in this regard is the comparison between the Greco and Liggio cousins on one hand and the patriarchs of the Greco and Navarra families on the other. Navarra, though unanimously considered the most important Mafia chief in Corleone, led a respectable life in his milieu. In 1948, at the age of twenty-three, Liggio became a fugitive from justice and from then on a great part of his life unfolded between prison and being on the run. Don Piddu u' Tinenti, despite his reputation as a Mafia chief, circulated freely in Palermo, surrounded by an aura of respectability. His sons and grandsons were able to circulate freely in Palermo only for several years; after that they became fugitives. But they were nevertheless able to become Palermo's conquering *cosca* and decisively take the route of the intensive exploitation of drugs. The combination of tobacco smuggling and drug trafficking were a crucial element for an understanding of the Grecos' activities. And their entry into this sector was particularly precocious if we recall that Salvatore Greco "the engineer" was involved in a deal of almost six kilos of heroin as early as 1952, traveling from Palermo to Milan. In 1955 and in 1957 he also was involved in the smuggling of tobacco; and finally in 1960 there was evidence of his connection with heroin trafficking in New York. All of this without there being a year between 1947 and 1963, when he became a fugitive, in which he is not charged with some crime. Undoubtedly, however, at the beginning of the sixties, the Grecos were the main operators in the field of drug trafficking in Palermo. In the sentence with which pretrial judge Cesare Terranova indicted the Greco cousins in 1965, it was stated: "Salvatore Greco, called ciaschiteddu, . . . is undoubtedly the member of a strong Mafia *cosca* devoted to the trafficking of tobacco and narcotics, as is proved . . . by the connections maintained with well-known elements of the international underworld."

And as for his cousin Salvatore Greco the "engineer," it was added that "his connections with notorious figures in the underworld are sufficiently brought to light by the information reported by the Guardia della Finanza, or Fiscal Police."[47]

At the time in which this sentence was issued, the Grecos could already be considered the preeminent group among the emerging *cosche* in Palermo; their position in the field of drug trafficking was dominant. But it had been attained after a war that had bloodied the streets of Palermo during the years between 1958 and 1963, when a great number of *cosche* struggling to gain control over the city were deployed on opposing fronts.

Intermezzo: Gangster-Mafiosi and the Struggles for Supremacy in Palermo

Since Palermo is a large urban center, its relations among Mafia *cosche* are much more complex than those in other towns. Indeed, in the city the zones of influence of each *cosca* are marked off with reference to the quarter, the peripheries, and the sectors of the various activities, but the risk of overlappings and interferences among the interests of the *cosche* is certainly greater than in smaller towns. During the fifties the city's rapid development caused an enormous increase in the possibility of enrichment for the Mafia groups, which applied old methods to the new activities. One example was the renewed extortions connected with property; the same method used in the past to force a *campiere* on the owner of landed property was now used to force the hiring of a guard at a building site. The expansion of opportunities for Mafia profit resulted in the increased overlapping of the activities of individual *cosche* both in terms of territorial division and of sectors of specialized activity. It was in this framework that new groups sprang up that ignited the bloody war, with alternating periods of intense conflict and of relatively peaceful equilibrium, which have characterized the life of the city of Palermo from the fifties down to the present day.

The first of these periods covered the years 1958–63, but its origins go back to the war of succession for the scepter of command over

Palermo that began in 1952.[48] In that year there took place in Palermo the death of Giuseppe D'Accardi, the most prestigious Mafia chief in the center of the city. Among the various candidates to the succession the upper hand was gained by Antonino Butera, who in fact was not well liked by everyone because he was not considered a man of action. In 1955 he was succeeded by Antonino Marsiglia, with Angelo La Barbera as his second in command and with the help of Bartolo Porcelli, Mafia chief in the Partanna-Mondello area. The most prominent member of this trio was undoubtedly Angelo La Barbera, a typical example of the urban gangster-mafioso. He and his brother Salvatore came from a very poor family. The father was an ex-convict, and by the time they were eighteen both brothers had had their first run-ins with the law, Salvatore for armed threats, Angelo for rape at knifepoint. The two brothers collected about fifty indictments for various crimes, from extortion to homicide, and from 1950 on scarcely a year went by in which they were not denounced or proposed for surveillance or *confino* (internal exile). Both introduced new customs in the Mafia way of doing things, replacing the shotgun with the automatic pistol and not observing the traditional restraint regarding the spilling of blood that underlay the Mafia's commercial principles. Their activity originated and was essentially centered in extortions—that is, the demand for payoffs, threatening letters, linked above all to the construction sector, in which they set up a company that, together with another trucking company, acted essentially as a screen for their extortion racket. Quite soon Angelo La Barbera, flanked by his brother and by Tommaso Buschetta, and utilizing his extortion enterprise in the building field—which he ran according to the new methods and with the assistance of young criminals under his orders—became the true chief of the center of Palermo.

Having become rich in so short a time, La Barbera set about constructing for himself the image of a rich entrepreneur and led a very modern and luxurious life—frequent travel; numerous, and expensive extramarital relationships; frenetic visits to first-class hotels and expensive night clubs. This type of behavior was in sharp contrast to the traditional antiexhibitionistic reserve of the mafiosi. During the second half of the fifties, the insertion of Sicilian Mafia groups into the international drug traffic had taken a decisive turn. And the obviously open manner in which the La Barberas displayed the fruits of their profits was certain to arouse the suspicion of the investigating authorities, whereas a curtain of silence and concealment should have been drawn around that very lucrative sector. This strategy of concealment, insisted on above all by the Grecos, clashed with the exuberant vitality of the La Barberas, and quite soon resulted in a conflict that began with the request of two mafiosi, Vincenzo Maniscalco and Giulio Pisciotta, to obtain a number of rooms from the builder Moncada in order to expand their furniture business. But Moncada was "protected" by the La Barberas, who extorted money and buildings from him as a reward. The two brothers asked Pisciotta and Maniscalco to desist. The latter was persuaded not to by members of other Mafia groups, who in this case saw an opportunity to curb the La Barberas' power. Since the conflicts seemed impossible to resolve, a meeting was set up to discuss the matter. It was the intention of the other Mafia groups to take advantage of the controversy to get rid of Angelo La Barbera. The La Barberas, true to their style, decided to eliminate the hostile *cosche*. From 1959 until 1962 the war between the La Barberas and the other groups produced numerous casualties.

Up until that time the Mafia wars had involved only minor figures. Further, it did not seem to have compromised the alliance between the Grecos and the La Barberas, above all in the sphere of drug dealing. It must also be added that the establishment of the parliamentary commission investigating the Mafia, and the public uproar aroused by the increasing number of murders, had induced the Mafia chiefs to avoid excessive bloodshed so as not to worsen the situation and to deflect public attention from the Mafia. The truce, however, lasted a very short time, because on December 26, 1962, the smuggler Calcedonio Di Pisa was killed in Palermo.

Di Pisa was one of the most skillful members of the Palermo Mafia in the field of smuggling and drug trafficking; connected with all the major members of the Palermo Mafia (his address book contained the telephone numbers of Rosario Mancino, Salvatore Greco "l'ingegnere," Gaetano Badalamenti, and Ninive Tancredi, Angelo La Barbera's brother-in-law), he operated under the orders of the La Barberas and, higher up, those of Salvatore Greco "ciaschiteddu." Together with Rosario Anselmo he had been ordered in February 1962 to pick up, off the coast of Porto Empedocle, a big shipment of heroin coming from Egypt and to transport it to Palermo, where it would be handed over to a steward on the ocean liner *Saturnia,* departing for the United States. However, when it was delivered to the Italo-American mafiosi to whom it was addressed the heroin turned out to be of inferior quality, and therefore the money that reached the Palermo mafiosi who had bought it—among them the La Barberas—was less than they expected.

The groups involved in the deal ascertained that neither the Americans nor the Egyptian smugglers nor the steward on the ocean liner had "cheated." The La Barberas then suspected that Di Pisa and Anselmo, in cahoots with Don Cesare Manzella of Cinisi, who was also involved in the deal and who had recommended them for the delicate task, had kept part of the drug in order to sell it themselves.

> So, toward the end of 1962, a meeting was set up in which participated those—all qualified mafiosi—who had a direct or indirect interest in the operation. . . . The "defendants" Di Pisa and Anselmo tried to prove that they had not taken advantage of the trust put in them and managed to convince most of those assembled. But the La Barberas and Rosario Mancini did not modify their intransigent and decidedly accusatory attitude.[49]

True to form, the La Barberas chose violent action over negotiations and reasoning. Having had Di Pisa killed, they turned their attention to a number of his friends, thus flouting the decisions of the summit in which they had participated. At this point almost all the *cosche* of Palermo and environs formed a coalition against the two brothers: They were the Grecos, the group from Corleone headed by Luciano Liggio, as well as the *cosche* of Partinico, San Giuseppe Jato, Carini, Casteldaccia, and Cinisi.

The first move in the conflict was to the advantage of the anti–La Barbera coalition: On January 17, 1963, Salvatore La Barbera mysteriously disappeared and his body was never found. A little less than a month later Angelo La Barbera answered by exploding a car filled with dynamite near the house of Salvatore Greco "ciaschiteddu," in the Ciaculli quarter. Approximately a month later a number of armed mafiosi burst into the slaughterhouse of the township of Isola delle Femmine, but they did not find the designated victim and left. This episode, too, was ascribed to La Barbera who was the target of an attempt on his life on April 1 when some hit men shot at him from a car inside the Impero fishmarket in Palermo. While a number of people were wounded, the intended targets of the attempt—Angelo La Barbera and his ally Vincenzo Sorce—managed to escape, being hidden in the back of the shop, where a large arsenal of weapons was found. Three days later, on April 4, 1963, Angelo La Barbera's revenge was aimed at Vincenzo D'Accardi, an old mafioso who had been asked to mediate among the rival *cosche.* But since the shooting at the Impero fishmarket had taken place half an hour after the end of the meeting during which a truce had been decided, La Barbera assumed that the truce was an ambush into which they were trying to lure him and that D'Accardi was a treacherous mediator. At that point his fury also turned against his former henchmen, who refused to carry out further executions and to participate in the struggle. On April 24 one of them was killed; barely two days later a car stuffed with dynamite was exploded on the estate of the Mafia boss Cesare Manzella, killing him together with his steward.

It was, however, evident that La Barbera was by now isolated. His *cosca* was decimated by murders and desertions and could no longer count on any hit men; furthermore, all the mafiosi of Palermo and the surrounding area were by now lined up against him. He therefore fled to Milan together with his remaining troops in an attempt to organize a counteroffensive, but on June 24 an attack against him took place in which he was wounded; he managed to escape but went from the hospital to the San Vittore jail.

The arrest of Angelo La Barbera marked his end as Mafia chief because the material foundations of his power had disintegrated during the course of the struggle against the rival *cosche*. But his disappearance from the scene did not put an end to the fights between the *cosche* or to the chain of killings. In fact, the problem of the drastically compromised equilibrium was still unresolved and, besides, the Palermo-center "family" remained without a chief.

Angelo La Barbera's exit from the scene opened the way to the pretenders to the Palermo-center throne, first among them Pietro Torretta, boss of the outlying Uditore quarter, and Buscetta, who had switched to the anti–La Barbera coalition. Nevertheless, as in all situations when a family remains without a chief, this position becomes attractive to the chiefs of the competing families, who try to place men they trust at the head of the organization. And Buscetta's candidacy was especially opposed by the Grecos, who considered him untrustworthy.

Buscetta, who became famous in the mid-eighties as the most important Mafia "pentito" (a man who repents and turns state's evidence), had begun his career by becoming part of the blackmail and extortion racket at the expense of building contractors, truckers, and merchants, but he soon combined his cigarette-smuggling activities with the more profitable one of drug trafficking. In 1958 the Guardia di Finanza, or fiscal police, established the existence of links between the Sicilian *cosche* and French traffickers through Buscetta's activities. As with the La Barberas, Buscetta's life-style also contained an element of dissoluteness that rendered him suspect and unacceptable to the traditional mafiosi, who were aware of the instability of his married life.

In the struggle for the succession to Angelo La Barbera, Buscetta allied himself with Torretta, who actually considered himself the legitimate heir of the dethroned boss. Faced by the wait-and-see attitude of the Grecos, who were temporizing in order to single out a trusted man to place at the head of the Palermo-center family, Torretta decided to begin violent and direct action against his opponents. In June 1963 two of them were killed in his house, where they had been lured by the request of a "discussion" in order to smooth out their disagreements. During June, too, tension rose, killings increased, and explosions of dynamite-stuffed cars multiplied, until on June 30 there was the massacre of Ciaculli. That day a telephone call warned the carabinieri that, on a farming estate in Ciaculli,

> a Julietta car was parked with open doors, presumably loaded with explosives because a section of burned fuse attached to a gas cylinder was visible. Bomb experts were called to remove the cylinder from the backseat; thinking that there was no more danger, a number of those present approached the car to find out the nature of the device and for further observation. At that precise moment there was a very powerful explosion. Seven members of the police and army were killed. . . . Their bodies, struck by the explosion, were literally torn to pieces.[50]

The Ciaculli massacre was followed by a period of relative calm in the struggle between the *cosche,* which lasted until 1969, and this came about partly due to arrests or to the application of the law of *confino* (internal exile) for almost all the Mafia chiefs. Among others arrested, almost a year after the event, was Luciano Liggio, who had been a fugitive for sixteen years. His arrest took place in a house in Corleone, under circumstances that gave rise to a dispute—neither the first nor the last—between the police and the carabinieri that pointed not only to the lack of coordination between the two forces committed to the anti-Mafia struggle but also to their deleterious rivalry. The credit for the arrest was claimed by both then Inspector (later Commissioner) Angelo Mangano and by the carabinieri, with statements on both sides that were at once contradictory and ridiculous. In fact, to support his claims, Inspector Mangano, four years after the arrest, submitted a report in which he accused the carabinieri of disloyalty during the stages preceding the operation and described Liggio's arrest as follows:

> I posted the men around the block and thereafter I approached the door to the apartment where the dangerous bandit was supposedly sheltered. The two lieutenant colonels (of the carabinieri) remained at a certain

distance under cover of the walls of adjacent buildings. . . . After having knocked at the door and opened it, I decisively went inside, climbed the flight of stairs, and on the landing I was startled by a locked door. I opened it and on a cot at the end of the room, in the dark, there was outlined the form of the dangerous bandit. Without hesitation I turned on the lights and in a flash I jumped on top of Leggio who, terrified [and] without hope of rescue, kept saying to me: "Inspector, I am the man you are looking for." After me there entered the other collaborators and, then, several minutes later, after I sent for them, came the two lieutenant colonels who had until then remained at a respectful distance, perhaps waiting to hear the burst of fire from the bandit's lethal weapon.[51]

Called by the Anti-Mafia Commission to give his own version of the events, the carabinieri-Colonel Milillo answered the question as to the manner of Leggio's arrest as follows: "It took place immediately and peacefully. When we entered the room, Liggio lay on a small bed at the end of the room. As soon as he saw me, he said: "Only to you, colonel, . . . would I give my gun and not to that clown." He was referring to the inspector, to whom he addressed other unpleasant epithets."[52]

While the forces of law and order wasted their time with disputes of this sort, all the mafiosi they had arrested were acquitted in the two trials at Catanzaro and Bari, where Liggio, the Grecos, La Barbera, Buscetta, Mancino, and Torretta were indicted and were found guilty of only minor crimes. Once again there was a victory for the Mafia strategy, based on the lack of evidence and witnesses and on the inability of a part of the magistracy to understand the Mafia's true criminal nature and its dangerousness. When the Bari trial ended in 1969 with the acquittal of Liggio, who would soon go into hiding and prove unfindable—all this due to serious mistakes made by the forces of law and order—gang wars once more began to bloody the streets of Palermo and were topped off by the massacre on the Viale Lazio.

New Relations between Mafiosi and Politicians

The Palermo of the fifties, theater of the bloody struggle between the La Barbera brothers and the Greco-Liggio alliance, was also the Palermo of rapid urban development, of building speculation, of the rise from nothing of the great financial and political fortunes that had fallen into the hands of the Gioia–Lima–Ciancimino trio with their ties to the banking system, a patronage system that determined hiring policies, and support on a national scale. It was the Palermo where, with builders like Vassallo, contractors like Cassina, and small and large local builders who were Mafia members or were forced to pay kickbacks and protection money to the Mafia, large areas opened up for the national real estate companies. In this city, but also in those of western Sicily, relations between politicians and mafiosi become close, almost to the point of amalgamation. In any event, examples of organic bonds between mafiosi and politicians are not lacking; indeed, they abound, in the sense that they belonged to the same Christian Democratic party. Aside from the cases of Vizzini, Genco Russo, Navarra, and Di Carlo, many others can be mentioned. Liggio's defense lawyer was a man named Canzoneri, a Christian Democratic deputy for the Sicilian region who, a few days after the Ciaculli massacre, took it upon himself to declare before the Sicilian Regional Assembly that Liggio was being judicially persecuted by the Communists. Ernesto Di Fresco, the president of Palermo's provincial administration, was often seen in public in the company of the known Mafia chief of east Palermo, Don Paolino Bontà. Tommaso Buscetta obtained a passport through the good offices of Di Benedetto, and Angelo La Barbera obtained his through the intercession of Barbaccia, both of them Christian Democratic deputies. And they needed the passports to better organize their smuggling and drug trafficking.[53] In the sentence the pretrial judge issued against La Barbera, there is documentation to prove that they had a close relationship with the deputy Salvo Lima, a relationship that he in fact acknowledged.

On what basis did the exchange between politicians and mafiosi take place? The primary merchandise was electoral support. Mafia chiefs were by tradition great vote-getters. They repaid favors by bringing in votes. In his autobiography Nick Gentile documents the support given Giuseppe La Loggia of the Christian Democratic party during the electoral campaign of 1951:

> I had decided to support La Loggia because of an old debt of gratitude. . . . I did not even know Peppino La Loggia; but I knew Commendatore Altieri, the father-in-law of Giuseppe La Loggia's brother Vincenzo. Commendatore Altieri was the mayor of Agrigento immediately after the Allied landing. When I was arrested and charged in 1927 and tried in 1929, Altieri and the Honorable Pandamo testified on my behalf in court. I owed [them] this debt of gratitude and decided to pay it

at all costs . . . for forty days I canvassed all of Agrigento province by car. In the course of that same electoral campaign I changed the color of the town of Burgio, which was red. The Communist deputy mayor, following the intervention of a relative of his who was grateful to me for favors I had done him in the past, abandoned Communism and joined La Loggia. La Loggia's success was great; he obtained more than 39,000 preferential votes [i.e., votes for a prechosen candidate].[54]

Electoral support is nothing new; but certainly with the introduction of universal suffrage and the high voter turnout during the period after World War II, it reached previously unknown and spectacular levels. Even the Anti-Mafia Commission pointed out the extent of this phenomenon and documented a series of cases brought to light by the study of the relationship between the percentage of expressed preferences and the list of voters in twenty-two communes in four provinces of western Sicily: Palermo, Agrigento, Trapani, and Caltanissetta. The wariness that typified the commission's work, to the point of not publishing the records of politicians found to be involved in Mafia practices, also resulted in the fact that politicians who found Mafia support advantageous were not named in the report. Yet the cases of even notorious mafiosi giving electoral support to politicians were quite numerous, often even the rule.[55]

Nevertheless, this traditional exchange mechanism kept the roles played by mafiosi and politicians quite separate, since their functions were not amalgamated. But during the fifties an amalgamation of these roles characterized the brazen management of power in the local agencies in Palermo and other Sicilian towns: The politicians entered a partnership of convenience with the entrepreneurs and mafiosi in order to participate in the distribution of public benefits. From the documentation of the Anti-Mafia Commission there emerges with unmistakable clarity the phenomenon of such partnerships operating in the field of public works, construction, and various franchises, which helped the public administrators to enrich themselves. This was made possible by the inextricable intertwining between the Christian Democratic party and the public administration through the system of irregular and clientele-oriented hirings, the nonobservance of administrative and legal norms, and the bending of public agencies to the service of party interests. In an environment like that of Palermo and mafioso areas in general, this led to a singular process of interpenetration between Mafia *cosche* and the party in power. The takeover of the functions of mediation by the Christian Democrats and the constellation of secondary associations that surround it—functions in the past typical of the mafiosi—caused the latter to pour into it. This explains why traditional mafiosi such as Vizzini, Genco Russo, and Navarra joined the Christian Democratic party. But just as the old Christian Democratic notables were replaced by Fanfani's "young Turks," so the young mafiosi, storming around with their automatic pistols instead of shotguns, and engaged in drug trafficking as the new means of enrichment, replaced the old brokers. Thus the new mafiosi and the new political class of Christian Democrats were born together: at the same historical moment, in the same territorial areas, and in the same political and economic circles (the intertwining among the region, the towns, and the policy that regulated hiring, economic development and urbanization, and public works and building speculation). They were therefore the offspring of a single process that quickly enveloped Sicilian society during the fifties. This was the fundamental reason why the connection between mafiosi and Christian Democratic politicians appeared so organic. The social mobility triggered by the enormous amount of public resources distributed by the state and by the territorial and economic development public agencies fostered the creation of new opportunities for the renewal of the leadership of the Christian Democratic party as well as of the Mafia groups. In other words Ciancimino and the La Barberas not only originated from one and the same process but had the same social roots and exploited, in different but closely connected fields, the same types of opportunities offered by an expanding system.

In this sense in the fifties the differentiation between mafiosi and politicians was particularly minuscule. Indeed, the degree of differentiation was determined by the level of specialization of activities. And the interconnection among mafiosi, politicians, and entrepreneurs makes it possible to label all three of them social entrepreneurs.

That is to say, the networks based on instrumental friendship were reconstituted, particularly inside those parties which have greater access to public resources. These networks permitted the resumption of the mediatory functions within a specialized agency such as the Christian Democratic party. Due to the persistence of the relationships of instrumental friendship and because of their strengthening, the borders separating roles disappear. The functional definition of a role in terms of the institutionalized tasks assigned to it tended to disappear and to be reformulated in informal terms with reference to friendship or kinship. Thus the man in charge of a technical office in a town, or a bank official, was defined within the web of kinship or instrumental friendship: He was in fact "a friend" or "a relative," and he was expected to respond accordingly to whatever request was made. In this manner the law, proper administrative procedures, and codes of bureaucratic behavior were manipulated, and functional attributes of roles and their distinctions disappeared. Through the manipulation of kinship and friendship, resources could be acquired. But manipulation was based on the ability to convert resources from one sector to another. Someone who owned a resource, for example a network of relationships, might utilize it to obtain jobs for his relatives. In so doing he spent, on behalf of these relatives, a share of the resources at his disposal. But he also gained resources consisting in the gratitude of those for whom he found jobs. These resources in turn can be converted into electoral support for the politician who got the jobs. In the second transaction, too, resources of gratitude are expended; in exchange credit is obtained with the politician. This credit can be cashed in by asking the politician to finance an enterprise one may want to launch. With the financing one again disposes of an amount of resources that can once again be manipulated and converted, as was done initially with the social resource that comprised acquaintances in high places. And the process continues ad infinitum to the extent that an individual is able to maintain and increase the initial capital through the conversion of resources.

In a fluid situation like this the functional specialization of roles disappears, and the only true specialization consists in being a social entrepreneur—that is, in combining, through the manipulation of relatives and instrumental friendship, the social relations that allow access to resources. Wherever this network of social relationships and this normative system reigns, the individuals who potentially aspire to the roles of social entrepreneurs address themselves to those sectors and situations where the opportunities are greatest. In these terms the concentration of mafiosi and politicians in the Christian Democratic party and the Mafia's intertwining with the public powers in Palermo and Sicily during the fifties can be explained. And for this reason it is difficult to say during those years which of the two (politicians or mafiosi) manipulated the other. The manipulation was reciprocal, the differentiation between the roles was functionally minimal. In a certain sense mafiosi and Christian Democratic politicians were both "Cosa Nostra."

8

THE ENTREPRENEURS OF CRIME

Amid the seeming confusion of our mysterious world, individuals are so nicely adjusted to a system, and systems to one another and to a whole.
—Nathaniel Hawthorne, *Wakefield*

We become what we are.
—Friedrich Nietzsche, *Ecce Homo*

Internecine Struggles and the War Against the Public Powers

After the 1963 Ciaculli massacre in Palermo, the outbreaks of violence seemed to subside until 1969. The chief Mafia bosses were brought to trial, while the partial decapitation of the *cosche* (only the Grecos and Rosario Mancino had remained at large, having become fugitives—the latter only until 1967) produced a temporary crisis in their activities. But during the same period conditions were created for the reorganization of their affairs and the dominance of the Grecos, who had remained the only ones active and thus without competitors. Full resumption of activities followed the disconcerting sentence of the trial after the Ciaculli massacre, in which almost all the bosses had been indicted. On December 28, 1968, the Catanzaro Court of Assizes acquitted practically all of them due to lack of evidence. Less than six months later, on June 10, 1969, the Bari Court of Appeals also acquitted Luciano Liggio, who had been charged with nine homicides, attempted homicide, and association with intent to commit a crime. Although the state attorney's office in Palermo had requested special surveillance for Liggio together with restricted residence, the order was never carried out, and only seven months after the request was made—that is, on January 19, 1970—a circular letter was issued for the arrest of Liggio, who in the meantime on November 19, 1969 had left the Roman clinic where he was hospitalized and had gone into hiding. He would be arrested again five years later.[1] Thus, during 1969 all the Mafia bosses and hit men were set free. In a report submitted to the Anti-Mafia Commission in 1973, Colonel Carlo Alberto Dalla Chiesa wrote:

> The head mafiosi . . . immediately resumed their ties with the groups . . . to which they belonged. The return to freedom of chiefs and qualified hit men meant . . . not only a resumption of criminal activities in accordance with the old canons and in the wake of the suddenly interrupted massive repressive action, but also the emergence of new reasons for conflict and a struggle for dominance of a particular area, group, activity, milieu. This background situation resulted in the prevailing and decisive affirmation of the "Greco group," which, because of the going into hiding . . . of some of its most prestigious opponents, had been able to continue its lucrative illicit activities (mainly the trafficking of drugs and the smuggling of tobacco) without being subjected to the "competition" of adversary groups, acquiring an ever-greater financial [resources] and prestige, thus creating the connective tissue and the "relations or understandings" that on one hand would guarantee the absorption of the followers of hostile groups and on the other, the decisive and ruthless elimination of the more obstinate adversaries and their followers.[2]

Internecine struggles soon began. Less than a year after the Catanzaro sentence, on December 10, 1969, five hit men disguised as policemen entered the Palermo offices of the Moncada Company on Viale Lazio, one of the thoroughfares that ran through the sites of the most ferocious building speculation, and opened fire on whoever was there. Two sons of the builder Moncada (who in the fifties had belonged to the La Barbera brothers' group) were wounded, and three people were killed, among them Michele Cavatajo, Pietro Torretta's lieutenant, who had aspired to succeed the La Barberas after their defeat by the Grecos.

The next two years saw the disappearance of the journalist Mauro De Mauro and the murder of the attorney general in Palermo, Pietro Scaglione, in May 1971, supposedly at the hands of Liggio. These events were completely unprecedented, because the Mafia had never before attacked judges and journalists. And they were not isolated episodes but the beginning of an escalation that would see judges, police officials, prominent party leaders, and important officials in the regional government fall under the bullets of the Mafia groups. The reasons for this escalation, which developed in the seventies and eighties, must be traced to the internecine conflicts among Mafia families and to the intensification of the clash with the state agencies following the expansion of Mafia interests.

At the beginning of the seventies the alliance among the families had reorganized, yet events would prove it a fragile one. The three principal groups that held sway in the Palermo Mafia were represented by a wing that included the Bontate, Badalamenti, Spatola, Inzerillo, and Buscetta families; by another headed by Liggio and composed of people from Corleone; and by a third composed of the Grecos from Ciaculli.[3] The coordinating summit among these families was formed by a triumvirate that included Bontate, Riina (Liggio's lieutenant), and Badalamenti. When Bontate and Badalamenti ended up in jail, the coordinating leadership was left to Riina alone—that is, to Liggio and the men from Corleone—and so the conflicts exploded. In 1971, in Palermo there was the kidnapping of Antonino Caruso, the son of the industrialist Giacomo Caruso, related through his wife to the boss of the Uditore quarter, Pietro Torretta (who in the sixties had been aligned with the La Barberas against the Grecos and Liggio), and also a protégé of Bernardo Mattarella. The same year the son of the real estate entrepreneur Francesco Vassallo was also kidnapped, while the next year the same fate was suffered by Luciano Cassina, the son of the entrepreneur who for decades held the monopoly of public works contracts for highway construction. In one of these cases Mattarella was struck directly, and in all three instances the prestige of Stefano Bontate (the son of Don Paolino Bontà, great vote getter for Ernesto Di Fresco, president of Palermo's provincial administration) was severely damaged. Bontate had inherited from his father the task of guaranteeing the alliances among the Mafia, the entrepreneurial class, and the political class in Palermo. In 1975 Stefano Bontate, who had in the meantime been released from jail, suffered a further serious defeat: the kidnapping of Luigi Corleo, father-in-law of Nino Salvo— one of the great Sicilian tax collectors—accused, with his cousin Ignazio Salvo, of being a member of the Bontates' *cosca*. Salvo entrusted Bontate and Badalamenti with the task of recovering his father-in-law's corpse by paying the ransom, but without success. Bontate's position within the Palermo Mafia began to weaken under the blows delivered by the men from Corleone. Finally, in 1978 Gaetano Badalamenti was ousted from the summit of the coordinating committee of the Mafia families, and from then on he continued to organize his drug trafficking from Spain and South America, but with an ever-decreasing influence over the Palermo *cosche*.

Meanwhile, in August 1977, in the Ficuzza forest in Corleone territory the carabinieri Colonel Giuseppe Russo was killed. According to the pretrial findings, the shooting was carried out by four Corleone members, while Stefano Bontate learned from Michele Greco, "the Pope," to whom he had gone to protest, that the head of the hit squad was Pino Greco, "Scarpuzzedda," an ally of the Grecos from Ciaculli. This was the first confirmation that in the internal Mafia war an alliance was being cemented between the Grecos and Liggio.

Stefano Bontate protested because the decision to kill Colonel Russo had been taken without prior agreement by all the families and at the initiative of the Corleone people and of Pino Greco, "Scarpuzzedda," thus exposing all the Mafia clans to police repression.

The murder of Colonel Russo showed how harsh the war between the *cosche* had become, even resulting in attacks on state authorities. It was also a violation of the principle of limiting bloodshed as much as possible. In other instances, however, the weapon of homicide had been (and would be) used by the mafiosi in a cautious manner, so as to deflect the suspicions of the investigating authorities, sending them off on false trails. A perfect example of this was the murder of the Mafia boss Giuseppe Di Cristina, the protagonist of the Sicilian Mining Agency-Verzotto-Gunnella affair. In April 1978 Di Cristina began collaborating with the law because he realized that his position inside the *cosche* was extremely shaky and he sensed that his alliance with the Stefano Bontate clan exposed him to retaliations by the men from Corleone, with imminent danger to his life. On May 30, 1978, he was killed in the Passo di Rigano, in territory under the control of the Mafia family of Salvatore "Totuccio" Inzerillo, an ally of Stefano Bontate. The murder was attributed to the people from Corleone, who not by chance carefully chose the site where it took place. It was in fact both an insult to the Inzerillo family, since it represented a violation of its sovereign territorial power, and a precise tactical choice, picked out to induce the investigators to suspect that the perpetrators of the crime were members of the family in whose territory it occurred. This use of murder to focus the attention of the investigators on competing Mafia families was not new. According to Di Cristina's own revelations, the murder of Attorney General Scaglione was decided by Liggio in order to make the investigators suspect that Rimi and Badalamenti, whom Scaglione was investigating, had committed the crime.

Until Di Cristina's murder, the war among the *cosche* had been indirect: the kidnapping, the killing of Attorney General Scaglione and Colonel Russo were all intended in various ways to cast discredit or accusations and suspicions upon the Bontate, Inzerillo and Badalamenti families. However, no prestigious member of any of the families had yet been struck down. But Di Cristina's murder marked a sort of official, direct opening of hostilities between the families, though it was followed by a truce that lasted almost three years.

In fact, the families had to address all their attention to the growing repressive activities of police and legal system. During the same year in which Di Cristina was killed, Inspector Boris Giuliano uncovered an illegal drug traffic, and his further investigations led to the discovery of money being laundered through the banks. The traffic involved a total of $820,000, and the Bontate and Marchese families were implicated. For the first time a series of judicial investigations began with the aim of identifying the banking channels through which illicit profits were channeled. Barely one year later, in July 1979, Inspector Boris Giuliano was murdered.

In Palermo 1979 was a year of bloodshed with unique characteristics: the systematic murders of politicians, judges, and police officials. Three months before the murder of Boris Giuliano in March 1979, the provincial secretary of the Christian Democratic party in Palermo, Michele Reina, had been killed. September 1979 saw the murder of Judge Cesare Terranova, who in the sixties had led investigations into the La Barberas, Grecos, and Liggio and who in the seventies, as a member of parliament, had sat on the Anti-Mafia Commission. His parliamentary experience over, Terranova had returned to Palermo to head the pretrial office at the Palermo courts. His death had been announced a year and half earlier by Di Cristina, who, in his revelations to the carabinieri, had said that the Honorable Terranova might be killed by Luciano Liggio's faction, both to cast the shadow of suspicion on the Di Cristina–Badalamenti faction (under investigation for the killing of Candido Ciuni) and to strengthen Liggio's supremacy within Mafia ranks by exploiting the setbacks that the investigators would inflict on the faction under suspicion.

On the basis of the findings of the Palermo judges, it appears certain that once again neither Stefano Bontate nor Salvatore Inzerillo had been given advance notice of the three "excellent" 1979 murders. In subterranean fashion, however, the war among the Mafia groups continued and remained intense. During that same year, if one is to judge by Buscetta's confessions, the power balances within what he defined as the "commission" showed substantial changes: The majority of the bosses were in Liggio's camp. Quite soon the alliance between the Grecos and Liggio's people from Corleone will be solidly cemented. In those years there appeared among the Mafia ranks a phenomenon similar to the one that sprang up in Palermo in the mid-fifties: the emergence in leadership positions of young men who were intolerant of the forms of mediation and caution typical of the traditional bosses and were ready to use arms wantonly and without restraint. Among Liggio's lieutenants were Totò Riina, Bernardo Provenzano, Leoluca Bagarella, and Pino Greco. Unlike the fifties and sixties, when the emerging group of the La Barberas was defeated in the internecine wars, now the young colonels in the end prevailed over the traditionalist wing. But in 1979 the game was still going on. The heroin refineries in Sicily produced deals in the millions, but heavy losses were inflicted on Bontate's organization, owing to the seizure of large amounts of dollars destined for payment of the heroin and on Liggio's organization too, with the discovery of the hideout of Leoluca Bagarella. The Bontate group underwent a complete financial and organizational restructuring, as proved by the contacts with Michele Sindona, who was in Sicily at that time in connection with his fake kidnapping. Sindona was an international banker with ties to the Vatican, to leading politicians in Italy, and to the Mafia—who pulled off one of the greatest bank swindles in recent history, stealing billions of dollars while laundering other billions of Mafia drug money. A few days after being convicted, he died in prison of strychnine poisoning, either at his own hands or at those of his disgruntled Mafia associates.

So 1979 was a decisive year in regard to both the Mafia's inner setup and the conflict with organs of the state. While on one hand the alignments of the Mafia front were being redefined, on the other the strategy of attacks against institutions—and all those who, within them, tried to refute the logic of those who said there was no Mafia—was being perfected. All this would be confirmed by events in the years to come.

The year 1980 began with the murder on January 6 of the president of the Sicilian regional government, Santi Mattarella. A member of the Christian Democratic party, the son of that Bernardo Mattarella who had been suspected of having connections with the Mafia world, he had tried to bring order and clarity into the assignment of contracts for public works and represented the new face of the Sicilian Christian

Democratic party. Mattarella's murder created havoc in the ranks of the Bontate–Spatola–Inzerillo–Gambino and Di Maggio families, whose principal spheres of activity were linked to drug traffic and to the system of contracts for public works and construction, which were also used as outlets for the laundering of dirty money. Mattarella's murder cast suspicion on the Bontate-Spatola-Inzerillo-Gambino clan, which had already suffered a severe blow due to the arrests of Rosario and Vincenzo Spatola, Inzerillo's cousins, and were implicated in Sindona's phony kidnapping. In May 1980 Emanuele Basile, a captain of the carabinieri, was murdered in Monreale, and a dragnet that had been prepared for some time led to the arrest of numerous members of this clan. The circle seemed to close around the "traditionalist" members: Their loss of prestige was enormous; the impact of decimation in their ranks began to be felt, and they were subjected to attacks by Liggio and the men from Corleone who were allied with the Grecos, as well as by repressive police and carabinieri operations. Police operations meanwhile continued and in August 1980 two heroin refineries were discovered and Gerlando Alberti and the chemist André Bousquet, the great international expert of heroin production, were arrested. But at the same time things were also happening in the offices of Palermo's judiciary, headed by District Attorney Gaetano Costa, who not only personally signed warrants for the arrest of the thirty-three bosses, backing up the police investigations despite the doubts of some of his deputies, but also initiated a series of bank investigations concerning money laundering.

At this point Totuccio Inzerillo, head of the Uditore *cosca,* realizing that he was surrounded, intended to prove to everyone that he still had power. On his own initiative and without informing the "commission," he decided to order the assassination of District Attorney Gaetano Costa, who was murdered on a Palermo street on August 6, 1980. This assassination, however, did not achieve the hoped-for results: the readjustment of power relationships in Inzerillo's favor. Instead of breaking the encirclement that gripped the Bontates, Spatolas, and Inzerillos, Costa's murder accentuated it; shortly thereafter the great slaughter of the gang wars began, with the murder in April 1981 of Pippo Calò, the most prestigious Mafia chief in the ranks hostile to the alliance of the Grecos, Liggio, and the men from Corleone. During that April, in fact, Stefano Bontate was gunned down by a Kalashnikov rifle; just a month later, Totuccio Inzerillo fell to bullets from the same weapon. And this started a bloody battle in which the prominent chiefs and mere followers of the Mafia *cosche*

188

struggling for dominance fell by the dozens. During 1981 the casualties of the Mafia war were more than one hundred, a stunning number never reached before in the city of Palermo. Among the famous names, besides those of Bontate and Inzerillo, were also those of the Mafaras, who were very active in drug traffic, and in a single year had exported heroin into the United States with a value of 270 billion lire and laundered the profits through real estate investments. Police and carabinieri reacted forcefully, and in November 1981 they carried out two important operations that led to the discovery of a Mafia summit and a secret Mafia safe in a house on the city's outskirts. Thousands of dollars and millions of lire were found that were used to finance the war under way between the gangs.

Nineteen eighty-two similarly began with a success by the police forces. In February they discovered a Palermo refinery with the productive capacity of 50 kilograms of heroin per week. But while the internecine struggle continued (with the murder, among others, of a prestigious boss such as Pietro Marchese, in Ucciardone jail), the mafiosi again set their aims high. On April 30, 1982, there was the assassination of Pio La Torre, regional secretary of the Italian Communist party, who had begun a courageous struggle against the Mafia and against the plan to militarize Sicily in connection with the Comiso missile bases, which offered great possibilities for infiltration by Mafia groups. La Torre's death made it necessary to speed up the installation of General Carlo Alberto Dalla Chiesa as prefect of Palermo. In June 1982, Alfeo Ferlito—a mafia boss from Catania who was being moved to Palermo from Enna jail—was killed on the bypass road encircling Palermo. With him were killed the driver and three carabinieri who were escorting him. Ferlito was aligned with the Bontates and the Inzerillos; his presumed assassin was the Catanian Nitto Santapaola, allied with the Grecos and the men from Corleone. Ferlito was killed by the same Kalashnikov that (the ballistics expert established) was used to kill Bontate and Inzerillo and would be used to murder Dalla Chiesa, who was killed on the evening of September 3 with his wife and his bodyguard, on his way home from his office in the prefecture.

Dalla Chiesa had in vain asked for the powers necessary to coordinate the struggle against the Mafia effectively. In vain he had urged on politicians and state authorities—even having recourse to the press, pointing to the pervasiveness of the Mafia phenomenon, its expansion beyond the confines of Palermo itself, the alliances between politicians and entrepreneurial groups, and the full participation of entrepreneurship and criminality in eastern Sicily in the game of connivances and Mafia activities. On Dalla Chiesa's arrival in Palermo, amid the blatant hostility or indifference of the local Christian Democratic party, the Mafia groups had initiated open defiance of the prefect, punctuated by murders that were followed by anonymous telephone calls to the local newspapers, announcing that the "Carlo Alberto operation" had begun, would continue, and would reach its conclusion. Called as a witness by the Palermo judges, Salvo Lima—a deputy in the European Parliament, a former mayor of Palermo, and a leader of the Andreotti wing of the Christian Democratic party in Sicily—maintained that he had learned of Dalla Chiesa's appointment as prefect of Palermo from the press, and declared:

> The Christian Democratic party on the island in no way contributed to the appointment of Carlo Alberto Dalla Chiesa as prefect of Palermo and it simply acknowledged his appointment, which was decided upon by the central government, without expressing either approval or perplexity in regard to said appointment. Not even during the polemics also fueled by Dalla Chiesa, with regard to the granting of powers that he considered necessary in the struggle against the Mafia, did the Christian Democratic party on the island take an official position in one sense or another, nor am I aware of any initiative in this regard on the part of single party members.[4]

The isolation whose victim Dalla Chiesa was produced further victims. Meanwhile, 1982 topped the 1981 record, with more than 150 murders. And, as mafiosi fell in the internecine battles, those who were in the front lines of the struggle against the Mafia continued to die. In June 1983 there was the assassination of Captain Mario D'Aleo, commander of the carabinieri in Monreale. On July 29 there was the murder of the pretrial councillor Rocco Chinnici: A car bomb exploded in front of his street door as the magistrate was about to get into the armored car to go to his office. In the wake of Dalla Chiesa's intuitions, Chinnici was also investigating the connections between the great Sicilian tax collectors, the cousins Ignazio and Nino Salvo, and the mafiosi groups in the Palermo and Trapani areas, as well as the involvement of the Catania entrepreneurial groups in Palermo public works contracts, and the relationships between the Mafia of Catania and Palermo and the entrepreneurs. The pretrial investigation initiated by Chinnici was concluded by the Palermo judges with a very complex series of inquiries in which the revelations made by a number of mafiosi such as Buscetta and Contorno played a prominent role. But meanwhile, as late as 1985, while the principal Mafia bosses were in jail—with the exception of Michele Greco, "the pope," who would be arrested a few months later—two more police officials, Inspector Montana and Deputy Commissioner Cassara, were killed in Palermo by the Mafia, proving that, despite the setbacks it had suffered, the Mafia was still not defeated.

Expansion of Drug Traffic

The roots of what happened during the last fifteen years within the Mafia ranks and in their conflicts with the state must be sought in the enormous opportunities for enrichment that evolved beginning in the mid-fifties with the great drug-traffic boom.

Italy's involvement in the narcotics traffic began shortly after the end of World War II, due to the activities of Lucky Luciano, who was in control of drug trafficking even during Fascism. It has been ascertained that starting in 1950 and for several years he was able to move substantial quantities of heroin, 450 kilos in only one year, produced by well-known pharmaceutical companies in northern Italy.[5]

Luciano returned to Italy in 1946, after a repatriation order from the United States, where he had been sentenced for crimes connected with the activities of Cosa Nostra. From Italy Luciano tried to move to Cuba, an excellent base for the direction of the traffic of narcotics. But in 1947 the American government succeeded in having him repatriated once again to Italy, where he settled down in the Campania region. From there until the mid-fifties Luciano became a chief, if not the most important, figure in the organization of the "stages" that move drugs from the production areas in the Middle and Far East to Europe and from there all the way to the final marketplace, which then was constituted almost exclusively by the United States.

Luciano's organization was not the only chief operator in drug traffic. Two other teams of drug traffickers were particularly active, and one of them used as its base of operation the village of Salemi in Trapani province, a traditional base for Mafia groups. Between 1949 and 1960 the fiscal police seized more than four hundred pounds of heroin; if we consider that the ratio between seizures and shipments that slipped through was 1 to 10, and that in the mid-fifties the price paid by the Cosa Nostra for heroin bought in Italy was $3,300 per kilo, we can estimate that during that decade the Italian traffickers were paid almost $15,000,000.[6]

During the fifties the presence of the Sicilian Mafia in the international drug trade was still marginal. It is true that Rosario Mancino, Luciano's right-hand man, was involved in the traffic; it is also true that even at the beginning of the decade the Grecos were active in tobacco smuggling and to a lesser extent in drug trafficking and that the Mafia in Salemi organized deals of considerable importance. But according to the United States Bureau of Narcotics, drug trafficking as a whole was controlled by the five Mafia families in the New York area—that is, the families of Joe Bonanno, Gaetano Lucchese, Carlo Gambino, Giuseppe Magliocco, and Vito Genovese; 95 percent of the heroin traffic of the United States was in their hands.[7] The principal role outside the United States fell to traffickers from Corsica and Marseilles, above all when it came to transforming the morphine base into heroin in laboratories concentrated in the Marseilles area, and the main operational base for drug entry into the United States was Cuba.[8] To this we must add that the main reference point in Italy for the traffic was Lucky Luciano, who lived in Naples. He had kept up his network of connections in the United States and harbored a certain mistrust for the Sicilian Mafia, which was still characterized by the predominance of personalities tied to the large estates, such as Genco Russo, Vizzini, and Navarra. Among Luciano's collaborators was Rosario Mancino, who was afterwards associated with the La Barberas and with Buscetta and Torretta; but these connections developed later on, when conditions on the world drug market changed and the premises were created for the integration of the emerging Mafia groups into the great network of drug trafficking.

These conditions came into being in the second half of the fifties and brought about a transformation in the modalities of drug trafficking. Some were caused by events external to the trafficking network; others were to be found within the criminal world.

The first was due to the fact that Cuba had lost its practical value as a support base for the sale of heroin in the United States. Castro's guerrilla warfare against the Batista regime, and the subsequent fall of the dictatorship completely eliminated the felicitous possibilities for smuggling in the Cuban paradise. The New York Mafia families were faced with the necessity of finding other support bases. What is more, the rapid growth of heroin consumption posed the need for centralization of the traffic and a reduction in the different stages in the transport of the merchandise from the places of production to those of distribution; hence the necessity to procure supplies directly from the areas of opium production. These conditions were accompanied by the fact that in the Mediterranean, together with the traffic of narcotics, the smuggling of tobacco was developing at a tremendous pace. This twofold expansion entailed the risk that many people might be attracted by the opportunities for profit and might enter the world of contraband with neither the experience nor the organizational abilities that would allow them to perform this activity successfully, thus exposing all the groups to the risk of discovery. It was therefore necessary to enforce tighter controls over the traffic, and to utilize the structure and organization of the tobacco contraband for the trafficking of drugs. And this was not in the sense of proceeding with both types of trafficking together, because it has always been a good policy to separate the distribution channels, since the relative value of each in relation to its bulk is too different for anyone to risk having drug shipments seized together with shipments of tobacco. But nevertheless there persisted the need to utilize in drug traffic consolidated experiences and organizational structures that had proved suitable for tobacco smuggling. This was one of the conditions that favored the integration of the emerging Mafia groups in the traffic of drugs. In fact, during the first half of the fifties a number of young Palermo mafiosi, among them Rosario Mancino, Pietro Davi, Tommaso Buscetta, and Salvatore Greco ("the engineer" or "the beanpole"), had made contact with one of the largest smuggling organizations in the Mediterranean, "the Franco-Corsican organization of Elio Forni and Marcello Falciai, which disposed of twenty-two smugglers' boats along the Tyrrhenian coast from Savona to Palermo."[9]

At any rate, the Grecos and Mancinos had been in the smuggling field since the end of the forties, while other emerging and impatient stars in the mafioso firmament, such as the La Barberas, Badalamentis, and Buscettas, became active in the fifties; the time had at last come for the request for help from the American mafiosi and the reply of the Sicilians, especially when France began a decisive repression of the Marseilles smuggling ring.

This rapprochement was heralded by a series of events; in smuggling in the mid-fifties there had erupted a Mafia war similar to the one that took place during the same years in Palermo over control of the wholesale markets. In the meantime two notorious Sicilian-American mafiosi moved to Italy from the United States: Frank Garofalo and Joe Adonis. The former, born in Castellammare del Golfo, was an "adviser" in New York of the family from Castellammare headed by Joe Bonanno. On August 10, 1955, Garofalo met a very important French smuggler, Pascal Molinelli, in Palermo. His presence was again reported in

Palermo during early October, in the company of Raffaele Quasarano, regarded as an international smuggler and drug trafficker. Finally in July 1957 Garofalo settled in Palermo, leaving the United States, and for many years and certainly until 1965, worked at setting up a drug trafficking organization, especially one that guaranteed the flow of capital to and from Switzerland in Italy and abroad. As for Joe Adonis, thought to be one of the heads of Cosa Nostra, he arrived in Italy in February 1956 and settled in the Val d'Aosta. From then until the early seventies an organized smuggling network, with connections in all the European nations, revolved around him.[10]

The increase in suspicious journeys by certain persons between Italy and the United States in the mid-fifties was the prelude to the Mafia summit that was held in Palermo from October 12 to 16, 1956, at the Hotel delle Palme. The Palermo summit had

> as its principal objective the establishment of an organization that will utilize enormous sums of American capital with the concurrence, and therefore with the sharing in profits, of the Sicilian Mafia, the definition of the role it is expected to play in this specific sector, leaving local problems to the various *cosche* . . . and, in particular, three important matters would be examined: (*a*) relations with the suppliers of drugs, generally the gangs in Marseilles . . . ; (*b*) relations with the Sicilian Mafia . . . ; (*c*) the movement of capital.[11]

The October 1957 gathering in Palermo that came shortly before the murder of Albert Anastasia in New York and the failed Appalachia summit, at which almost all the members of the American Mafia families were arrested, had two important results. On one hand Lucky Luciano lost his preeminence in the drug trafficking organization in Italy; on the other, despite Genco Russo's reluctance to get involved in drug trafficking, vast territories were opening for the emerging *cosche,* which would gradually become integrated in the heroin traffic, occupying increasingly important positions.

We have already seen how the conflict between the La Barberas and the Grecos had been caused by a controversy related to the sale of a heroin shipment. Therefore, as early as the second half of the fifties, several groups of mafiosi were particularly active in the drug traffic. And this is confirmed by what we read in the report on the drug traffic issued by the Anti-Mafia Commission. On the basis of a report by the fiscal police, the report asserted that in 1958 in Sicily the acquisition of merchandise is monopolized by the two organizations which, respectively, are headed by Pietro Davi and Salvatore Greco. . . . But whereas Davi is personally active, the Greco group is already in a position to have its "buffers," and they are Tommaso Buscetta, Antonio Camporeale, and Francesco Rizzuto. . . . The difference in rank is considerable and proves that the Grecos, even though operating within the ambit of the organization and in accordance with its directives, attain, if not actually increasing autonomy, the right to be . . . heard at the summit.[12]

At the end of the fifties the Greco clan therefore already occupied a dominant position within the Mafia *cosche*. This position was further reinforced in the sixties, when the Grecos were the only ones who did not fall into the hands of the police and were therefore able to "weave . . . the dense web of international smuggling that will become consolidated around 1969–70 in what will be the 'realm' of the new Mafia, with capillaries extending throughout the entire country."[13]

The events of the seventies and of the first half of the eighties are too recent to be reported without the risk of falling into a simple recital of current crime news, especially on a subject as delicate as that of drug traffic. A number of things, however, are certain: for one thing, the enormous increase in the demand for heroin, whose consumption during the fifties found its major market in the United States and spread through Europe and Italy. The traffic expanded incredibly fast, making it possible for the new group to step forward and enter the market, using the money derived from tobacco smuggling or from other forms of legal or illegal accumulation typical of Mafia activities. The large-scale availability of capital allowed the Sicilian Mafia groups to undertake a rationalization of drug traffic, at the same time exploiting the crisis of the traffickers in Corsica and Marseilles. On one hand an effort was made to eliminate as many intermediaries as possible from the chain of traffic by obtaining supplies at the sites of production. On the other hand the transformation of morphine into heroin took place directly, through the establishment of laboratories along the coastline from Trapani to Palermo.[14]

During the seventies and in the early eighties, therefore, a clear-cut predominance of the Sicilian Mafia *cosche* was established in international drug trafficking. But this predominance entailed a series of organizational problems and a number of profound changes in the configuration of the Mafia groups, whose equilibrium was upset by the copious flow of money.

Excess Liquidity

According to the computations made by the fiscal police in 1970, the cost of one thousand cases of contraband cigarettes was 42 million lire at the port of departure; 75 million on the open sea; 100 million at the port of debarkation; and 120 million when delivered on land.[15]

During the course of the smuggling operation the value of the merchandise was therefore almost tripled. And since the average cargo of a smugglers' ship varied between three thousand and six thousand cases, the capital used ranged from a minimum of 126 million lire (three thousand cases purchased at the port of departure) to a maximum of 720 million lire (six thousand cases delivered on land). These figures give us an idea of the capital needed to finance the contraband of foreign tobacco. The initial amount of capital entailed the need to bring together several forces and several financiers, and thus the need to make alliances with other families. Tobacco smuggling resulted in the emergence of the elements of a crisis in the rigid delimitation of territories belonging to each Mafia family and in the various sectors of activity. And obviously, by definition, the alliances also entailed conflicts. The inevitable consequence of the increase in traffic and earnings was an increase in the tensions among the families.

These same considerations applied all the more to the situation produced by the traffic in drugs. In 1965 ten kilos of opium, from which could be obtained one kilo of the morphine base needed to produce one kilo of 80 to 85 percent pure heroin, cost, at the site of origin (Turkey or Syria), $350. Through a series of transformations, cuts, and adulterations with lactose, quinine, and other substances added to the glassine envelope sold at retail, the kilo of heroin was changed into sixteen kilos of 5 percent heroin in 45,000 thirty-five-gram glassine envelopes that are sold at $5 each for a total value of $225,000.[16] Therefore if the value of a shipment of contraband cigarettes tripled, that of a heroin shipment from the opium base to the retail sale multiplied 640 times. It is estimated that during the early seventies ten to fifteen tons of heroin entered the United States every year, with a net profit of at least ten billion dollars for the traffickers.[17] The dimensions of the drug business require a sizable initial capital and the procuring of this capital usually involves risks. First among them is that of losing the money invested if the merchandise is seized. Furthermore, as the sphere of those who participate in the deal expands, the possibility of the operation being discovered increases. In fact, the links in the chain that runs from opium producer to heroin consumer includes about twenty different hands that pass the merchandise along. Obviously, with each transfer the risk increases. What is more, the greater the number of people involved, the greater the necessity for the existence of a climate of mutual trust among the participants. It is true, of course, that those who put up the money can remain relatively anonymous. An American congressman tells us:

> To acquire several shares in a deal under way and no questions asked, a financier was offered a minimum profit of two million dollars within six months for a contribution of one hundred thousand dollars. Of course, he ran a risk, that of losing his money; but the shares were negotiable. Should he suddenly be short on cash, he would be able to resell them. The financial transaction had the banal appearance of a routine operation; but this, however, involved a shipment of heroin from the Middle East to the United States. [18]

And certainly the idea of multiplying one's investment twenty times over in the course of six months cannot fail to be attractive. But if, in the financing of an operation, one may have recourse to anonymous financiers, this is not possible for the operations involved in the transformation of opium into heroin or for its transfer from the areas of production to the areas of consumption. In these instances the trust system must be based on relationships of a personal type, on direct contacts, on reliance that goes beyond pure economic interests and is based on shared membership in a group, on shared values, or on the fear of incurring revenge and paying with one's life for betrayal. And yet, it is precisely the size of the traffic and the temptations offered by the great profits that can be made from it that form many potential obstacles to the construction of a network of trusted relationships of a personal kind. In fact, on one hand, it is possible to eliminate only a certain number of the stages through which the heroin must pass. On the other, the considerable amounts of capital necessary for large-scale operations attract possible "investors" from among the Mafia groups. While this reduces the necessity of turning to "outside financing," it also increases the complexity of the network of interests at stake. Every alliance carries within it the potential seeds of suspicion. It increases the need to be informed about the movements of one's ally, who is still a competitor and a potential adversary. Nevertheless, the network for the conveyance of the merchandise must constantly be kept alive, avoiding as much as possible repeated substitutions of men and organizational structures, which entail not only additional costs but, above all, damaging interruptions in the flow of supplies.

All these conditions add particular complexity to the organizational network that must be set up for the traffic to be successful and escape the action of the law-enforcement agencies. It is therefore necessary to combine business methods that are typical of market anonymity and relationships of a fiduciary nature based on personal connections and on family and kinship solidarity. If in one way these "criminals . . . operate like businessmen and employ the same methods,"[19] in another they must rely on relatives and friends, put spies and informers inside the other Mafia families, corrupt officials of the police and legal system, and make use of the threat of violence to keep their organization running smoothly. Above all, they must reconcile the need of one family to realize a profit with the maintenance of a network of alliances and the demands of a centralized management of the traffic.

Organizational Changes

The events of the last fifteen years cast light upon these changes in the Mafia power structure. Together with the prolonged attack on the powers of the state, there in fact emerge new organizational modalities, above all based on the revelations made by those who have turned state's evidence, such as Buscetta and Contorno. Revelations which, repeating in great part those made by Joe Valachi as regards the organizational structure of the American Cosa Nostra,[20] seem to call into question a number of acquired notions about the Mafia's organizational structure. On the basis of the confessions of Buscetta and Contorno, the judges conclude that

> Cosa Nostra is organized with rigidly vertical structures and has its epicenter in Palermo, the seat of the directorial organism of the association, which is called *cupole,* or "commission." Contrary to a widespread belief, the Mafia on the island is not a structure composed of independent associations often at loggerheads with each other, but it is an organization that, though articulated and complex, has a substantial uniqueness of its own.[21]

The confessions of Buscetta and Contorno highlight the following organizational structure of Cosa Nostra:

• The family constitutes the basic cell in the organization. This is a structure with a territorial base that controls a quarter or an entire inhabited center.

• Each family is made up of "soldiers," men of honor coordinated in groups of ten by a *capodecina* (head of ten).[22] The members of the family elect a family head. He is assisted by a counselor, usually an older person or someone held in high esteem because of his wisdom, and assisted by one or more vice chiefs chosen by him.

• Three or more territorially contiguous families make up a *mandamento* (district) and nominate a district chief who can be a family head or a different protagonist.

• The district chiefs make up the collegial organism called the "commission" or "cupola," which has a provincial sphere of action and the task of insuring respect for the rules of Cosa Nostra and of settling disputes between the families.

• The commission is presided over by one of the district chiefs who is called "secretary" or "chief."

• Finally there exists, though on this point the information is not quite clear, a superior liaison organism called "interprovincial," which has secret and mysterious features, and about which even Buscetta is unable to say much more. As for relations between the Sicilian Cosa Nostra and the American Cosa Nostra, Buscetta positively excludes that there might be any form of stable organizational connection.[23]

This description strongly emphasizes the stable, monolithic characteristics that are accentuated by further revelations about the initiation procedures and rituals into Mafia families. In fact, still according to these depositions, it is established procedure that before a new member takes his oath to enter a family, the other family heads must be informed. Thus the commission not only assumes the functions of coordination, supervision, and settlement of disputes between the single families, but the families are in fact nonautonomous articulations of the commission, since they are unable to recruit without controls.

The recruitment then takes place through an initiation ritual that consists in taking an oath of fidelity to Cosa Nostra. In the presence of three persons of the family—according to Buscetta's version, or of the entire family, according to Contorno's—the neophyte holds in his hands the picture of a saint, touches it with the blood that drips from a finger pricked by a pin, sets fire to the image and holding it in his hands as it burns concludes his oath with this sentence: "May my flesh burn like this image if I do not keep faith with my oath."[24]

The existence of these rituals qualifies the Mafia organization as a secret society with iron rules, strictly formalized in rituals shared by all families. And the formula of the oath reported to us by the *pentiti* (those who repented) almost seems to demonstrate their detailed knowledge of the positivistic literature on criminology.[25]

The content of these depositions and the conclusion reached by the Palermo judges based on them are in sharp contrast to the theory according to which the Mafia organization has a fluid, impermanent character, and the so-called criminal associations are nothing but networks of social relations.[26] According to this theory, within the family or the Mafia *cosca,* the organizational pattern rests on a dyadic-stellar structure, dominated by the chief: "The father . . . is the symbolic figure who . . . holds together (the members of a family). He is the coordinator and conciliator. He is mediator and judge. He is in charge of the connections. He is the man who puts things in order when life becomes complicated."[27]

Externally, however, that is, in the relations between *cosche,* the operative principle is one of rigid territorial compartmentalization. Each family has an exclusive and monopolistic domination over a particular territory. The other families, if they want to undertake operations or carry on business activities in that territory, must ask permission of the family that rules it.[28]

This organizational model in its internal and external dimensions is subject to continuous, recurrent tensions whenever new opportunities for profit open up for the Mafia *cosche* and the innovative processes that lead to renewal of Mafia leadership are set in motion. In particular, two elements seem to be most prominent in its crisis: the spreading of the Mafia in urban situations that are subject to processes of social differentiation, with the consequence of a continued reshaping of territorial boundaries and spheres of reciprocal influence. Second, new opportunities for "making money" drive the emerging mafiosi to defy the rules solidified by tradition that have been established by the ruling family heads. These conditions bring out the weaknesses of the family head, so that rival families can exploit these internal divisions in order to appropriate sections of territory or spheres of business that belong to families undergoing a crisis. The alternation of phases of ruthless, violent competition with an increase in murders and retaliations, and phases of relatively stable *pax mafioso* is a constant in Mafia history. Traditionally, during the phases of acute conflict the most authoritative family head was asked to mediate or settle the controversies. But this was possible only as long as the territorial area of Mafia interests and activities was sufficiently limited, coinciding with a quarter, a single large estate, or a township. The development of Mafia activities on a large scale has brought with it a crisis in the traditional territorial demarcations. While the families continue to maintain a territorial social basis, the kinds of traffic in which they are involved, particularly the drug traffic, compel them to deal with situations that involve transgressing territorial boundaries. This is the reason for the organizational changes that we observe in the Mafia, and from them derives the need for coordination among the families. In the United States this need arose in the thirties, and the first meeting of the "commission" was held in New York in 1931. But the commission "was not an integral part of the . . . tradition; no organ of this sort existed in Sicily. The commission was born of a need to adjust to American reality."[29]

In Palermo the same need arose in the fifties, when building speculation, tobacco smuggling, the beginning of drug trafficking, and the movement to town of mafiosi who had until then been active inland (Liggio's is a representative example) suddenly heightened the clashes among competing *cosche* in order to corner the new opportunities for enrichment.

These changes have taken place, but it would be a gross error to believe that they radically changed the Mafia's organizational structure by transforming it into a sort of unique enterprise or association perhaps having a formally structured organizational chart like that of a bureaucratic organization, as one often gathers from journalistic accounts or from the image presented by the mass media. In fact, the similarities in procedures and functions—which according to the testimony of Mafia members seem to be shared by the Mafia and formal associations—are largely only superficial.

Let us begin with the "electoral" procedure for the appointment of the family head. It would be a mistake to consider this procedure as an actual casting of votes similar to that which takes place in an association or a democratic political system. In fact, the purpose is not to decide who among several contenders should assume the scepter of command. And usually there actually is only one candidate; it would make no sense to appoint as head of a family a candidate who has obtained 51 percent of the votes over another candidate who has obtained one vote less. The purpose of the vote is something more symbolic; that is, it gives the measure of the family's unity and indicates the extent of real consent. Also, the functions that are typical of the various roles in the Mafia family are profoundly unlike those in a formal organization.

The relations between the families therefore are absolutely not comparable by analogy to those between the offices or the organizational functions of an enterprise whose directorial summit might be constituted by the commission. On the contrary, they have more similarities to the relations among states. This is in fact a true and proper system of sovereignties in competition with each other, as proved by several indicators, among which the most important is the widespread practice of infiltrating one's men as spies into competing families.[30] And, as with all relationships between competing sovereignties, the organism that regulates the competition, establishes its norms, and prevents destructive conflicts is born, dies, and is resurrected in connection with changes in the power relationships among the Mafia families and in relation to the more or less conflictual nature of internal competition and the state's agencies. Not by chance, as we gather from the pretrial findings of the judges in Palermo, the Cosa Nostra commission was formed, then entered a crisis, and did not exist for a period and subsequently, in the mid-seventies, it came together again.[31] Nothing confirms better than these episodes that we are not dealing with the organizational structure of a single monolithic organization, but with one (whose procedures have a certain degree of formality) that serves to regulate an ever-changing system of alliances among the families that make up the basic mainstay of the Mafia's entire economic and political power system.

But the complications within the organization of Mafia families do not arise only at this level. Other, no less relevant problems exist with regard to the investment of the cash accumulated as a result of the trafficking.

The availability of enormous sums of money obtained through illegal operations increases immeasurably the need to launder the profits. The laundering consists in eliminating traces of the money's origins by investing it in legitimate economic activities—an operation that poses considerable problems. The traditional method of laundering dirty money through the banks often entails the need for accomplices and is dangerous since because of banking controls the laundering may be discovered. No method is safe, and many are used together with, or as an alternative to, laundering through the banks.

As for the necessity of investing the profits from the traffic of heroin, it results in increased pressure on public agencies to obtain contracts, building concessions, and public works that make it possible to invest capital obtained through illicit activities. Therefore it is not true, as one might be inclined to think, that the development of drug trafficking, with the high profits it entails, induces Mafia groups to attach less importance to relationships with the political sphere and thus with the possibility of obtaining benefits through public expenditures. On the contrary, precisely because of the needs that arise from the expansion of drug trafficking, such relationships assume new and more important aspects. In order to reconcile the two needs, that of recycling and laundering dirty money and that of investing it in legitimate productive activities, the Mafia groups set up complex networks of enterprises whose functions are not always of a productive nature.

Mafia Enterprises and Recycling Strategies

The modern enterprise is an organization oriented to the realization of profit by means of formally peaceful methods. Moreover, the activity must consist in the production of goods and services that are not prohibited by law. These are therefore two criteria by which we can decide whether an enterprise is Mafia inspired: The first relates to the kind of productive activity that is being performed—that is, whether it is a legal or illegal activity; the second concerns the methods used in economic competition—that is, whether the profit is obtained by formally peaceful or with violent methods. In defining whether or not an enterprise is a Mafia enterprise, reference to the origins of the accumulated capital is really irrelevant. Money does not carry identification tags, thus what matters is how it is used in terms of production and competitive methods.

On the basis of these criteria we have four types of enterprises. The first three can be considered to be those in which the Mafia enterprises should be listed:

1. Enterprises that perform illegal production activities and employ violent methods to discourage the competition.
2. Enterprises that perform illegal production activities and employ formally peaceful methods (of a type that cannot be easily detected).
3. Enterprises that perform legal production activities and employ violent methods to discourage the competition.
4. Enterprises that perform legal production activities and employ formally pacific methods.

The importance of this typology lies not only in the possibility of distinguishing among which types of enterprises those of the Mafia can be placed, but in the observation that the difference between the third and fourth types resides simply in the methods being employed, and therefore the passage from one kind to another is not difficult to carry out, above all if one takes into consideration the influence of the environment and the prevailing methods through which the competition among enterprises is expressed. In this way the typology sets up a discrimination in respect to the frequent tendency of lumping all Sicilian enterprises together by utilizing the term "Mafia" as an umbrella to cover them all. This tendency is open to criticism, but it has a basis in the fact that the borderlines between these two types of enterprises is extremely changeable, and as a result the non-Mafia enterprises, in order to survive, are often forced to face a competition carried out with violent methods, so they, too, must have recourse to these methods.

Alongside these enterprises there exists another type—the "screen enterprise," which does not perform, or performs to a minimum extent, production activities, and whose main service it is to recycle capital of illegal origin and dirty money. In this case the importance of the network of enterprises that serves as the overall recycling system assumes greater importance than the single enterprise.[32]

The majority of the enterprises set up by Mafia groups operate essentially in four sectors of activity: construction, construction materials, services, and agriculture. These sectors are characterized by very low technological levels and by a high ratio of births and deaths; many enterprises fail, and there is a continuous creation of entrepreneurial initiatives. The dimensions are medium or small, in terms of company capital, labor force employed, and overall business volume. The sectors in which such enterprises operate are those in which public intervention in support of Sicilian economy is most evident and ample. A further characteristic consists in the high, often seasonal variation in the volume of activities, both in terms of billing and employment. Finally, there are enterprises with scant organizational complexity: They often function with a single manager, few officials, low company capital, and small offices.

So the main function of these enterprises, which is performed through two distinct and separate organizational modes, does not fall within a productive category but fulfills the need to recycle dirty money and reintroduce it into normal channels of circulation. This takes place in two different ways, which are aimed at avoiding completely or at least partially the need to turn to the banking system on which the investigators' attention is chiefly focused.

The first of the two modalities consists of refinancing the companies through increases in company capital that are not justified by economic or commercial exigencies, given the low volume of business. A variant of this modality lies in the acquisition of costly assets that are almost never utilized by the companies in question. Instead, a different strategy is to have the partners advance a money loan to the company; the company then applies for a loan, so that, when the bank's financing is obtained, the dirty money contributed by the partners, which has already been put into circulation, is replaced by clean money that is returned to the partners.

The strategies used by Mafia groups who introduce money of illicit origin into normal financial channels gives rise to questions connected with the limited organizational articulation of their enterprises. The modern enterprise is an extraordinarily complex organizational structure; in the case of Mafia enterprises this organizational complexity is not encountered at the level of the single enterprise but rather at the level of the network of enterprises headed by a single family.

The organizational complexity of the enterprise network is demonstrated above all by their number. The mafioso group headed by the Badalamenti family had established ten companies (and these are only the ones about which the court was able to gather information), almost all of them exclusively aimed at recycling dirty capital. The same applies, perhaps to an even greater extent to another group, the group headed by the Bontate family, composed of eleven companies whose exclusive purpose was also the recycling of monies of illicit provenance. The Inzerillo-Spatola group had twenty-three companies. The fractioning and multiplication of these companies answered functional needs aimed at differentiating the laundering sites and thus avoiding the possibility that the identification of one company might lead to the identification of the others through a domino effect.

In the face of a strategy of this kind one consideration emerges, that is, the enormous amount of organizational and entrepreneurial abilities that are employed in pursuit of the concealment and recycling of tainted money. These entrepreneurial abilities are, so to speak, "deflected" from their normal use: Instead of being used for the building up of companies with productive purposes, they are exploited for the formation of organizational structures with illegal aims.

But a further point must be emphasized with regard to the organizational modality of the network of companies, and this concerns the role played by the persons involved. In the Badalamenti group only two persons controlled the ten enterprises that formed the organizational

Fig. 3. Network of Companies Owned by the Bontate Family

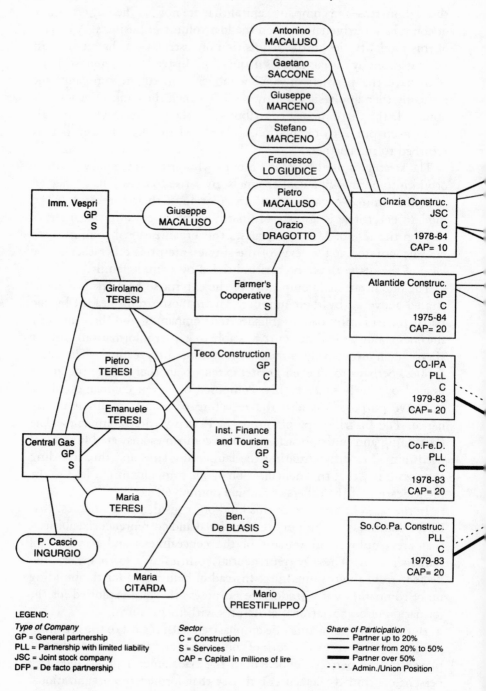

LEGEND:

Type of Company	Sector	Share of Participation
GP = General partnership	C = Construction	——— Partner up to 20%
PLL = Partnership with limited liability	S = Services	▬▬ Partner from 20% to 50%
JSC = Joint stock company	CAP = Capital in millions of lire	▬▬ Partner over 50%
DFP = De facto partnership		- - - - Admin./Union Position

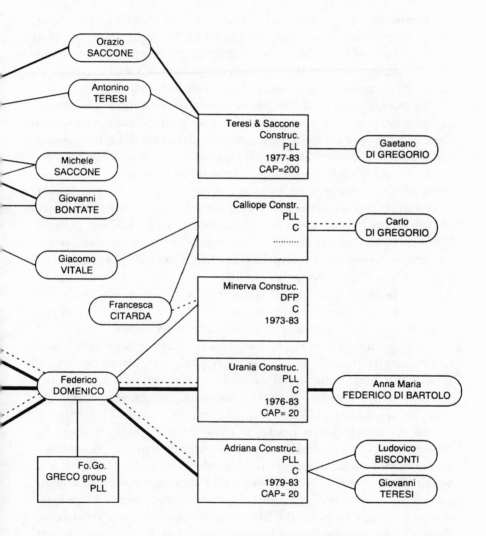

Source: Civil and Penal Tribunal of Palermo, Decrees Ordering the Application of Special Surveillance by Police and Fiscal Measures in Regard to Domenico Federico (registered 10/14/83), Michele Saccone (3/71/84), Carlo Teresi (3/20/84), Giovanni Teresi (3/24/84), and Orazio Saccone (5/19/1984).

network. And they controlled them by owning a majority of shares or by being their managing directors. In the enterprises of the Bontate group a single person controlled no fewer than seven of the eleven companies belonging to the group by owning a majority of the shares and filling the role of managing director in most of them. That this role was filled mainly by single partners in the companies is proof of the persistence of a traditional characteristic of Mafia groups—their being centered on the pivotal role played by the leader. The fact that Mafia groups use the form of the commercial enterprise does not mean that the impersonal role typical of such organizations will prevail, but rather it combines modern and archaic forms of personal power.

The modern market system has institutionalized a form of economic competition—among enterprises and among individuals—in which there is room only for formally peaceful modes of confrontation among the subjects. Therefore commercial enterprises operate within an institutionalized network of exchange relationships founded on trust. Formally peaceful competition and trust make it possible for the market to perform one of its fundamental functions: to allow for the possibility of calculation by the individuals who operate in it, making possible long-term investments and therefore giving the organizational structures of the commercial enterprises the chance to solidify in impersonal forms. What characterizes the system of Mafia economy, and thus the relations between commercial enterprises and individuals inside the system and with the economy as a whole, is its accentuated competition; but the basic weapon of this competition is violence. The form of commercial enterprise is instrumental for the Mafia groups with regard to the pursuit of illicit goals, and these goals are pursued by having recourse to both commercial and violent transactions; as a result, violence is not eliminated by the economic enterprise; the market relationships do not unfold in formally peaceful ways but by means of intimidation and violent practices. However, the profits that can be realized in the illegal sphere result in the fact that the individuals' aspirations of social mobility are channeled inside the Mafia system, which offers tremendous opportunities for enrichment, though accompanied by greater risks as compared to the normal system of the legal economy. The system of the Mafia enterprises socializes in violence those who have ambitions and entrepreneurial abilities. This prevents formally pacific relationships from becoming established in the Sicilian economy. In addition, in recent years the increasing socialization of individuals who turn their entrepreneurial abilities to violent, predatory, and felonious activities has resulted in a progressive degeneration of the Sicilian economy.

Illicit Economy and Hidden Power

In recent years the sector of the illicit economy has become a considerable part of the Sicilian economy, and its dangerousness does not consist only in its growing and by now considerable dimensions, but also and to a greater extent in its ability to socialize potentially mobile individuals in forms of predatory and violent behavior.

One reason for the growth of this sector is the existence of an entrepreneurial sector formed by the successful companies established by entrepreneurs who originate locally in both eastern and western Sicily. These enterprises have gained such strength and such ability to bring pressure to bear on the political powers as to assure for themselves the lion's share of public funds. Since access to the legal sector of the Sicilian economy is hindered by the existence of these groups, potentially emerging entrepreneurial figures do not find an outlet in this sector and are faced by two alternatives: an activity in the legal sector that does not appear particularly promising from the point of view of economic success and profitability, or entry into the illicit sector, which is highly competitive and guarantees great profits. In this way it then becomes possible to transfer capital and activities from the illegal to the legal sector, and to compete in this manner with the groups that are already established in this sector.

The coexistence of these two sectors, and their relationships, which are perverted in both their mechanisms and their effects, can also supply an explanation for Sicily's low industrial development during the 1971–81 decade. Among the southern regions that have displayed the lowest rates of industrial development when compared to the average in the South in those years, Sicily occupies last place. And the other two regions that have shown trends below the southern average are Calabria and Campania[33]—that is to say, regions that, like Sicily, are characterized by the massive presence of organized crime. This confirms the fact that the Mafia's economic system is incapable of promoting economic development.

The deterioration of Sicilian economy goes back to the fifties, when we see the emergence of private entrepreneurial groups and initiatives that are not based on the selective functioning of the market but on a massive policy of government financing. Emerging entrepreneurial initiatives are stimulated by the concession of considerable credit incentives and nonreturnable contributions to companies set up on Sicilian territory. The effects of this policy are such as to create an entrepreneurial class strongly connected by relationships of political-clientele-oriented exchange with the party system (and in particular with the Christian Democratic party) and with the political-administrative system. [34] This is a phase during which, while union activists and leaders of the labor movement are still being murdered, death by immersion in concrete is emblematically reflected by the modern buildings that spring up like mushrooms in the urban centers or along their peripheries.

The coming into existence of subsidized entrepreneurship is shared by all traditional Mafia areas in Sicily and by those that had not been touched by the Mafia. Its expansion in market terms has resulted in growth in the practices of Mafia behavior. In the course of the seventies the subsidized entrepreneurs operating in the areas of eastern Sicily, traditionally considered untainted by the Mafia phenomenon, begin to enter the markets of western Sicily. Consequently they must come to terms with the practices ruling relationships between economy and politics that exist on the spot. The differences are not great; it is merely a matter of adjusting clientele-oriented practices in a Mafia–clientele-oriented direction. In this fashion an entrepreneurship that seemed to have arisen in "clean" ways, untainted by Mafia practices, becomes "polluted" by those practices following the conquest of new markets. This is due to the fact that in order to be able to compete with the Mafia enterprises operating locally, one must perforce use the same weapons. The complementary phenomenon is to be seen with entrepreneurs that have been Mafia from the start. [35] Their expansion in markets that had not originally been infested by the Mafia brings about a shift of the local political systems in a Mafia-clientele direction. This produces an expansion of Mafia practices throughout Sicily and a homogenization of the relationships between the economic and political systems in a Mafia-clientele direction. This phenomenon is important because it involved not only changes of quantity and degree in Mafia activities. We are in the presence of a process of depersonalization of Mafia power.

The traditional configuration of Mafia power was of a personal nature. This was due in the first place to the mafiosos' function as brokers. All mediation activities demand skill and connections, the ability to persuade and influence—abilities that are typically personal. This was all the more true since Mafia power manifested itself in the ambit of a community in which, once his power was institutionalized as being legitimate, the mafioso took on the tasks of settling controversies, administering de facto justice, and representing the community to the outside. This communitarian aspect was connected with the territorial demarcation of Mafia power.

The crises of mediatory functions and the organization of modern economic entrepreneurial activities conflict with the personal characterization of Mafia power. The establishment of Mafia enterprises that specialize in long-distance traffic causes a crisis in the communitarian aspect of their power and, together with this—due to the logical expansion and conquest of markets—in its territorial limitations as well. In the eyes of the people, Mafia power, even personified by an individual, tends to be seen as an anonymous power in the market.

This tendency is limited by the increase in the use of violence as a regulatory instrument of economic competition among Mafia groups. Nevertheless, we must not forget a number of factors that bolster this tendency and that consist in purely economic, and thus financial, links between Mafia enterprises and other economic subjects—the companies to which jobs are subcontracted and with which agreements are made or cartels formed; the banking and financial system into whose coffers capital of Mafia origin flows in the form of deposits and checking accounts; and the numerous individuals who draw their incomes and work from this chain of business deals. Thus is formed a constellation of interests on which an impersonal Mafia power over the market tends to rest. This tendency is accompanied by an accentuation of the hidden aspects of Mafia power.

Traditional Mafia power, even though surrounded by silence, was not hidden; it manifested itself openly for all to see. And this was true during both periods in the development of the Mafia, that is, the period of violent revolt against the established order, and the period of institutionalization, when it was legitimatized by acceptance on the part of the population. In the first instance it was true because everyone knew who had committed the crime but no one talked. In the second instance there was nothing to hide. The illicit activities that were typical of the first stage of a mafioso's career had served to acquire wealth and conquer high position in society.

In both instances the open display of power on the part of the mafioso came from the combination of his function as mediator and the authority granted him by the state to exercise violence in its stead. In order to perform his function as a mediator the mafioso had to enjoy a high social reputation; he had to be considered a man of respect, and this social consideration derived from his having demonstrated that he was adept in the use of violence. Having acquired this reputation, the mafioso could rule without having recourse to open violence, and he could procure income through the performance of normal economic activities.

Both these processes of transition, from the use of violence to the legitimatization of power and from illicit to licit economic activities, are no longer part of the new picture that is being delineated beginning with the fifties. The need for social control through traditional methods having become less pressing, both the assignment of the monopoly of violence by the state and the mediatory functions by the men of respect have ceased. The Mafia has lost its role as a pragmatic extension of the state, and consequently we observe a growing tendency to its taking on the configuration of a hidden power.

Adjustment to the Cultural Codes

The end of the mafiosi as power brokers is an anthropological phenomenon of extraordinary importance. But this change does not lie in the development of entrepreneurial activity previously nonexistent in the mafioso behavioral universe. The element of novelty resides in the fact that, as a result of the changed context of economic and political relationships, the entrepreneurial activities lose the cultural framework that encased them. In this manner the utilization of the market mechanism and of a privileged relationship with the apparatuses of the state in order to build economic empires founded on the combination of legal and illegal activities is further developed in comparison with what happened before, and makes it possible for the Mafia groups to attain a scope that is an nth proof of their ability to combine the old and the new, the modern and the traditional. Thus an old model is repeated: Traditional values do not disappear, but their function changes; consequently their meaning also changes. This is also the case with honor, violence, and instrumental friendship.

The mafiosi, having become full players in the game of economic market competition, must adjust to its rules. The function of instrumental friendship that allowed for trust and predictability in economic transactions to a great extent disappears, and is replaced by judicial and commercial guarantees. But to a great extent the problem remains, especially in an economy characterized by the inability to invest in advanced production sectors, whose markets are subject to strong fluctuations due to outside competition. The problem of predictability is solved through public intervention, whose funding, by systematically favoring certain sectors of economic activity, makes it possible for the entrepreneurs to identify low-risk investment opportunities. On the plane of predictability, instrumental friendship is in an increasing measure transformed on the one hand into a clientele-oriented exchange relationship among entrepreneurs and politicians and on the other into the formation of groups and alliances among economic subjects, political subjects, and segments of the state apparatus. Thus it loses all traces of an emotional-symbolic nature and becomes a purely instrumental relationship linking various interests.

As for the problem of trust, while the need to have recourse to instrumental friendship in the legal sector of the economy diminishes sharply, this need becomes all the more pressing in the illegal sector. Here, however, in view of the size of the interests at stake, instrumental friendship proves that it is no longer able to offer sufficient guarantees. By its very nature the operation of illegal traffic cannot rest on transactions that take place in full daylight and are based on normal relationships of trust typical of the market. Since the traffic unfolds in a hidden fashion, the only system that allows for the functioning of the illicit machine lies in creating a network of totally special fiduciary relationships. For these reasons the mafioso groups are organized to recover a series of traditional values. The organization of the criminal Mafia enterprise is based on the family, on relations of kinship or quasi kinship. But no matter how far these bonds may be extended through matrimonial strategy, godfather, and best-man relationships and so on, it is nevertheless still necessary to have recourse to individuals alien to the networks of kinship or quasi kinship. In these instances, which are very numerous, above all in the not-infrequent hypothesis of alliances among different *cosche,* recourse to the traditional code of honor proves to be of fundamental importance. Respect for commitments made and compliance with decisions arrived at within the *cosca* are modes of behavior that conform to the code of honor. Therefore this code becomes a principal instrument on which relationships of organizational trust in illegal economic activities rest. Honor loses its previous functions as a cultural norm regulating the competition for social ascent. Now that the mafiosi are also more intent on accumulating capital than on acquiring respect, honor serves exclusively as a means of internal cohesion within the Mafia groups.

At any rate, this cohesion is not easy to maintain because the temptations offered by the illegal market are many. A single successful operation is enough to make someone rich, it is enough to keep for oneself the money brought in by the sale of a drug shipment instead of handing it over to the promoters of the operation or to appropriate a part of a payoff not authorized by the organization. This increases the importance of violence in the competition among mafiosi. Not only that, but now the violence assumes a new, more open significance, stripped of ideological incrustations and justifications. Until the fifties it is legitimized by three factors: the state's authorization to exercise violence on its behalf, the communal character of Mafia power as control of public order, and the title to its monopoly, justified in terms of the social attribution of honor. Now that the conditions for the existence of these three factors have vanished, the exercise of violence shows itself for what it is, even in the substitution of the automatic pistol and dynamite for the traditional shotgun—a pure, brutal, often indiscriminate demonstration of the predominance of physical force.

Thus, in the transformation of the Mafia during the last forty years, an upheaval and a readjustment of the traditional cultural codes takes place. Instrumental friendship loses its delicate balance between its instrumental aspects and its aspects of symbolism and solidarity. The former is transformed into financial and exchange relationships among individual and collective confreres and specialized agencies. The latter aspects, where Mafia groups are concerned, tend to be replaced by honor. This last word loses its connotation as an idiom in which the language of material wealth is spoken and as an instrument regulating the competition for social ascent. So the ambivalent duplicity of the honor concept disappears. Replaced by wealth as the criterion of social stratification and symbol of power, honor tends to assume the functions of the institutionalization of trust in the delicate business relationships that accompany the organization of an illegal economy. Its previous competitive function is assumed by violence. Violence in its actual exercise and in the threat of having recourse to it regulates not only the competition among Mafia groups but tends to present itself as a normative system in the relations between the Mafioso economic sector and the nonmafioso sector of the economy. The discouragement in various ways of the competition of non-Mafia companies by Mafia companies is a far from negligible example of this attempt to impose violence as a regulatory norm in the competition on the market.

Pollution of the Political System

Mafia violence, by now deprived of its symbolic disguise of honor, does not present itself only as an instrument regulating economic competition. In an increasing measure the Mafia tends to become a political force and to enter into open conflict with the powers of the state, by killing magistrates, police officials, officers of the carabinieri, political men, and members of the government.

What are the causes behind this phenomenon? The expansion of an illegal economy, the round of business affairs fueled by mafioso trafficking, the national and international dimensions of the financial interests involved, have made it necessary for Mafia groups to seize directly the most crucial sectors and segments of the state apparatus and openly combat those apparatuses that are opposed to the spreading of the Mafia. The persistence of violence within economic competition has in its turn resulted in the pollution of the Sicilian political system. The regional government and the agencies in charge of the promotion of local development and of public intervention were and are not alien to the complex of economic relationships; on the contrary, they are among the principal protagonists of the Sicilian economy and consequently are responsible not only for the formation of a class of entrepreneurs but also for the proliferation of Mafia groups. The functional relations among institutions and public development agencies and businesses both in legal and illegal economies have resulted in an increased intertwining and a progressive interconnection, in which the political system has become involved with violent and predatory practices. The commingling of interests and the continued practice of relationships with Mafia groups has produced a parallel between the criteria regulating the mafioso economic system and the criteria regulating relationships in the political system. Also within the latter system violence tends to become common practice, as shown by recent episodes in which physical or moral assassination has been the weapon employed for the resolution of political competition. In this manner the circle closes: The political system greatly responsible for the affirmation and expansion of the principle of violence in the economy is in turn overtaken by it in serious and profoundly destructive form.

The process of taking over political apparatuses is not a new phenomenon. But in the past it took place with the state's consent in order to manage power at the periphery in the interest of the local ruling class. Now, however, the state holds the monopoly of violence, and illicit economic activities are of a scale that goes far beyond the interests that prevalently belong only or chiefly to the periphery, and are instead characterized according to national and supranational dimensions. Consequently the profound difference between present Mafia power and its traditional model lies in the fact that, from being a phenomenon typical of the periphery, it tends to involve the entire Italian political system. From the periphery where it had arisen, Mafia power has moved toward the center in an attempt to achieve domination over it. Crimes against the state can only be regarded as part of a violent struggle among power groups that nestle in the very apparatus of the institutions and struggle to gain control of them. And it is due to these reasons that the fight against the Mafia is still far from being won.

Nevertheless, even though it has greatly expanded during the last fifteen years and even though its strength and its spheres of activity have grown enormously, the Mafia is not invincible. As has happened with terrorism, it, too, can be largely eliminated. But we must underline at least two elements of difference between terrorism and the Mafia that must impact on the way in which the battle against the latter is conducted. What characterizes the Mafia families is the competition on the markets of legal and illegal economic activities. Consequently the single groups have a great interest in employing the police and magistrature for their internecine struggles, supplying information, even false information, about rival groups. In fact, whenever the Mafia families do not coexist peacefully, any weakening of the competitor favors the family that supplies the information, since new spaces are opened in the market and the attention of investigating agencies is then focused on those who are the object of the information or "squealing," deflecting it from the other Mafia groups. This strategy, aimed at confusing the investigative authorities, is substantially alien to terrorism, which—considering the state as the fundamental enemy to be fought—was less (if at all) interested in this dangerous utilization of repressive methods.

In the second place, there is a difference in social roots. The Mafia, unlike terrorism, combines criminal activities with normal, legal economic activities. If on one hand it sows death, on the other it distributes wealth. As the Palermo magistrates point out:[36] There is a climate of "contiguity" that causes a large number of persons to collaborate with the mafiosi.

> The Mafia waters are much higher and deeper than the waters of terrorism, Stajano points out. The economic possibilities [of] the profits, the trafficking of all kinds, the web of availability, the economic interests . . . involve an infinite number of persons. . . . The phenomenon is ample and widespread, it concerns not only the hotbeds of the underworld and the front companies, but numerous economic activi-

216

ties and numerous individuals, salespeople, retail and wholesale merchants, professionals, small companies, building constructors, owners of building sites . . . the bureaucrats and professional politicians and the owners of enterprises who go so far as to consider it more convenient . . . to take the leap, to pass over into the ranks [of,] and [be] at the service of, Cosa Nostra rather than be subjected to the generalized payoffs or authority codes of the various Mafia families.[37]

The social roots of the Mafia are much more extended and deeper than those of terrorism, which was defeated above all because of its progressive isolation, which was followed by the phenomena of disassociation and loss of members and *pentitismo* (or recanting).

This does not mean that court trials like those in Palermo (despite all the procedural difficulties connected with their size), the confessions of the mafiosi, and the capture of the fugitive Mafia chiefs are not inflicting defeats on the Mafia organization. We only intend to underline the peril that can result from excessively emphasizing these successes and from an uncritical reading of the trials' consequences. If the Mafia is considered as a single, monolithic association, with possibly a stable organizational structure like that of a commercial enterprise, we may run the risk of thinking that a megatrial like that in Palermo is sufficient to mark its true defeat. But this is a dangerous illusion because the Mafia is not a single association but rather a system of deeply rooted alliances with close ties to the political power system. Therefore, unless there is a radical cleanup of the state apparatus and the organs of government in Sicily, it will not be possible to break up the intertwining that has historically occurred between the public hand and the invisible hand that is progressively corrupting the Sicilian economy and society by employing violence.

The history of the struggle against the Mafia has been characterized by the continuous illusion that from time to time the decisive blow had been delivered, only to reveal a few years later its renewed expansion. Trials and repressive activities can inflict a severe defeat on the Mafia, but they are not enough to eradicate it.

NOTES

Chapter 1. An Obscure Object of Inquiry

1. G. Alongi, *La maffia* (Palermo: Sellerio, 1977; 1st ed. 1886), pp. 72–73. H. Hess, *Mafia* (Bari: Laterza, 1973), p. 176, adds contraband to the types of illicit earnings listed by Alongi.
2. Hess, *Mafia*, p. 177.
3. For numerous examples of the various types see Alongi, *La maffia*, pp. 82 ff., 97 ff.; L. Franchetti, *Condizioni politiche e amministrative della Sicilia* (Florence: Vallecchi, 1974; 1st ed. 1876) cites as cases of the illicit acquisition of positions of monopoly those of the Mulini and Posa associations (pp. 6–7). The first, in the form of a legal consortium among the proprietors of flour mills, in reality had the purpose of keeping the price high and extorting kickbacks from the members. The second, masquerading as a mutual aid society, was in reality an instrument for exercising a violent monopoly over the labor force.
4. P. Alatri, *Lotte politiche in Sicilia sotto il governo della Destra (1866–74)* (Turin: Einaudi, 1954), pp. 212, *passim*.
5. The text of the play has been republished in G. G. Loschiavo, *Cento anni di mafia* (Rome: Bianco, 1962). The first time that the term was used by a public authority in its present meaning was in 1865, when Prefect Gualtiero sent from Palermo, on April 25, a report to the minister of the interior in which he spoke of the "so-called *Maffia* or criminal association" (cited in Alatri, *Lotte politiche*).
6. To prove this one has only to read the prefects' reports and the declarations of the judges of the period, some of which have been published in N. Russo, ed., *Antologia della mafia* (Palermo: Il Punto, 1964). In general on this period and on the confusion concerning the nature of Mafia, opposition, and banditry, see Alatri, *Lotte politiche*.
7. G. Montalbano, *La mafia*, in "Nuovi Argomenti," 1953 (5), pp. 165–204. On the "romantic" conception of the mafioso as a folk hero, and on its origins and its developments, see S. F. Romano, *Storia della mafia* (Milan: Sugar, 1963), pp. 31–76.
8. See Russo, *Antologia della mafia*, pp. 22–23.
9. *Relazione della Giunta per l'inchiesta sulla condizione della Sicilia (Relazione Bonfadini)* (Rome, 1976), partially republished in Russo, *Antologia*, pp. 182–83 (italics added).

10. L. Barzini, *Gli italiani* (Milan, 1970), p. 327 (italics added).

11. In "Giornale di Sicilia," August 6, 1966 (italics added).

12. Hess, *Mafia,* pp. 17 ff.

13. G. Pitre, *Usi, costumi, credenze e pregiudizi del popolo siciliano* (Palermo: Pedone Lauriel, 1889), pp. 289–90.

14. L. Sciascia, *Appunti su mafia e letteratura,* various authors. (Bologna: Boni, 1970), p. 73.

15. P. Martino, *Storia della parola* " *'ndrangheta,"* in "Quaderni calabresi," 44, 1978, cited in P. Arlacchi, *La mafia imprenditrice* (Bologna: Il Mulino, 1983), p. 22. For other, perhaps less reliable, etymological explanations of the word *mafia,* see Hess, *Mafia,* pp. 3–5.

16. Pitre, *Usi,* p. 291.

17. Ibid., p. 289. It should be kept in mind that in the play *I Mafiusi della Vicaria di Palermo* (The mafiosi of Palermo's Vicariate), when reference is made to the organization, the term *camorra* is used. The characters are described as *cammoristi* or "head cammorista." What is more, if one examines the literature on the subject during the first thirty years after the Unification, Mafia and *camorra* are used as synonyms, signifying an extension to the Mafia of characteristics connected with the *camorra,* whose origins seem to reach further back in time. However, there is no doubt that Pitré was quite close to the mark in regard to the informally associational nature of the Mafia. The associational tie in the *camorra* appears to be much more explicit and important, as is shown by its strong subcultural quality, which even today persists and can be seen in the explicit declarations of membership and affiliation to *camorra* families and organizations.

18. According to Zingarelli, *Vocabulario della lingua italiano* (Bologna: Zanichelli, 1979), the word *omertà* means humility, from the root *humus* (earth, soil), from which would come the word's meaning as subordination (abasement, humiliation) to an organization, agreement, or institution to which a man considers himself subject. However, in the most commonly accepted usage the word supposedly derives from the root *"omu"* ("man" in Sicilian) and would signify a glorification of the gifts of a "true man" according to the Sicilian ideal, that is, a man who has blood in his veins, who is conscious of his existence, and who does not tolerate offenses. For this definition see Pitré, *Usi,* p. 294. According to Alongi, who leans more to the first solution (*La maffia,* pp. 55–56), one should not exclude the fact that the two meanings could coexist. That would confirm the coexistence of the Mafia spirit and the organizational component in Mafia groups.

19. Romano, *Storia,* p. 76. On Sicilianism and Mafia see N. Dalla Chiesa, *Il potere mafioso* (Milan: Mazzotta, 1976), pp. 168–264.

20. On Florio's episode see F. Renda, *Socialisti e cattolici in Sicilia, 1900–1904* (Caltanissetta: Sciascia), p. 405. Pitré's thesis is presented in Dalla Chiesa, *Il potere mafioso,* p. 174. On the Notarbartolo case see my discussion in Chapter 5.

21. L. Capuana, *L'isola del sole,* Catania, Giannotta, 1898, pp. 85–86.

22. Cited in Romano, *Storia,* p. 232.

23. Cf. Dalla Chiesa, *Il potere Mafioso,* pp. 181 ff.

24. Romano, *Storia,* p. 76.

25. See S. M. Lipset and S. Rokkan, eds., Introduction to *Party Systems and Voter Alignments* (New York: The Free Press, 1967), pp. 1–64.

26. Sciascia, *Appunti,* pp. 71–72.

27. G. M. Puglia, "Il "mafioso" non è associato per delinquere," in Russo, *Antologia,* pp. 603–13.

28. Loschiavo, *Cento anni,* pp. 61 ff. By the same author, see also "La mafia e il reato di associazione per delinquere," in Russo, *Antologia,* pp. 615–42.

29. *Atti dell'Inchiesta agraria e sulle condizioni della classe agricola (Inchiesta Jacini),* vol. xiii, nos. I and II, partly presented in Russo, *Antologia,* pp. 416–17 (italics added).

30. Mosca, *Che cosa è la mafia,* in *Partiti e sindicati nella crisi del regime parlamentare* (Bari: Laterza, 1949), pp. 215, 224, 227.

31. In Russo, *Antologia,* pp. 23, 25–26.

32. Ibid., pp. 12, 14.
33. Ibid., pp. 15–16.
34. Alongi, *La maffia*, p. 50.
35. In Russo, *Antologia*, p. 18.
36. *Inchiesta Jacini*, cited in Russo, *Antologia*, pp. 416, 419 (italics added).
37. *Inchiesta parlamentare sulle condizioni dei contadini nelle provincie meridionali e nella Sicilia*, vol. iv. part ii, cap. 9 (Rome, 1910), partially republished in Russo, *Antologia*, p. 516 (italics added).
38. Ibid., p. 517.
39. Mosca, *Che cosa è la mafia*, pp. 229–30.
40. *Inchiesta parlamentare sulle condizioni dei contadini*, cited in Russo, *Antologia*, p. 517.
41. Cutrera, *La mafia e i mafiosi* (Palermo: Reber, 1900).
42. P. Villari, *Le lettere meridionali e altri scritti sulla questione sociale in Italia* (Naples: Guida, 1979; 1st ed., 1878), pp. 55–56.
43. Ibid., pp. 58, 59.
44. S. Sonnino, *I contadini in Sicilia* (Florence: Vallecchi, 1974; 1st ed., 1876), p. 68.
45. Franchetti, *Condizioni*, p. 94.
46. In Russo, *Antologia*, p. 12.
47. Alongi, *La maffia*, pp. 106–7.
48. Mosca, *Che cosa è la mafia*, p. 241. On the practice of fencing for stolen goods, see Franchetti, *Condizioni*, pp. 31–33.
49. The classic analysis is that of A. Tocqueville, *Democracy in America*. It is further taken up by R. Bendix, *Stato nazionale e integrazione di classe* (Bari: Laterza, 1969).
50. Mosca, *Che cosa è la mafia*, p. 242.
51. Franchetti, *Condizioni*, p. 34.
52. Romano, *Storia*, p. 222.
53. J. Schneider and P. Schneider, *Culture and Political Economy in Western Sicily* (New York: Academic Press, 1976), p. 173.

Chapter 2. Careers in Killing

1. See E. J. Hobsbawm, *I ribelli* (Turin: Einaudi), 1966, p. 60.
2. In Russo, *Antologia*, p. 34; on the theme of the protection furnished by the Mafia see also F. Ferrarotti, *Rapporto sulla mafia* (Naples: Liguori, 1978), pp. 18–19.
3. Franchetti, *Condizioni*, p. 25.
4. E. Sereni, *Il capitalismo nelle campagne, 1860–1900* (Turin: Einaudi, 1948), p. 178.
5. A. Blok, *The Mafia of a Sicilian Village* (New York: Harper & Row, 1974), p. 61.
6. Alongi, *La maffia*, p. 84.
7. *Relazione Bonfadini*, in Russo, *Antologia*, p. 218.
8. Blok, *The Mafia*, p. 146.
9. Concerning these threats, and in particular the gunshot of the *chiacchiaria*, see Sonnino, *I contadini*, p. 68; Mosca, *Che cosa è la mafia*, pp. 232–38; Romano, *Storia*, p. 147.
10. Hobsbawm, *I ribelli*, p. 65.
11. Blok, *The Mafia*, p. 161.
12. Alongi, *La maffia*, p. 106.
13. Ibid., p. 104.
14. Cf. Hess, *Mafia* pp. 116–17; Alongi, *La maffia*, pp. 62–81.
15. See D. Novacco, *Inchiesta sulla mafia* (Milan: Feltrinelli, 1963), pp. 164–65.
16. For significant examples see Hess, *Mafia*, pp. 164–65. Interesting cases of relations between Mafia and banditry in an area of inland Sicily are reported in Blok, *The Mafia*, pp. 108–9, 130–34, and *passim*.
17. Hobsbawm, *I ribelli*, pp. 32 ff.

18. Romano, *Storia*, p. 83.
19. Hobsbawm, *I ribelli*, pp. 32–82.
20. Blok, *The Mafia*, pp. 99–102. For a discussion between Blok and Hobsbawm in regard to banditry, see A. Blok, "The Peasant and the Brigand: Social Banditry Reconsidered," in *Comparative Studies in Society and History*, 14 (1972), pp. 495–504; E. J. Hobsbawm, "Social Bandits, A Comment, pp. 504–7. For an evaluation of the debate, see S. Lupo, "Storia e società nel Mezzogiorno in alcuni studi recenti," in *Italia contemporanea*, 154 (1984), pp. 71–93.
21. Hobsbawm, *I ribelli*, p. 53. It should be noted that, for Hobsbawm, the Mafia is also a manifestation of primitive forms of social revolt, and the juxtaposition of the two phenomena therefore takes place (contrary to Blok) on the side of social rebellion.
22. Ibid., p. 65.
23. An emblematic example is the career of Salvatore Miceli of Monreale, whose armed squads took the side of the patriots against the Bourbons in the Palermo revolt of 1848; he later became a captain in the Bourbon army in 1850, subsequently took his men to fight alongside Garibaldi in 1860, and died in the Palermo revolt of 1866. See Cutrera, *La mafia e i mafiosi*, pp. 170–74.
24. A fuller description of the bandit Giuliano is given in Chapter 6.
25. Franchetti, *Condizioni*, p. 93.
26. Hess, *Mafia*, pp. 96–97.
27. Ibid., pp. 54–55.
28. Cf. F. G. Bailey, *Stratagems and Spoils: A Social Anthropology of Politics* (Oxford: Basil Blackwell, 1969), p. 40; Blok, *The Mafia*, pp. 62, 172–73.
29. Blok, *The Mafia*, pp. 154–56, 173–74.
30. Mosca, *Che cosa è la mafia*, pp. 216–17. On the "contemptuous" nature of crimes in Sicily, see also Alongi, *La maffia*, pp. 40–41.
31. C. Mori, *Con la mafia ai ferri corti* (Milan: Mondadori, 1932), p. 125.
32. D. Dolci, *Spreco* (Turin: Einaudi, 1962), pp. 63–64.
33. Schneider and Schneider, *Culture*, p. 179.
34. Franchetti, *Condizioni*, p. 126.
35. E. R. Wolf, "Aspects of Group Relations in a Complex Society: Mexico," in *American Anthropologist*, 58 (1956); p. 1075.
36. Cf. S. F. Silverman, "Patroni tradizionali come mediatori fra communità e nazione: il caso dell'Italia centrale (1860–1945)," in L. Graziano, ed., *Clientelismo e mutamento politico* (Milan: Franco Angeli, 1974), p. 291.
37. Blok, *The Mafia*, p. 8.
38. I. Montanelli, *Pantheon minore* (Milan: Longanesi, 1958), p. 282.
39. Blok, *The Mafia*, p. 177.
40. Alongi, *La maffia*, p. 108.
41. Cf. Franchetti, *Condizioni*, pp. 126–27; Blok, *The Mafia*, pp. 147, 152–53, 177, and *passim*.
42. Renda, *Funzioni e basi sociale della mafia*, p. 47.
43. For several examples see Blok, *The Mafia*, pp. 161, 176.
44. For an accurate description of agrarian agreements and the ways in which—by exacting various tolls and kickbacks and by a policy of harassment—the major part of their produce was taken from the peasants, see Sonnino, *I contadini*, pp. 24 ff.
45. Ibid., pp. 107–10.
46. Franchetti, *Condizioni*, p. 49.
47. Hess, *Mafia*, p. 182.
48. Sereni, *Il capitalismo*, pp. 184–85.
49. M. Weber, *Economia e società* (Milan, Communità, 1961), vol. I, p. 195.
50. S. Cammareri Scurti, "Crispismo in Sicilia," in *Critica Sociale*, April 16, 1898, cited in Romano, *Storia*, p. 78.

51. See Arlacchi, *La mafia imprenditrice.*
52. Hess, *Mafia,* pp. 174–76.
53. For many examples see Sonnino, *I contadini,* p. 164; Novacco, *Inchiesta,* p. 142; Blok, *The Mafia,* p. 77.
54. Hess, *Mafia,* pp. 65 ff. Hess criticizes the assertion of Cutrera and Hobsbawm that Mafia chiefs were found among the *gabelloti* and owners but never among the peasants.
55. Hess, *Mafia,* p. 87.
56. Dolci, *Spreco,* p. 69.
57. For this analysis see Hess, *Mafia,* pp. 69–106.
58. Arlacchi, "Mafia e tipi di società" in *Rassegna italiano di sociologia,* XXI (1980), p. 8.
59. This is a characteristic of the mafioso phenomenon on which all scholars agree, from Blok, who describes the never-ending change in the dominant groups at Contessa Entellina, to Arlacchi, who underscores the fact that in Piana di Gioia Tauro, "the society of permanent transition" is characterized by continual instability.
60. Blok, *The Mafia,* p. 47.
61. The term "social entrepreneur," coined by F. Barth in *The Role of Entrepreneur in Social Change in Northern Norway* (Oslo: Universitets forlaget, 1963), has been utilized in the analysis of the networks of social relations in a commune of western Sicily by F. Cossentino, "Imprenditori sociali e processi di cambiamento nella Sicilia occidentale," (thesis, University of Modena, 1982–83).
62. Russo, *Antologia,* pp. 18, 23.
63. Franchetti, *Condizioni,* p. 114.
64. Russo, *Antologia,* p. 14 (italics added).
65. According to the definition offered by Schneider and Schneider, *Culture,* pp. 11, 55, 103.
66. Franchetti, *Condizioni,* p. 98.
67. Alongi, *La maffia,* p. 50. The expression "to feel oneself the head artichoke" is used in Sicily to this day to denote bravery.
68. Blok, *The Mafia,* p. 126.
69. Cf. Hess, *Mafia,* pp. 108–17.
70. Novacco, *Inchiesta,* p. 27; Hess, *Mafia,* p. 188.
71. Franchetti, *Condizioni,* pp. 37–38 (italics added).
72. Blok, *The Mafia,* pp. 137, 147; Hess, *Mafia,* p. 188.

Chapter 3. Prelude: Conflicts of Honor

1. V. Titone, *Storia, mafia e costume in Sicilia* (Milan: Edizioni del milione, 1964, p. 256.
2. L. Sciascia, *Il giorno della civetta* (Turin: Einaudi, 1961), p. 113.
3. J. Davis discusses the duplicity of the concept of honor in *Antropologia delle società mediterranee: un'analisi comparata* (Turin: Rosenberg & Sellier, 1980), pp. 101–14; from this discussion I take the materialistic interpretation of honor as a social idiom connected to the allocation of resources. By comparison, the point of view expressed by Arlacchi in *Mafia e tipi di società,* pp. 5 ff.—wherein he emphasizes exclusively the competition for honor and neglects the other aspect—seems unilateral.
4. Cf. Davis, *Antropologia,* pp. 104, 11. The safeguarding of women's honor leads to their exclusion from productive activities that are performed outside the home. Sicilian women do not work in the fields. Cf. Sonnino, *I contadini,* pp. 58–59; Sereni, *I capitalismo,* pp. 181–83.
5. Davis, *Antropologia,* p. 105; Schneider and Schneider, *Culture,* pp. 100–101.
6. Davis, *Antropologia,* p. 110.
7. On the equating of integrity with honor, see Davis, *Antropologia,* p. 111; J. K. Campbell,

Honour, Family and Patronage (Oxford: Clarendon Press, 1964), p. 269. On the relationship between honor and status, see also J. Pitt-Rivers, "Honour and Social Status," in J. G. Peristiany, ed., *Honour and Shame: The Values of Mediterranean Society* (London: Weidenfeld & Nicholson, 1965), pp. 19–78.

8. Hobsbawm, *I ribelli*, p. 56.

9. This tradition is clearly expressed in a medieval English quatrain: "The rich man in his castle/ The poor man at his gate/ God made them high or lowly/ And ordered their estate" (quoted in S. Ossowski, *Struttura di classe e coscienza sociale* (Turin: Einaudi, 1966, p. 24); it is even more explicitly described in a Sicilian proverb: "In this world half of the people are rich and half are poor, and the latter are the servants of the former, while the former help the latter to survive" (*"Intra la munnu la mità sunnu ricchi e la mità poviri, e chisti servinu a chiddi, chiddi fannu campari a chisti,"* quoted in E. Pontieri, *Il tramonto del baronaggio siciliano* [Florence: Sansoni, 1943], p. 69).

10. It is no accident that the mafiosi are found in these ". . . occupations that are changeable and flexible and, with the possibility of a rapid ascent combine a great margin of risk. . . . [They choose to be] entrepreneurs and mediators, activities located between the peasant and the rich landowner . . . [also] bailiffs, guardians of the truck gardens and of the water in the area of the *latifondi*, dealers in cereals and livestock, mediators of all kinds, butchers who also act as fences for stolen cattle. Mafiosi are also often carters. . . . Among the professions they prefer to be lawyers, pharmacists, doctors." See Hess, *Mafia*, p. 82. Although Hess does not mention it, this characterization in occupational terms of the mafiosi is found in Mosca, *Che cosa è la mafia*, pp. 229–40.

11. On the relationship between means and ends in regard to the study of individual behavior, the classic analysis is that of R. K. Merton, *Teoria e struttura sociale* (Bologna: Il Mulino, 1971), vol. ii, pp. 297–401.

12. In Russo, ed., *Antologia*, p. 18.

13. On the incongruence or imbalance of status, see G. Germani, *Sociologia della modernizzazione* (Bari: Laterza, 1971), pp. 104 ff.; W. G. Runciman, *Ineguaglianza e coscienza sociale* (Turin: Einaudi, 1972), pp. 42–43.

14. In the pages that follow I have based several observations on the studies of Schneider and Schneider, *Culture*, in particular pp. 41–109, and of M. Aymard, "La transizione dal feudalesimo al capitalismo," in *Storia d'Italia*, Annale 1: *Dal feudalismo al capitalismo* (Turin: Einaudi, 1978), pp. 1131–92.

15. Cf. M. Aymard and H. Bresc, "Problemi di storia dell'insediamento nella Sicilia medievale e moderna," in *Quaderni Storici*, 24 (1973), p. 946.

16. Aymard, *La transizione*, pp. 1136–37.

17. The idea of Sicily as the granary of the Mediterranean, enunciated by F. Braudel in *Civiltà e imperi del Mediterraneo nell' età di Filippo II* (Turin: Einaudi, 1976), pp. 624, 649–653, has been taken up again and documented notably in the following studies of M. Aymard: "Amministrazione feudale e trasformazioni strutturali tra '500 e '700, in *Archivio storico per la Sicilia orientale,"* vol. I (1975), pp. 17–42; "Il commercio dei grani nella Sicilia del '500, in *Archivio storico per la Sicilia orientale*, vols. i–iii, pp. 7–40. On the characterization of the fief, see H. Bresc, *Il feudo nella società siciliana medievale*, in S. Di Bella, ed., *Economia e Storia: Sicilia–Calabria XV–XIX secolo* (Cosenza: Pellegrini, 1976). On land settlements, see Aymard, and Bresc, *Problemi di storia dell'insediamento*, pp. 945–76; C. Klapisch-Zuber, "Villagi abbandonati ed emigrazione interne," in *Storia d'Italia: I documenti* (Turin: Einaudi, 1973), vol. v, t. II, pp. 309–64. For an analysis of the relationship between the structure of the settlements and the feudal model of cereal production on the *latifondo*, see M. Verga, "La 'Sicilia dei feudi' or 'Sicilia dei grani' dalla 'Wüstungen' alla colonizzazione interne," in *Società e storia*, n. 3 (1978), pp. 563–79.

18. Aymard, *La transizione*, pp. 1184–85.

19. Ibid., pp. 1187–88. For a Polish model cf. W. Kula, *Teoria economica del sistema feudale: Proposta di un modello* (Turin: Einaudi, 1977).

20. Cf. E. R. Wolf, "Peasant Rebellion and Revolution, in N. Miller and R. Aya, eds., *National Liberation: Revolution in the Third World* (New York: The Free Press, 1971), pp. 49–50.

21. It is to this type of dualism that Arlacchi probably refers when he maintains that the Mafia comes into existence in a particular type of social formation that he defines as "a society in permanent transition" (cf. *Mafia, contadini e latifondo*, pp. 81–129). The society in permanent transition is a commercial society that "revolves around itself"—a definition that seems to be the logical basis for the preceding one but is not much of an explanation. With this statement Arlacchi counters the thesis that the Mafia supposedly came into existence on the *latifondo*. The problem, however, is that in Sicily the Mafia arose both in the areas of large estate and in the urban environment, that is, in Palermo. Even though Arlacchi says he has demonstrated that the Mafia arose in societies that were in permanent transition—cf. *La Mafia imprenditrice*, pp. 10–11—we do not find in this last volume (despite declarations on p. 11) an analysis of western Sicily as a society in permanent transition. In reality, Arlacchi's postulate reflects the flaws of a schematic application of the Weberian model of ideal types. In his description of the *latifondo* in the area of Crotone, Arlacchi overlooks the existing historical research into the large southern estate or *latifondo* (see M. Aymard, *La transizione*), and he stresses the aspect of class conflict that derives from the salaried labor relationship. Furthermore, Arlacchi concludes, because he does not find the Mafia in the Crotone area, that the Mafia did not come into existence on the large estate. But this contradicts the fact that the Mafia's crucible in Sicily is to be found also in the *latifondo*, whose characteristics, as we have seen above, are much more similar to the general characteristics of the southern large estate. At any rate, the true challenge is not to establish whether the Mafia did or did not originate on the *latifondo*, but—once it is ascertained that they did appear there as well as in cities and small landed properties—to identify the reasons for their genesis.

22. This analysis has been carried out by Schneider and Schneider, *Culture*, pp. 94 ff. The authors draw their inspiration from the model of I. Wallerstein based on the center-periphery model and on the differences between the capitalist economy and empires.

23. See Pontieri, *Il tramonto*, pp. 10 ff.

24. D. Mack Smith, *Storia della Sicilia* (Bari: Laterza, 1970), pp. 191–201.

25. On the significance of the code of *omertà* see Mosca, *Che cosa è la mafia*, pp. 217–18; Hess, *Mafia*, pp. 146–47; A. Blok, *The Mafia*, pp. 211–21.

26. C. Johnson, *Revolutionary Change* (London: The University of London Press, 1968), p. 8.

27. The distinction between instrumental friendship and affective friendship has been set forth by E. R. Wolf, *Kinship, Friendship, and Patron–Clients Relations in Complex Societies*, in M. Banton, ed., *The Social Anthropology of Complex Society* (London: Tavistock, 1966), pp. 10–18.

28. Cf. F. G. Bailey, ed., *Gifts and Poison: The Politics of Reputation* (Oxford: Basil Blackwell, 1971), p. 19. On friendship as the voluntary exchange of favors see Blok, *The Mafia*, p. 150.

29. Cf. M. Mauss, *Saggio sul dono*, in *Teoria generale della magia e altri saggi* (Turin: Einaudi, 1956).

30. For a description of banquets as forms of rituals symbolic of the glorification of friendship see Schneider and Schneider, *Culture*, pp. 105–7.

31. Cf. Blok, *The Mafia*, p. 146. In general on this theme see J. Boissevain, *Friends of Friends, Networks, Manipulators and Coalitions* (Oxford: Basil Blackwell, 1973).

32. On the functions of instrumental friendship in Sicily, see Schneider and Schneider, *Culture*, pp. 102–9; J. Boissevain, "Rapporti diadici in azione: parentela, amicizia e clientela in Sicilia," in L. Graziano, ed., *Clientelismo e mutamento politico*, pp. 265–78.

33. On the concept of reciprocity see M. D. Sahlins, "La sociologia dello scambio primitivo," in E. Grendi, ed., *L'antropologia economica* (Turin: Einaudi, 1972), pp. 99–146; K. Polyani, *La grande trasformazione* (Turin: Einaudi, 1974), pp. 62 ff.

34. On the instability of the *ad hoc* coalitions, see P. Schneider, "Coalition Formation and Colonialism in Western Sicily," in *European Journal of Sociology*, 13 (1972), pp. 256–67.
35. Blok, *The Mafia*, p. 171.
36. Cf. Schneider and Schneider, *Culture*, p. 109.
37. For a picture of the syntheses of the administration in Sicily under the Spanish rule see Mack Smith, *Storia della Sicilia*, pp. 145–52.
38. Hess, *Mafia*, pp. 42–43.
39. Schneider and Schneider, *Culture*, p. 109.
40. For the characterization of the market as the place alien to violence see M. Weber's preliminary observations to *L'etica protestante e lo spirito del capitalismo* (Florence: Sansoni, 1965), p. 67.
41. For this observation, and in general on the problem of the relationship between faith and economic development, see an unpublished paper by D. Gambetta, "Trust as a Pre-Condition for Economic Development," in particular p. 7.
42. Schneider and Schneider, *Culture*, pp. 10–14.

Chapter 4. The State and the Market of Violence

1. C. Tilly, Foreword to Blok, *The Mafia*, pp. xvii–xix.
2. On these two aspects of the relations among the mafiosi, landowners, and the state see Franchetti, *Condizioni*, pp. 109–10; Tilly, Foreword, p. xix.
3. On these three processes and on the problems attending the formation of the national state see S. Rokkan, "Formazione degli stati e differenze in Europa," in C. Tilly, ed., *La formazione degli stati nazionali nell' Europa occidentale* (Bologna: Il Mulino, 1984), pp. 397–437.
4. Cf. Pontieri, *Il tramonto*, pp. 13–14, 17–19.
5. Ibid., pp. 34, 93. It should be pointed out that several of these aristocratic titles were concentrated in the hands of a few persons who had accumulated them. That fact led Pietro Colletta to declare that "in no place on earth is a title or a decoration more precious than in Sicily" (cited in Pontieri, p. 92).
6. Sicilians who tilled the soil using their own means of production were called bourgeois, regardless of whether they were peasants or capitalist landowners. Cf. Sereni, *I capitalismo*, p. 177.
7. R. De Saint-Non, *Voyage pittoresque ou description des Royaumes de Naples e de Sicile* (Paris, 1785), vol. iv, no. i, p. 156; Graf Zu Stolberg, *Reise in Deutschland, Schweitz, Italien und Sicilien* (Koenigsberg, 1974); vol. iii, p. 316; both are cited in Pontieri, *Il tramonto*, p. 55.
8. Our elaboration on the basis of data reported in E. Pontieri, *Il tramonto*, p. 8.
9. On this subject, see G. Poerio, cited in Pontieri, p. 368.
10. Pontieri, *Il tramonto*, p. 369.
11. See Sereni, *Il capitalismo*, p. 175.
12. Cf. Sonnino, *I contadini*, p. 102.
13. Attorney General Morena, *Relazioni statistiche sull'amministrazione della giustizia per gli anni 1877–78*, cited in Alongi, *La Maffia*, p. 18.
14. Sonnino, *I contadini*, p. 11.
15. Ibid., p. 17; Sereni, *Il capitalismo*, p. 176. The fief that was the object of Blok's analysis in *The Mafia*, pp. 58 ff., had an extension of around 2,100 hectares.
16. Pontieri, *Il tramonto*, p. 56.
17. Sonnino, *I contadini*, p. 103.
18. Pontieri, *Il tramonto*, p. 10.
19. Sonnino, *I contadini*, p. 103.
20. Mack Smith, *Storia della Sicilia*, p. 527.

21. Sonnino, pp. 131–32. For a description of the contracts and the systems of rotation of cultivations see Sonnino, pp. 117–57: Sereni, *Il capitalismo*, pp. 176 ff.; Blok, *The Mafia*, pp. 58 ff.
22. For the definition of rent capitalism I am indebted to H. Bobek, "The Main Stages in Socio-Economic Evolution from a Geographical Point of View," in P. L. Wagner and M. K. Mikesell, eds., *Readings in Cultural Geography* (Chicago: The University of Chicago Press, 1962), pp. 234–37.
23. Sonnino, *I contadini*, pp. 130–31.
24. See P. Bevilacqua, *Le campagne del Mezzogiorno tra fascismo e dopoguerra* (Turin: Einaudi, 1980). On the salaried day laborers in agriculture in Sicily see Sonnino, *I contadini*, pp. 152 ff.
25. On demographic growth in the first half of the 19th century, cf. E. Pontieri, *Il riformismo borbonico della Sicilia del Sette e dell'Ottocento* (Naples: ESI, 1961), p. 46; A. Saba and S. Solano, "Lineamenti dell'evoluzione demografica ed economica della Sicilia dall'Unificazione ad oggi," in P. Sylos Labini, ed., *Problemi dell'economia siciliana* (Milan: Feltrinelli, 1966), p. 12. On the increase in competition on the labor market see H. Hess, *La mafia*, p. 57.
26. Franchetti, *Condizioni*, p. 72.
27. Ibid., p. 91. For the preceding analysis see pp. 88–90. Also, on the independence of the mafiosi from the landowners, see Blok, *The Mafia*, p. 181.
28. Franchetti, *Condizioni*, pp. 83–84.
29. Cf. Alatri, *Lotte politiche*, p. 187.
30. Franchetti, *Condizioni*, pp. 152–53.
31. G. Ciotti, *I casi di Palermo* (Palermo, 1889), cited in Romano, *Storia*, p. 81.
32. Villari, *Le lettere meridonali*, p. 60. On the events involving the field guards and the mounted militia, cf. Alatri, *Lotte politiche*, pp. 187–89. On the *componende* or "arrangements," see D. Tajani, "Discorso pronunciato nella tornata dell' 11 e 12 giugno 1875 alla Camera dei Deputati, in Russo, *Antologia*, pp. 141–42.
33. *Relazione del prefetto di Palermo Rasponi in data del 1 settembre 1874*, Camera dei Deputati, Session 1874–75, *Documenti relativi al progetto di legge sui provedimenti straordinari di pubblica sicurezza*, n. 24, p. 5, cited in Franchetti, *Condizioni*, p. 155. On the functionaries sent from the north and on their characteristics, see Alatri, *Lotte politiche*, p. 347; also C. Tommasi-Crudelli, "Intervento pronunciato nella tornata del 7 giugno 1875 alla Camera dei deputati," in Russo, *Antologia*, p. 110.
34. See the text of the proposal, in article 8 of the provisions for Sicily, in Russo *Antologia*, p. 94.
35. Franchetti, *Condizioni*, p. 179. The business of giving good conduct certificates to well-known mafiosi is hardly new; see Arlacchi, *La mafia imprenditrice*, pp. 202 ff.
36. Franchetti, *Condizioni*, p. 193.
37. Cf. Sereni, *Il capitalismo*, p. 291.
38. For a documented study of medium-sized landownership, see G. Astuto, "Agricoltura e classi sociali in Sicilia, 1860–1880, in *Annali 80* (Department of Historical Sciences, Faculty of political sciences, University of Catania: Galatea, 1981), pp. 177–253.
39. Alatri, *Lotte politiche*, p. 67.
40. Sonnino, *I contadini*, p. 164.
41. The data on the Bourbon land registry and on the distribution of land owned by the Church is dealt with by Astuto, *Agricultura e classi sociali*, p. 238. For further concrete examples see Blok, *The Mafia*, pp. 116–17; also Parliamentary records, Chamber of Deputies, legislature v, Doc. xxiii, no. 2, Parliamentary commission of inquiry into the Mafia phenomenon in Sicily, *Relazione sui lavori svolti e sullo stato del fenomeno mafioso al termine della V legislatura, Allegato 1 (Relazione Brancato)*, Rome, 1972, pp. 206–7.
42. Sereni, *Il capitalismo*, p. 292. On the development of bourgeois landownership more at the expense of mortmain than because of erosion of the barons' property, see ibid., pp. 169–70.

43. Cf. Blok, *The Mafia*, p. 96.
44. Franchetti, *Condizioni*, pp. 196–97; Sonnino, *I contadini*, pp. 263–64.

Chapter 5. Social Hybridization

1. P. Cala Ulloa, "Considerazioni sullo economico e politico della Sicilia," cited in Pontieri, *Il riformismo*, pp. 222–25.
2. Cited in Alatri, *Lotte politiche*, p. 207.
3. Among the eliminated offices were the State Secretary, the Court of the Comptroller and Auditor General, the Council of State, the General Treasury, the Office of Clearance, the General Superintendence of Statistics, the General Superintendence of Public Spectacles, the Supreme Court of Appeal of Palermo, and Departmental Superintendence of the Public Debt. See Alatri, *Lotte politiche*, p. 211.
4. Cited in ibid., p. 284.
5. Cited in ibid., p. 289.
6. *Relazione Bonfadini*, in Russo, *Antologia*, pp. 190–91.
7. Sonnino, *I contadini*, pp. 71–72 (italics added).
8. Franchetti, *Condizioni*, pp. 122–23.
9. On banditry see F. Molfese, *Storia del brigantaggio dopo l'Unità* (Milan: Feltrinelli), 1964.
10. Franchetti, *Condizioni*, pp. 124–25.
11. Ibid., p. 104.
12. E. Ragionieri, *Politica e amministrazione nella storia dell'Italia unita* (Bari: Laterza, 1967). Here and in the next paragraph I present in revised form material from my two articles "Potere e politica locale in Italia," in *Quaderni di sociologia*, xxiv, 4 (1975), pp. 273–322, and "Struttura sociale, sistema politico e azione collettiva nel Mezzogiorno, in *Stato e mercato*, 8 (1983), pp. 105–49.
13. Cf. S. Tarrow, *Tra centri e periferia* (Bologna: Il Mulino, 1979), pp. 50 ff.
14. Ragionieri, *Politica e amministrazione*, p. 121.
15. See R. Fried, *The Italian Prefects: A Study in Administrative Politics* (New Haven: Yale University Press, 1963); G. Salvemini, *Il ministro della malavita e altri scritti sull'Italia giolittiana* (Milan: Feltrinelli, 1962), pp. 135–44, in *Scritti sulla questione meridionale* (Turin: Einaudi, 1955), pp. 148–51.
16. Franchetti, *Condizioni*, p. 102.
17. Villari, *Le lettere meridionali*, p. 60.
18. See M. Shefter, *Patronage and Its Opponents: A Theory and Some European Cases*, Cornell University, Western Societies Program, 1977, Occasional Paper no. 8.
19. Cf. Graziano, "Clientela e politica nel Mezzogiorno," in P. Farneti, ed., *Il sistema politico italiano* (Bologna: Il Mulino, 1973), pp. 214–20.
20. Salvemini, *Scritti sulla questione meridionale*, pp. 149–50.
21. Alongi, *La maffia*, p. 32.
22. Ibid., pp. 98–99.
23. Franchetti, *Condizioni*, p. 196–97, 213.
24. On this matter, see Alatri, *Lotte politiche*, pp. 247–48.
25. Ibid., pp. 310, 573, and *passim*.
26. Franchetti, *Condizioni*, pp. 11, 13.
27. Cited in Alatri, *Lotte politiche*, p. 208.
28. Ibid., p. 222.
29. Ibid., p. 212.
30. For an account of the debate see Alatri, *Lotte politiche*.
31. N. Colajanni, "Nel regno della magia," in Russo, *Antologia*, pp. 491–92.
32. Romano, *Storia*, pp. 159–60.

33. Cited in ibid., p. 158.
34. Mosca, *Che cosa è la mafia*, p. 243.
35. Colajanni, "Nel regno," in Russo, *Antologia*, p. 493.
36. B. King, cited in Mack Smith, *Storia della Sicilia*, p. 665.
37. Romano, *Storia*, p. 162.
38. See the notations of F. S. Merlino, cited in Romano, *Storia*, p. 163.
39. N. Colajanni, "Nel regno," pp. 494–98.
40. For a synthetic exposition of the important elements in the Notarbartolo case see Romano, *Storia*, pp. 164 ff.
41. See Mosca, *Che cosa è la mafia*, pp. 253–55.
42. Blok, *The Mafia*, p. 109.
43. G. Pagano, *La Sicilia nel 1876–1877* (Palermo, 1878), pp. 25–26.
44. See G. Carocci, *Agostino Depretis e la politica interna italiana dal 1876 al 1887* (Turin: Einaudi, 1956), p. 135.
45. See Hess, *Mafia*, pp. 43 ff.
46. Cf. Blok, *The Mafia*, p. 6.
47. See Schneider and Schneider, *Culture*, p. 183.
48. Romano, *Storia*, pp. 176–77. In general, for a reconstruction of the events and characteristics of the movement of the Sicilian Fasci, see Romano, *Storia dei Fasci siciliani* (Bari: Laterza, 1959); F. Renda, *I fasci siciliani 1892–94* (Turin: Einaudi, 1977), as well as the essays by divers hands published in *I Fasci siciliani* (Bari: De Donato, 1975).
49. Romano, *Storia*, pp. 171, 175. On the relationship between the Mafia and the Fasci see also Romano, *Storia dei Fasci*, pp. 360 ff.
50. Cf. Blok, *The Mafia*, pp. 124–25. Vito Cascio Ferro was accused of having killed in 1909 the American agent Joe Petrosino, who had come to Palermo to investigate the Sicilian Mafia groups. Regarding this episode see M. Pantaleone, *Mafia e politica* (Turin: Einaudi, 1962), pp. 45–46, and A. Petacco, *Joe Petrosino* (Milan: Mondadori, 1972), pp. 111 ff.
51. Hobsbawm, *I ribelli*, p. 131. The use of the associations through patronage was already noted by Franchetti, *Condizioni*, p. 199.
52. See Pantaleone, *Mafia e politica*, pp. 100–101, 117–18.
53. Franchetti, *Condizioni*, pp. 109–10. On the concept of the unconditional granting of benefits see C. Lindblom, *Politica e mercato* (Milan: Etas, 1979), p. 41.
54. The characteristics of the South as a precontractual society have been underscored by L. Graziano, *Clientela e politica nel Mezzogiorno*, pp. 211–377.
55. For an analysis of attempts at the development of modern economic initiatives in Sicily, (though with excessive emphasis on "modern" aspects of the Sicilian economic reality), see G. Barone, "Stato, capitale finanziario e Mezzogiorno"; also S. Lupo and R. Mangiameli, "La modernizzazione difficile: Blocchi corporativi e conflitto di classe in una società arretrata," both in the collection entitled *La modernizzazione difficile* (Bari: De Donato, 1983).

Chapter 6. Hibernation and Reawakening: From Fascism to the Postwar Period

1. On the first manifestations of the Mafia of Sicilian origin in America—New Orleans, in 1889—see E. Reid, *La mafia* (Florence: Parenti, 1956), pp. 152–79. For a succinct overall picture, cf. Romano, *Storia*, pp. 209–27. On the expansion of Mafia dealings on a large scale, see an account of the fleet of fishing boats owned by Vito Cascio Ferro, which, according to Pantaleone, was used for smuggling (*Mafia e politica*, p. 43). However, according to Blok, *The Mafia*, pp. 125–26, Pantaleone exaggerates the importance of Cascio Ferro and the power he enjoyed.
2. For several examples, cf. Romano, *Storia*, pp. 193–202; Blok, *The Mafia*, pp. 131 ff.

3. An anecdote told by R. Candida, *Questa mafia* (Caltanissetta: Sciascia, 1960), p. 101, is particularly significant. During Mussolini's trip to Sicily in 1924, in a commune (possibly Piana dei Greci), the mayor, a noted mafioso, seeing the array of police and carabinieri lined up by the state authorities as an escort for the head of the government, complained to Mussolini himself that there was no need to bring along "so many bravos" when in this mayor's company. For other examples see Blok, *The Mafia*, pp. 178–79; Loschiavo, *Cento anni*, pp. 143, 172.

4. Cf. Romano, *Storia*, p. 202.

5. On the Fascist squads and the struggle with the bands in Madonie and Caronie see the testimony presented by A. Spano, *Faccia a faccia con la mafia* (Milan: Mondadori, 1978), pp. 14–36. On the need to defeat the Mafia on its own terrain see Mori, *Con la mafia ai ferri corti*, pp. 243–46.

6. Cf. Romano, *Storia*, pp. 195–98.

7. See the text of the ordinance published in Russo, *Antologia*, pp. 589–98. In particular the ordinance subjected the activities of the *campieri*, guards, and overseers of the estates to rigid controls, and made it mandatory that those who exercised such activities had to reside permanently on the estate. Furthermore it established the need for a declaration of consent by the owner of the estate in regard to the *campiere*, and the obligation of the latter to report twice a month to the police or to the carabinieri. Provisions were also made for the dismissal of any *campieri*, guards, and overseers who refused to take up the jobs of persons who had been denied consent by the landowner. Regarding prevention of the theft of livestock, special regulations were enforced for carters, goatherds, and shepherds, including proofs of identity and a prohibition forbidding goatherds and shepherds to carry arms or to assemble in groups larger than three when working at their trade with the animals in the countryside. Branding and identification tags were also reinstituted for horses and cows. Traders were subjected to rigorous controls and were made to present monthly declarations concerning their commercial activities and to keep records of their purchases, which had to be declared to the police authorities within forty-eight hours. The ordinance was so minutely detailed as to stipulate that cane groves could not be planted at less than one hundred meters from the edge of the road and existing cane groves were to be extirpated as necessary to remove the conditions favorable for ambushes.

8. On this episode see Mori, *Con la mafia ai ferri corti*, pp. 364–65. For a summary review of police methods used by Mori, cf. Pantaleone, *Mafia e politica*, pp. 56–57; for a general reconstruction see A. Petacco, *Il prefetto di ferro* (Milan: Mondadori, 1975), as well as S. Lupo, "L'utopia totalitaria del fascismo," in *Storia d'Italia: Le regioni dell'Unità ad oggi: la Sicilia* (Turin: Einaudi, 1987), pp. 373–482.

9. Mori, *Con la mafia ai ferri corti*, pp. 370–71.

10. Cf. Pantaleone, *Mafia e politica*, p. 59; Romano, *Storia*, pp. 205–7. On Cucco see Lupo, *L'utopia*.

11. Cf. Mori, *Con la mafia ai ferri corti*, p. 354, and for other testimonies in the same sense see pp. 355 and *passim*.

12. See Blok, *The Mafia*, pp. 186, 189.

13. Pantaleone, *Mafia e politica*, p. 53.

14. For this analysis and for that which follows see F. Renda, *Movimenti di massa e democrazia nella Sicilia del dopoguerra* (Bari: Donato, 1979), pp. 17 ff.

15. Cf. Giorgetti, *Contadini e proprietari nell'eta moderna* (Turin: Einaudi, 1974), pp. 479–80. The length of time of the contract (18 years) was in fact too short to introduce effective improvements; there were ample possibilities for the proprietors to cancel a contract in advance, and the pay for a peasant's work toward improving the land amounted to only 35 percent of the average salary of a day laborer.

16. On the crisis of the Sicilian agrarian bloc see Renda, *Movimenti*, p. 21.

17. There does not yet exist a sufficiently reliable and well-founded reconstruction of the role

the Mafia played in assisting the Allied invasion of Sicily. Pantaleone recounts an uncon-
firmed anecdote (in *Mafia e politica*, pp. 62–64) according to which Lucky Luciano
collaborated with Don Calogero Vizzini on methods of identification for the Allied
invasion and the advance of the American troops in Sicily (a famous yellow scarf was
supposedly dropped from an American plane at Villalba, the Sicilian mafioso's home-
town). F. Sondern, Jr., believes that Lucky Luciano's contribution to the landing in Sicily
"was . . . probably negligible. . . . There is reason to believe that he was in no way
connected with American war plans. The Sicilian Mafia, from time to time, was quite
helpful to the American forces; it supplied trustworthy fishermen for exploration of the
terrain, skillful, reliable people of all sorts, 'support bases' from which agent provocateurs
operated. But the New York Mafia chiefs had nothing to do with all this" *La Mafia Oggi*
(Milan: Bompiani, 1960), p. 115. However, in support of Pantaleone's thesis, see F.
Gaia, *L'esercito della lupara* (Milan: Area, 1962), pp. 113 ff. For a critical evaluation of the
events see R. Mangiameli, "Le allegorie del buon governo: Sui rapporti tra Mafia e
Americani in Sicilia nel 1943," in *Annali 80*, pp. 607–29.

18. Cf. Parliamentary records, Chamber of Deputies, legislature vi, doc. xxiii, n. 2: Parliamentary commission of inquiry on the Mafia phenomenon in Sicily, *Relazione conclusiva
(Relazione Carraro)* (Rome: Senate printing press, 1976), p. 114.

19. On the appointment of Vizzini as mayor see Pantaleone, *Mafia e politica*, p. 71. The
phenomenon of mayors appointed from among the mafiosi has led some to maintain that
"the authorities in the town governments created by the Allies, when they were not
Mafiosi, were Separatists (90% of the 350 communes in Sicily)." Cf. Romano, *Storia*, p.
232. In the same sense see G. C. Marino, *Storia del separatismo siciliano* (Rome: Editori
Riuniti, 1979), p. 30, where some cases are cited. G. Giarrizzo, "Sicilia politica, 1943–
45: La genesi dello Statuto regionale," in *Archivio storico per la Sicilia orientale*, lxvi (1970),
pp. 10–11, maintains that this is a claim without any foundation, but he does not present
any proofs for his own opposing claim. Just as some former Fascist mayors became mayors
under the Allied occupation, as confirmed by A. Blok (*The Mafia*, p. 194), it is not
improbable that other mafiosi besides Vizzini were appointed to the post.

20. Pantaleone, *Mafia e politica*, p. 73.

21. Sondern, *La mafia oggi*, p. 129.

22. The titles of separatist pamphlets circulated in Sicily are emblematic: in Catania the title
of the pamphlet written by Canepa under the pseudonym "Mario Turri" was "Sicily to the
Sicilians." In Palermo a pamphlet written by Baron Tasca, the same person who later
successfully proposed the alliance of the separatist movement with the bandits, bore the
title "Eulogy of the *latifondo*." In Canepa's pamphlet there was an explicit criticism of
Fascism; Tasca's pamphlet, however, sang the praises of the *latifondo*, insisting that in
that system lived rich and prosperous peasants, and that primitive methods of cultivation
were preferable to the mechanization of agriculture. Cf. F. Renda, "Il movimento
contadino in Sicilia," in the collection entitled *Campagne e movimento contadino nel
Mezzogiorno d'Italia* (Bari: De Donato, 1979), vol. I, p. 574; F. Gaja, *L'esercito della
lupara*, pp. 199–203, 123, and Appendix I, where Canepa's text is included.

23. See Romano, *Storia*, pp. 232–33.

24. Ibid., pp. 233, 237; F. Gaja, *L'esercito della lupara*, p. 235; M. Pantaleone, *Mafia e
politica*, p. 92.

25. On this episode see V. Sansone and G. Ingrascì, *Sei anni di banditismo in Sicilia* (Milan: Le
edizioni sociali, 1950), pp. 62–63. Gaja, *L'esercito della lupara*, pp. 221–22; Pantaleone,
Mafia e politica, pp. 103–4; Mangiameli, "Gabellotti e notabili nella Sicilia dell'interno,"
in *Italia contemporanea*, 156 (1984), pp. 60–62. The trial for the shoot-out at Villalba
dragged on for fourteen years, when the defendants were either given absolution or
pardoned by the president of the Republic—with the exception of Don Calò, who in the
meantime had died.

26. Our elaboration on the INEA data, *La distribuzione della proprietà fondiaria in Italia: Tavole*

Statistiche Sicilia (Rome: Edizioni italiane, 1947). In general, on the agrarian reform see G. E. Marciani, *L'esperienza di riforma agraria in Italia* (Rome: Giuffre, 1966).

27. Renda, *Il movimento contadino,* p. 622.
28. Cf. Blok, *The Mafia,* pp. 245, 251–52.
29. See Renda, *Il movimento contadino,* p. 622.
30. For example, in Puglia, on which see F. De Felice, "Il movimento bracciantile in Puglia nel secondo dopoguerra, 1947–69, in *Campagne e movimento contadino,* vol.I, pp. 253–414.
31. On the *jacqueries,* or peasant agitations for the land in the South, see in general S. Tarrow, *Partito communista e contadini nel Mezzogiorno* (Turin: Einaudi, 1972), pp. 246 ff.; P. Villari, Introduction to P. Villani and N. Marrone, eds., *Riforma agraria e questione meridionale* (Bari: De Donato, 1981), pp. 6 ff. For Sicily see F. Renda, *Il movimento contadino,* pp. 569–70, 599, 656 *passim.*
32. Cf. Renda, *Il movimento contadino,* pp. 613 ff., to which I return in the remainder of this paragraph.
33. Cf. Villani, *Introduzione,* p. 17.
34. See Renda, *Il movimento contadino,* pp. 618–19.
35. For these data and comparisons see ibid., pp. 624–26.
36. These aspects are emphasized especially in P. Villani's Introduction, pp. 6, 18. On certain failings of the movement Renda (*I movimento contadino*) also agrees, but he underscores the fact that in Sicily the Gullo decrees had distanced the peasants from the Separatist movement (p. 628).
37. Parliamentary records, Chamber of Deputies, legislature V, Doc. xxiii, n.2, Parliamentary commission of inquiry into the Mafia phenomenon in Sicily, *Relazione sui lavori svolti e sullo stato del fenomeno mafioso al termine della V legislatura (Relazione Cattanei),* Rome, 1972, p. 117.
38. On an overall view of these events see Marino, *Storia del separatismo,* pp. 138 ff.; Gaja, *L'esercito della lupara,* pp. 234–89; Romano, *Storia,* pp. 235 ff; Spano, *Faccia a faccia,* pp. 85–210; G. Maxwell, *Dagli amici mi guardi Iddio* (Milan: Feltrinelli, 1957); Parliamentary records, Chamber of Deputies, legislature V, Doc. xxiii n. 2, Parliamentary commission of inquiry into the Mafia phenomenon in Sicily, *Relazione sui rapporti tra mafia e banditismo in Sicilia,* Rome, 1872, pp. 24–35.
39. Romano, *Storia,* pp. 234–43.
40. *Relazione sui rapporti tra mafia e banditismo,* p. 110.
41. Sassone and Ingrascì, *Sei anni di banditismo,* p. 110.
42. See ibid., pp. 113–15; Gaja, *L'esercito della lupara,* p. 304; S. Di Matteo, *Anni roventi: La Sicilia dal 1943 al 1947* (Palermo: G. Denaro, 1967), p. 448.
43. On the massacre at Portella della Ginestra see Gaja, *L'esercito della lupara,* pp. 347–54; Di Matteo, *Anni roventi,* pp. 514–19, and the authors cited in note 38.
44. *Relazione sui rapporti tra mafia e banditismo in Sicilia,* pp. 56–57. The obscure aspects of the death of Salvatore Giuliano and the end of his band are so well known that there is no need to repeat them here. For a documentation, see the authors cited in the preceding notes, and above all the sentence of May 3, 1952, of the Court of Assizes of Viterbo (which concluded the trial of the Giuliano band), published in the *Appendix* to *Relazione su mafia e banditismo in Sicilia,* pp. 89–402.
45. A list of murders is presented in *Relazione Carraro,* pp. 154–55.
46. For an account of episodes of this sort see A. Sorgi, "Quindici anni di lotte contadine," in *Il Ponte,* xv (1959), pp. 628–31.
47. *Relazione Carraro,* pp. 119–20.
48. Cf. Blok, *The Mafia,* pp. 77–81, 252.
49. See Parliamentary records, Chamber of Deputies, legislature VI, Doc. xxiiii, n. 2: Parliamentary commission of inquiry into the Mafia phenomenon in Sicily, *Prima relazione di minoranza (Relazione La Torre),* allegato I, Doc. 131 (Rome: Senate printing press, 1976), p. 624. See also Pantaleone, *Mafia e politica,* pp. 678–79.

50. Renda, *Il movimento contadino*, pp. 678–79.
51. National Institute of Rural Sociology (INSOR), "Dieci tesi sulla riforma fondiaria del 1950," in *Rivista di Economia agraria*, xxiv (1979), p. 701.
52. Renda, *Il movimento contadino*, pp. 678–79.
53. INEA, Annuario dell'agricultura italiana, Rome, vol. xvi (1962) and xix (1965).
54. *Relazione La Torre*, p. 576.

Chapter 7. Survivors, Pistoleros, and Innovators

1. On the institutionalization of the rights of social citizenship as an aspect of the formation of the State and the nation see T. H. Marshall, *Cittadinanza e classe sociale* (Turin: Utet, 1976); Bendix, *Stato nazionale;* Rokkan, *Formazione degli stati e differenze in Europa.*
2. Cf. A. Del Monte and A. Giannola, *Il Mezzogiorno nell'economia italiana* (Bologna: Il Mulino, 1978); A. Graziani and E. Pugliese, eds., *Investimenti e disoccupazione nel Mezzogiorno* (Bologna: Il Mulino, 1979), pp. 7–65; A. Graziani, Introduction to A. Graziani, ed., *L'economia italiana dal 1943 ad oggi* (Bologna: Il Mulino, 1979), pp. 11–129.
3. Cf. G. Gribaudi, *Mediatori* (Turin: Rosenberg & Sellier, 1980).
4. For the analysis of the transformations of the patronage system see Tarrow, *Partito communista e contadini;* on the relations of "kinship" between party and State see J. La Palombara, *Clientela e parentela* (Milan: Communità, 1967).
5. For empiric examples of these practices see P. A. Allum, *Potere e società a Napoli nel dopoguerra* (Turin: Einaudi, 1975); M. Caciagli et al., *Democrazia cristiana e potere nel Mezzogiorno* (Florence, Guaraldi, 1977); F. Cazzola, ed., *Anatomia del potere DC* (Bari: De Donato, 1979).
6. Cf. Gribaudi, *Mediatori*, pp. 23–28.
7. *Relazione Carraro*, p. 124.
8. Ibid., p. 125. See also Parliamentary records, Chamber of Deputies, legislature VI, Doc. xxxiii, n. 2., *Seconda relazione di minoranza, parte terza (Relazione Niccolai)*, enclosure no. 5, *Relazione "mafia ed enti locali" (Relazione Alessi)*, Rome, Senate printing press, 1976, pp. 1205–6.
9. See V. Ottaviano, "L'assunzione del personale da parte della Regione, in P. Sylos Labini, *Problemi dell'economia siciliana*, pp. 961–85.
10. Cf. *Relazione Carraro*, pp. 205–6.
11. *Relazione Alessi*, p. 1211.
12. *Relazione Carraro*, p. 206.
13. Cf. *Relazione La Torre*, enclosure no. 1 (Doc. 131), pp. 639–47.
14. See Gunnella's letter printed in *Relazione Niccolai*, pp. 1097–98, as well as the statements made by Gunnella himself in ibid. (enclosed in n. 2), pp. 1125–26.
15. Cf. *Relazione Niccolai*, enclosed in n. 2, p. 1149.
16. *Relazione Niccolai*, allegato n. 4, p. 1164 (italics added). The subject of the responsibilities borne by the opposition of the Left for the politics of assistance to the South is too vast to be dealt with here. For this see E. Reyneri, *La catena migratoria* (Bologna: Il Mulino, 1979).
17. Cf. *Relazione Niccolai*, allegato n. 4. In the matter of the rules of godfatherhood, it is common practice for the mafiosi to have politicians as witnesses at weddings. A scandalous example was that of the son of Genco Russo, at whose wedding in 1950 witnesses ranged from Don Calogero Vizzini to the Honorable Rosario Lanza, Christian Democrat, regional deputy, and president of the Sicilian Regional Assembly. The episode is reported in Parliamentary records, Chamber of Deputies, legislature V, Doc. xxiii, n. 2, Parliamentary commission of inquiry into the Mafia phenomenon in Sicily, *Relazione sull'indagine riguardante casi di singoli mafiosi (Relazione Della Briotta)*, Rome, 1971, p. 43.

18. Cf. Parliamentary records Chamber of Deputies, legislature VI, Doc. xxiii, n. 2, *Relazione sul traffico mafioso di tabacchi e stupefacenti nonche sui rapporti tra mafia e gangsterismo italo-americano* (*Relazione Zuccala*), allegato n. 1, p. 479.
19. See *Relazione Carraro*, p. 213.
20. Cf. S. Stajano, ed., *Mafia: L'atto d'accusa dei giudici di Palermo* (Rome: Editori Riuniti, 1986), pp. 16–17. This volume carries in part the ordinance-sentence of the pretrial penal instructions of the Palermo office, on the basis of which the most important Sicilian mafiosi (the Grecos, Liggio, Calò, Santapaola, etc.) were tried in the so-called mass trial of the Mafia beginning in 1986. See also G. Di Lello, "La presenza mafiosa in Sicilia: Cronologia e interpretazione di una "escalation" di violenza," in G. Borre and L. Pepino, eds., *Mafia 'ndrangheta e camorra* (Milan: Franco Angeli, 1983), p. 73.
21. *Relazione Alessi*, pp. 1202–3. An explosive case of embezzlement by a regional assessor—only partly documented in the records of the Anti-Mafia Commission but destined to burst wide open some years later—is the case of the Honorable Salvino Fagone, deputy to the Sicilian Regional Assembly for the Independent Socialist Party, assessor of Public Works, Industry, and Commerce, and later Parliament deputy; on this case see *Relazione Niccolai*, pp. 1081–89.
22. Parliamentary records, Chamber of Deputies, legislature V, Doc. xxiii, n.2, Parliamentary commission of inquiry on the Mafia phenomenon in Sicily, *Relazione sulle risultanze acquisite sul Comune di Palermo* (*Relazione Pafundi*), allegato n. 1, Rome, Senate printing press, 1971, p. 18.
23. *Relazione Pafundi*, allegato n. 1, pp. 16–17 (italics added).
24. *Relazione La Torre*, pp. 577–78.
25. See S. Tarrow, *Partito communista e contadini*; P. A. Allum, *Potere e società*; M. Caciagli et al., *Democrazia cristiana*.
26. *Relazione Carraro*, p. 227.
27. *Relazione La Torre*, allegato n. 4, Doc. 133, p. 842.
28. J. Chubb, *Patronage, Power, and Poverty in Southern Italy: A Tale of Two Cities* (Cambridge: Cambridge University Press, 1982), p. 133. This is an essential book for the understanding of Palermo's recent history.
29. Cf. *Relazione Carraro*, p. 228. Sixteen hundred building permits were given to a certain Salvatore Milazzo, who hired out as a mason by the day, had never been active as a builder, and did not own any buildings or real estate; seven hundred licenses were given to a certain Michele Caggeggi, a mason receiving a social security pension, who did not work at his trade due to bad health; and two hundred licenses went to a certain Lorenzo Ferrante, who was also on pension.
30. *Relazione Pafundi*, allegato n. 1, p. 18.
31. *Relazione Pafundi*, allegato n. 6, p. 23.
32. Cf. *Relazione La Torre*, pp. 589–90, for the charges against Lima, who has never been sentenced. On Vassallo's connections see the report of the Fiscal Police which recounts in detail how Vassallo, for the construction of a building, had acquired a plot of land from Prof. Cusenza, and that the latter, "while not a member in the literal sense of the word, seems not to have been immune to the influence of the local Mafia." Subsequently, when the Honorable Gioia became Undersecretary of Finance, the writer of the report, Colonel Giuseppe Lapis, denied in part this last statement. On the entire episode see *Relazione Pafundi*, allegato n. 18, p. 79, Appendix, pp. 101–2.
33. *Relazione Carrao*, p. 232. On the entire Ciancimino episode cf. ibid., pp. 221–37. Francesco (Frank) Garofalo was the right hand man of Joe Bonanno (called Joe Bananas) head of one of the five Mafia families in New York.
34. *Relazione La Torre*, p. 599.
35. *Relazione Zuccala*, p. 438 (italics added).
36. *Relazione Carraro*, p. 197. For the facts relating to the presence of convicted felons in the wholesale markets see Parliamentary records, Senate of the Republic, legislature v, Doc.

xxiii, 2-bis, Parliamentary commission of inquiry into the Mafia phenomenon in Sicily, *Relazione sui mercati all'ingrosso,* Rome, Senate printing press, 1971, p. 13. What is more, in the wholesale markets there was a pronounced domination of certain families—for example, the three contractors for the fish market belonged to the same family; two were at the same time auctioneers and bidders. Of the thirteen wholesale meat merchants, five belonged to one family and five to another. Cf. *Relazione La Torre,* allegato n. 4, p. 862.

37. *Relazione Carraro,* p. 197; *Relazione sui mercati all'ingrosso,* p. 62.
38. For a biography of Licari see *Relazione Della Briotta,* pp. 213–40. The quantitative data relating to the biographies of mafiosi have been the work of Sara Romano.
39. For the biography of Di Carlo cf. *Relazione Della Briotta,* pp. 271–87.
40. On events relating to the biography of Genco Russo see *Relazione Carraro,* pp. 181–91; *Relazione Della Briotta,* pp. 39–44; *Relazione La Torre,* pp. 604–5, 624–31; *Relazione Zuccala,* pp. 329, 373, 376 *passim.*
41. *Relazione Della Briotta,* p. 75.
42. Cf. M. Pantaleone, *Mafia e politica,* p. 134. In 1951 Filippo Collura, the son of Vincenzo ("Vincent") Collura, was killed. Filippo had been in America, where he was Frank Coppola's best man, and the crony (*compare*) of a well-known boss such as Joe Profaci. On his return to Corleone after the war he refused to become one of Navarra's soldiers, and the latter, when called to inspect his corpse, "stated that his death was caused by the kick of a mule." Another doctor from Corleone, summoned by the commandant of the carabinieri station at Roccamena, where the death had occurred, "diagnosed the death as the result of a shot from a firearm, of which there existed entry and exit wounds." See *Relazione Della Briotta,* p. 77.
43. Cf. Pantaleone, *Mafia e politica,* pp. 136–42. Vanni Sacco, *gabelloto* on a fief of 3,200 hectares along the Belice river, also joined the Liberal party, and later decided to go over to the Christian Democrats. The secretary of the local party section, Pasquale Almerico, was opposed to his acceptance as a member, which both the local clergy and the party chiefs had urged. Almerico was murdered in a typical Mafia ambush on the evening of April 25, 1957. In his corpse were found seven pistol bullets and one hundred four submachine gun bullets. Ibid., pp. 146–48.
44. *Relazione Della Briotta,* p. 115.
45. For the biography of Liggio see idem., pp. 103–30; Pantaleone, *Mafia e politica,* pp. 139 ff. The activities of both Liggio and the Grecos after 1970 have yet to be reconstructed.
46. *Relazione Della Briotta,* p. 123.
47. Ibid., pp. 141–42. For the biography of the Grecos see pp. 131–52.
48. For the struggles of the 1958–63 period in Palermo see M. Pantaleone, *Mafia e droga* (Turin: Einaudi, 1966), pp. 109–17; also *Relazione Della Briotta,* pp. 153–200.
49. *Relazione Della Briotta,* p. 175.
50. Ibid., p. 183.
51. Parliamentary records, Chamber of Deputies, legislature VI, Doc. xxiii, n. 2, Parliamentary commission of inquiry into the Mafia phenomenon in Sicily, *Seconda relazione di minoranza, parte seconda (Relazione Pisanò),* p. 1015.
52. Ibid., p. 1016.
53. The passport of Angelo La Barbera was valid for Nationalist China, Japan, Afghanistan, Nepal, Colombia, Pakistan, Israel and Libya, all key countries for the traffic of drugs.
54. N. Gentile, *Vita di capomafia* (Rome: Editori Riuniti, 1963), p. 172.
55. Cf. *Relazione Carraro,* pp. 147–53.

Chapter 8. The Entrepreneurs of Crime

1. *Relazione Carraro,* pp. 274–79; *Relazione Pisano,* pp. 1020–44.
2. Cited in *Relazione Zuccalà,* p. 406.

3. The reconstruction of events of the seventies and eighties is based on the pretrial inquiry of the judges of Palermo, published in part in C. Stajano, *Mafia;* for a further reconstruction of events see also the articles of A. Calabro in "L'Ora," republished in *Segno*, xii, 66 (1986), pp. 193–259, as well as G. Di Lello, *La presenza mafioso in Sicilia*, pp. 73–76. On the contacts among the Mafia bosses and Sindona during his faked kidnapping see the sentence-ordinance that sent him to trial, partially published in M. De Luca, ed., *Sindona: Gli atti di accusa dei giudici di Milano* (Rome: Editori Riuniti, 1986), pp. 57–121.

4. C. Stajano, *Mafia*, p. 235. For the reconstruction of the entire episode involving Prefect Dalla Chiesa at Palermo see N. Dalla Chiesa, *Delitto imperfetto* (Milan: Mondadori, 1984).

5. See *Relazione Zuccalà*, p. 343; Pantaleone, *Mafia e droga*, p. 35.

6. Cf. Relazione Zuccalà, pp. 351, 355, 366–67.

7. Parliamentary records, Chamber of Deputies, legislature VIII, Doc. xxiii, n. 1/vii, *Documentazione allegata alla relazione conclusiva della commissione parlamentare d'nchiesta sul fenomeno della mafia in Sicilia*, vol. iv, tome xiii, part 1, Document 414, *Organized Crime and Illicit Traffic in Narcotics (Relazione McClellan)*, Rome, Senate printing press, 1980, p. 64.

8. For information in regard to production, transformation, and sale of drugs, see, besides the sources cited in preceding notes 6 and 7, C. Lamour and M. R. Lamberti, *Il sistema mondiale della droga* (Turin: Einaudi, 1973).

9. *Relazione Zuccalà*, p. 367.

10. Ibid., p. 371. On the role of Joe Adonis and in general on Mafia criminality in America until the beginning of the fifties see E. Kefauer, *Il gangsterismo in America* (Turin: Einaudi, 1953).

11. *Relazione Zuccalà*, pp. 363–64. At the Hotel delle Palme there gathered Joe Bonanno (who arrived with two second-in-command bosses from his family, Camillo Galante and Giovanni Bonventre, and with his adviser Frank Garofalo); Joseph Palermo, representative of the Lucchese family of New York; Santo Sorge, representative of Cosa Nostra, charged with creating ties to the Sicilian Mafia; Vito Di Vitale and John Di Bella, representatives of the Vito Genovese family; Vito Vitale, from the John Priziola family of Detroit; Lucky Luciano; Giuseppe Genco Russo; Gaspare Magaddino, Mafia chief of Castellamare del Golfo, and related to the family of the same name in Buffalo, New York.

12. *Relazione Zuccalà*, p. 391.

13. Ibid., p. 399.

14. The sentence-ordinance of the pretrial judges of Palermo highlights quite effectively the characteristics of these new tendencies, pointing to numerous cases of the discovery of clandestine laboratories for the refinement of heroin as well as direct relations between the Silician Mafia *cosche* and traffickers of the Far East. See Stajano, *Mafia*, pp. 139 ff., *passim*.

15. *Relazione Zuccalà*, p. 391.

16. See *Relazione McClellan*, pp. 63–65.

17. Cf. Lamour and Lambert, *Il sistema mondiale della droga*, pp. 81, 82.

18. Cited in Lamour and Lambert, p. 80. For an interpretation of recent activities of mafiosi in the field of financial activity see U. Santino, "La mafia finanziara: Accumulatione illegale del capitale e complesso finanziario-industriale," in *Segno*, xii, 69–70 (1986), pp. 7–49.

19. Ibid.

20. Cf. *Relazione McClellan*, pp. 12 ff.

21. Stajano, *Mafia*, p. ix.

22. *Relazione McClellan*, pp. 13–14, reports that Valachi would have talked about a *caporegima*, that had the same functions as the *capodecina* to which Buscetta and Contorno referred—that is, Valachi might have used the term *capodecina* (head of ten) interchangeably with *caporegima*, which, in Italian-American pronunciation, is very similar and, for that matter, has no meaning in Italian, English, or Sicilian.

23. Cf. Stajano, *Mafia*, pp. 41–42, 63.

24. Ibid., pp. 42–43, 64.
25. This formula is presented in the same terms by Alongi, *La Maffia*, p. 102, which cites a study by Colacino. Oaths that are very similar are described in Lombroso, *L'uomo delinquente*, vol. 1°, pp. 639–41, which cites a study by Lestingi. A complex ritual for induction into the Calabrian *'ndrangheta* is described in G. G. Loschiavo, *100 anni di mafia*, pp. 372–91. Yet there are those who deny the existence of such rituals: Candida, *Questa mafia*, pp. 202–7, maintains that the rituals are not typical of the Mafia as a whole, but only of particular small Mafia groups of secondary importance; J. Bonanno, *Uomo d'onore* (Milan: Mondadori, 1985), pp. 81–82, describing his entry into the Castellamare family in Brooklyn, does not mention such rituals.
26. Cf. Blok, *The Mafia*, p. 145.
27. Bonanno, *Uomo d'onore*, p. 207.
28. Arlacchi, *La mafia imprenditrice*, p. 177; Bonanno, *Uomo d'onore*, p. 275. For the reasons that, according to a mafioso like Buscetta, lead to this rule, see Stajano, *Mafia*, pp. 17, 23–24, 72–75.
29. Bonanno, *Uomo d'onore*, p. 172.
30. In the pretrial inquiry of the Palermo judges there are some examples of this attitude. See Stajano, *Mafia*, p. 21. This casts doubt on Buscetta's assertion that some families give other families advance information on the identity of new members.
31. Ibid., p. 62. Moreover, on p. 92 the judges declare that at present "the structures of Cosa Nostra have become a formal simulacrum of ratification and support of one group, headed by the people from Corleone" (that is, by Luciano Liggio). Notably, in other parts of the pretrial inquiry (see for example pp. 24–26) the judges from Palermo emphasized that within Cosa Nostra there were "fiercely hostile alignments" and had proof (p. 28) that at one Cosa Nostra meeting "they came to realize the impossibility of a unified operation in smuggling tobacco . . . and they decided that each member could work with whomever he wished." But presumably the freedom to make alliances meant also the freedom to make war against opposed alignments.
32. The investigation into Mafia enterprises, conducted with the collaboration of Sara Romano, reviewed the provisions taken until 1985 by the Palermo Tribunal in applying the Rognoni-La Torre law.
33. Cf. Istat, *6° Censimento generale dell'industria, del commercio, dei servizi e dell'artigianato*, 1981, vol. ii, tome 2, regional folder.
34. Cf. R. Catanzaro, ed., *L'imprenditore assistito* (Bologna: Il Mulino, 1979).
35. For notable anecdotes concerning the Salvo cousins, the great Sicilian tax collectors indicted in the mass trial at Palermo (July 1986), also concerning the successful contractors at Catania (Costanzo, Graci, and Rendo) and their relations with mafioso families and personages in Catania and Palermo, see Stajano, *Mafia*, pp. 103 ff., 313 ff.
36. See Stajano, *Mafia*, p. 83.
37. Ibid., p. xvi.

INDEX

INDEX

242